PRAISE FOR
L. DOUGLAS KEENEY

"Doug Keeney takes this pivotal, if wrongly forgotten, 36-day episode in World War II and captures the reader with a true tale of suspense and drama. At the last possible moment, the 1943 Big Three Conference in Teheran forged the winning strategy for the most powerful, and the most difficult military alliance in modern history. All know the Three: FDR, Churchill, Stalin, plus, in the wings, Eisenhower. Keeney adds the rest, whose loud arguments, tenacity and surprising diplomacy starts the countdown for D-Day and victory in Europe. Marshall, King and Arnold along with the British and Russian chiefs have it out in an exotic setting complete with spies and assassins, all amid the chess moves of their political leaders. A great read and great history. Keeney has done his research and now serves it up with all of his skills as a wonderful writer."

—ROBERT BRUCE ARNOLD
author and grandson of General Hap Arnlod, for *The Eleventh Hour*

"An extraordinary look at the men and decisions that determined how WWII was going to be fought . . . and won. Should be on every WWII history buff's shelf."

—STEPHEN COONTS
New York Times bestselling author, for *The Eleventh Hour*

"A jolting year-by-year history of Strategic Air Command's transformation into a massive worldwide force primed to launch bombers within 15 minutes of the order."

"A chilling and unsettling account of accidents, oversights, errors in planning, and other mistakes and misjudgments by the military and its civilian masters . . . sobering and recommended."

"Such dedication to dangerous work . . . deserves to be recognized and honored. Thanks to Mr. Keeney, it now is."

"Brilliantly written, and engrossing . . . Keeney's book shows us the world beyond the press-releases of American propaganda . . . a must-read for anybody interested in the Cold War."

"The power of Keeney's book lies in his determination to avoid excess emotion and stick to the facts—facts that, God knows, are themselves emotive enough. You finish this book a little numbed, though with a strange sense of hope: If mankind can get through years like these and learn the lessons, perhaps it can get through anything."

"Keeney's well-written history is aimed at a general audience, but experts will find it an enjoyable read."

"I enjoyed this book immensely. It was fast-paced, exciting, filled with the untold yet in no way unglamorous adventures and perilous day-to-day existence of the United States Air Force . . . This is one of the best historical books I have read."

" . . . comes from a historian who considers the politics and personalities of *The Pointblank Directive* and how it became one of the most amazing military come-backs in history."

"A thoroughly satisfying read: informative and entertaining . . . *Pointblank Directive* shows quite clearly what the airwar leading up to D-Day cost both sides of the conflict. More impotantly, it fills a needed gap in knowledge of exactly how critical the proper air campaign can be in determining the ground conflict. Historians and students of World War II history alike will be well-served reading this book."

THE ELEVENTH HOUR

OTHER BOOKS BY L. DOUGLAS KEENEY

LOST IN THE PACIFIC:
Epic Firsthand Accounts of
WWII Survival Against Impossible Odds

15 MINUTES:
General Curtis LeMay and the Countdown
to Nuclear Annihilation

THE POINTBLANK DIRECTIVE:
Three Generals and the Untold Story
of the Daring Plan that Saved D-Day

LIGHTS OF MANKIND:
The Earth at Night as Seen from Space

BUDDIES:
Men, Dogs and World War II

THIS IS GUADALCANAL:
The Original Combat Photography

GUN CAMERA WORLD WAR II

DOOMSDAY SCENARIO - HOW AMERICA ENDS:
The Official Doomsday Scenario Written By the United
States Government During the Cold War

GUN CAMERA PACIFIC

SNAKES IN THE COCKPIT:
Images of Military Aviation Disasters

DAY OF DESTINY:
The Photographs of D-Day

THE ELEVENTH HOUR

**HOW GREAT BRITAIN, THE SOVIET UNION, AND THE U.S.
BROKERED THE UNLIKELY DEAL THAT WON THE WAR**

L. DOUGLAS KEENEY

WILEY

Turner Publishing Company/Wiley General Trade

424 Church Street • Suite 2240 • Nashville, Tennessee 37219

445 Park Avenue • 9th Floor • New York, New York 10022

www.turnerpublishing.com

The Eleventh Hour

Cover design: Susan Olinksy
Front cover photographs: Courtesy of the National Archives
Book design: Taylor Reiman

Library of Congress Cataloging-In-Publication Data

Keeney, L. Douglas.
The Eleventh Hour: How Great Britain, the Soviet Union, and the U.S. Brokered the Unlikely Deal That Won the War / l. douglas keeney. pages cm

Includes bibliographical references and index.
ISBN 978-1-118-26986-2
1. Teheran Conference (1943) 2. World War, 1939-1945--diplomatic history. 3. World War, 1939-1945--diplomatic history--sources. 4. Roosevelt, Franklin D. (Franklin Delano), 1882-1945. 5. Churchill, Winston, 1874-1965. 6. Stalin, Joseph, 1879-1953. 7. Iowa (battleship) 8. Meetings--Iran--Tehran--History--20th Century. 9. World War, 1939-1945--Iran--Tehran. i. Title.

d734.k33 2015
 940.53'141--dc23
2014046897

ISBN: 978-1-11826-986-2

Printed in the United States of America
14 15 16 17 18 19 0 9 8 7 6 5 4 3 2 1

TO ARTHUR H. KEENEY, MD AND RICHARD E. JOHNSON

CONTENTS

THE ELEVENTH HOUR

FOREWORD

Soviet Marshal Joseph Stalin asked a simple question laced with frustration. "Will [D-Day] take place or not?" asked Soviet Marshal Joseph Stalin. "If it takes place, that is good, but if not, I wish to know in advance … This is the important question."[1]

The answer to Stalin's question was not an easy "yes" or "no" and the story why began on a cold, rain swept morning in November of 1943 on the wide decks of the battleship USS *Iowa*. Owing to a deep and bitter dispute among the Allies over the course of the war against Germany, Franklin D. Roosevelt and his Joint Chiefs of Staff secretly departed Washington, D.C. on a trip that would take them nearly halfway around the globe to Oran, Algeria, where they would board a four-engine military transport and fly across the rim of North Africa to Cairo and from Cairo up to Tehran, Iran. In Tehran, a place as desolate and as impoverished as any city could possibly be, Roosevelt would meet with British Prime Minister Winston Churchill and Joseph Stalin, and together they would attempt to come to an agreement on a war plan to relieve the Soviet front and defeat Adolf Hitler's Third Reich.

There, in the shadow of the Alborz Mountains, one hundred miles south of the Caspian Sea, three of the world's most powerful leaders met, discussed, argued, fumed, deceived, reconciled, drank—even danced—and ultimately agreed on a unified military strategy to invade the European continent. It was in Tehran that the unexpected became the norm, where good was bad and bad was good. An old Bulgarian proverb seemed to sum it up just right, saying, *"My children, it is permitted you in time of grave danger to walk with the devil until you have crossed the bridge."*

Through hundreds of pages of formerly classified minutes, from the pages of once secret personal diaries and official correspondence, we are given an insider's view into one of the most pivotal weeks in the history of World War II. Through the prism of these historic records we are also given the opportunity to see these three world leaders as never before. The mercurial and petulant, bratty Churchill, whose powerful oratory fails him. The larger-than-life but indecisive Roosevelt, who comes in like a lion but recedes—uncharacteristically—like a lamb. And Stalin, the brutal, abrupt, ruthless Stalin, who for four days is deft, insightful, and decisive, who in the end brokers the deal that unites the Allies and leads to the defeat of Hitler. "Everything else is just a distraction," said Stalin of the British and American plans presented in Tehran, and the others could only agree.

Between November 10 and December 16, 1943, Roosevelt quietly slipped from public view to attend these pivotal meetings. Both Churchill and Stalin made similar journeys. For each, no trip would be so dangerous, no meetings so vital, no divide deeper than the ones that culminated in Tehran. Said Charles E. Bohlen, First Secretary of the Moscow Embassy: "[They were] the most critical diplomatic negotiations the United States had ever engaged in."[2] Another historian summed it up well: "A final showdown over basic European strategy was in the offing. The whole strategy of the global war, the 'Beat Germany first' concept, the roles of the United States, Great Britain, the USSR, and China in the coalition effort—all were in the balance."[3]

And it would come about with an ending that no one expected.

ACKNOWLEDGMENTS

The happy circumstance of finishing a book is occasioned by the opportunity to thank those who helped along the way.

First, to David Way and Robert Kent of the Pacific Battleship Center, San Pedro, California, for the generosity of their time. In particular, my thanks to David Way who clarified details regarding the voyage to Oran via several email exchanges and during a private tour of the great battleship USS *Iowa*. Because of his tour I was able to see where the president and his Joint Chiefs were quartered and held their meetings. Also, my thanks to the Pacific Battleship Center for supplying several of the photographs in this book, as cited. (The Pacific Battleship Center is a non-profit organization that operates the USS *Iowa* as a museum, berthed in San Pedro, California.)

My thanks to Navy reservists and my good friend Will Duke— Commander Will Duke, USN, that is. Will read many of the passages in this book and helped me understand how Navy ships were handled during certain maneuvers. Will also gave me the background I needed to understand some naval traditions and he clarified many of the terms used by the principals in their diaries. I take full responsibility for any misuse or abuse of Will's counsel.

I would also like to thank Editor in Chief of *Yachting Magazine*, co-author of *Outrageous Yachts*, and friend Kenny Wooten who also helped me with nautical terms and whose library included an odd but very useful history of the *Delphine* née USS *Dauntless*.

I thank Kevin Burge, Archivist at the Air Force Historical Research Agency, for his help with research and accessing records related to General Tom Handy, Hap Arnold, and the bombing missions of World War II.

Also many thanks to Robert Arnold, Hap Arnold's grandson, for copies of previously unpublished notes, photographs, and letters sent or received by Arnold; and for his advice and comments, which often clarified some aspects of Arnold's life as depicted in this book.

My thanks to the staff of the George C. Marshall Foundation for numerous oral histories including those of George Marshall, Thomas Handy, and Helen McShane Bailey, and for various documents including copies of the minutes from the meetings of the Joint Chiefs of Staff held on the *Iowa*.

My thanks to Julia Tobey, step daughter of Admiral John McCrea for her permission to cite several passages from an unpublished copy of her forthcoming book, Captain McCrea's War: A Memoir by Franklin D. Roosevelt's Naval Aide and USS *Iowa*'s First Commander.

I am indebted to The Franklin D. Roosevelt Library and, in particular, the Grace Tully Archives for details related to the president's trip to Tehran and the president's daily log.

I was generously helped by the staff at the Library of Congress as I accessed various papers and diaries including the papers of Admiral Ernest King and Admiral William D. Leahy, plus various collections of media reports during World War II including photographs of the facilities where the Joint Chiefs of Staff met in Washington, D.C., which helped me describe them in this book.

A very special thanks to the staff at National Archives for the photographs cited herein, and also for the movie clips of several meetings during the Cairo and Tehran Conferences, and for clips of FDR's visits to various military installations. Using these, I was able to observe small things like how dignitaries were assembled at various official receptions, certain mannerisms including toasting, saluting, and smoking, and get a general feel for the atmosphere during the conferences by means of sight, sound, and motion.

I recommend and am grateful for the United States Department of State's collection titled the Foreign Relations of the United States. I was able to use the more than eight hundred pages of minutes, papers, diaries, and letters related to the Tehran Conference as compiled by the Historian's Office, which I collectively cite as "FRUS."

I would also like to thank the staff of The Naval Historical Center at the Washington Navy Yard. The Navy Department Library contains excellent histories of the ships mentioned here and several studies of World War II and the navy's participation in it, particularly, as regards to this book, the Battle of the Atlantic.

I thank Tom Helvig who writes and edits the *The Iowan History Letter* and keeps the spirit of the USS *Iowa* alive through the remembrances of those who served on her. His newsletters are excellent and are available at the Library of Congress.

And finally, many thanks to my agent and friend Doug Grad of Doug Grad Literary and my editors Christina Roth and Kelsey Reiman of Turner Publishing Company.

CHAPTER 1: WINTER 1943

The night was cold and wet with low hanging clouds that blanketed Washington, D.C. in a drab grayness that was a sure sign that winter had arrived. It was nine o'clock at night, a dark evening by any measure. The city was all but shut down, the deserted sidewalks and streets long ago emptied, the war subduing any fleeting moments of optimism.

The White House residence was quiet. President Franklin Delano Roosevelt was making his final preparations before being driven down to the Marine Corps base at Quantico, Virginia, where he would board the presidential yacht *Potomac* for a six-hour trip to the Chesapeake Bay. There he would transfer to the battleship USS *Iowa* for the Atlantic Ocean crossing to attend a war conference with Winston Churchill and Joseph Stalin.

It was Thursday, November 10, 1943. A pair of hanging lights faintly illuminated a line of cars waiting under the North Portico and upstairs the windows glowed around the edges of the blackout curtains. "Arthur," said Roosevelt, pointing at the staircase. "See who's coming up the stairs." Arthur was FDR's valet, Arthur S. Prettyman, who, at that moment, was holding the president's wheelchair while they waited for the elevator doors to open. The residence was mostly empty, the air somewhat stuffy and stale. It had been six or seven years since a fresh coat of paint had been applied to the walls or new carpets had been laid, and the warren of rooms on the second floor was cluttered with years of neglect. Not that Roosevelt paid much attention to such things. The creaky floors and sagging beams could wait; the war needed people for other things, and Washington was no exception. In less than two years the city had grown from a small, Southern town to a packed metropolis swollen by 250,000 new arrivals, many of them "government girls", the typists and secretaries who had qualified under exams administered nationwide and were now the arms and legs of the war machinery that kept the troops supplied.

Roosevelt waited as the rain tapped a soft beat against the windows. He had his hat in his lap, a cigarette in his hand, and his trademark cape over his shoulders. It had been a long day, the weather bad, but, really no more than an inconvenience. He started the morning with the annual wreath laying ceremonies at the Tomb of the Unknown Soldier, and then had a joint meeting with his vice president and some congressional leaders before leaving for a lunch with Secretary of State Cordell Hull, just returned from Moscow. He went back to his office for a four-hour war conference, then was wheeled back to the residence to eat a bland dinner served from a steamer cabinet with his wife Eleanor Roosevelt and his assistant Grace Tully. After dinner, he excused himself to pack his suitcases, black tie for state dinners, business suits for the plenary sessions, and his favorite wardrobe, a pair of old khaki trousers, a well-worn work shirt, and a floppy fishing hat that only a president could be forgiven for wearing.

One floor below, his travel companions were arriving and bundling into the cars—Admiral Ross T. McIntire, his personal physician; Harry Hopkins, his friend and former Secretary of Commerce and now a close political confidant; two military aides; and the thoughtful and much respected chairman of the Joint Chiefs of Staff, Admiral William D. Leahy. Waiting for them to arrive on the USS *Iowa* were the three other members of the Joint Chiefs, Army General George C. Marshall, Navy Admiral Ernest J. King and Army Air Forces General Henry A. "Hap" Arnold.

Roosevelt beckoned to Prettyman to see what was causing the rustle of papers and thumping of feet. It was the watch officer from the White House Map Room now running up the stairs with an urgent cable in his hand. The cable was from Prime Minister Winston Churchill, and it required an immediate response. Roosevelt read it and nodded. Both Roosevelt and Churchill were prolific writers of cables—some would say they wrote too many, and, considering the press of a global war, perhaps even they would agree with that. In the last several months, more than thirty of them had gone back and forth, almost all of them regarding their attempts to schedule a face-to-face meeting with Stalin, almost all of them about problems that were preventing that from happening. As Roosevelt took the cable he assumed a new problem had arisen and indeed one had, but it had to do with protocol, not war strategy. The crux of the message was this: Stalin had confirmed that he could go to Tehran just the day before, on the 10th, but Roosevelt had failed to tell Churchill.[1] Churchill had learned about it anyway, which had hurt his feelings. "I rather wish you had been able to let me know direct," he said in the cable just delivered to the president, and Roosevelt knew he could not leave it at that. He called downstairs to hold the motorcade while he dictated a response. He briefly explained his slip-up by saying that he had just confirmed his availability to meet with Stalin in Tehran, and had not cabled Churchill because he was unsure if the timing would work out, but, now that it was on, he was delighted. Of course there was more to it than that—Roosevelt was not above tweaking Churchill's nose, and the presidential slight well may have been intentional—but Roosevelt closed the cable with a personal note and that was that. "I am just off," he said in his typically frothy fashion. "Happy landings to us both."[2]

At 9:30 P.M. the motorcade pulled out from under the *porte-co-chère* and into the chilly rain. Behind it, a gust of wind snapped open the flag that flew over the White House to indicate the president was still in residence. No one—not his staff, not his Cabinet and no one in Congress—was to know of his trip lest something leak and the Germans be alerted. To explain Roosevelt's absence, the press was to be given the cover story that he was indeed in the Washington area, but merely taking a short vacation cruising the Virginia Tidewaters on the *Potomac*. That would hold long enough to shield the most dangerous part of the trip—the Atlantic crossing.[3]

The motorcade sped down to Quantico, passing through the gates and out to the docks with only the base commandant knowing what was going on. The president was lifted onto the ship and into a small elevator that inched between the decks. Roosevelt was tired anyway so he thanked his crew, then promptly went to his stateroom and in a moment was fast asleep. Just six minutes had elapsed in the boarding; it was precisely 10:38 P.M.

Prettyman left Roosevelt and went to his own quarters as the *Potomac* gunned her engines and swung out into the stream. To her starboard, the Navy submarine chaser USS SC-664 cast off her lines and pulled abeam, and together they churned the brownish river into a soft boil and headed downstream as armed lookouts and Secret Service agents scanned the dark banks for anything suspicious.[4] "During the night we passed and exchanged calls with the USS *Dauntless* and the USS *Stewart*, bound up-river for Washington," wrote FDR's naval aide Lt. William D. Rigdon. "They were returning there after having transported members of the Joint Chiefs of Staff party and their baggage to the *Iowa* on Thursday." Some five hours later, at 3:30 A.M., they pulled over to the side of the river and came to a halt. "The *Potomac* anchored off Cherry Point, Va., near the mouth of the Potomac River, to await the transfer of the President and his party," wrote Rigdon in his trip log. "Some five miles distant, farther out in the Bay, the massive *Iowa* could be seen riding at anchor."[5]

And there they waited for dawn.

CHAPTER 2: THE *IOWA*

Although acerbic, short-tempered, and known to stand on formality to the point of some occasional ridicule, United States Navy Commander in Chief and Chief of Naval Operations Admiral Earnest J. King, 64, was possibly the most gifted naval strategist of World War II. Tall and thin with penetrating eyes and a long face, King would often say that any navy foolish enough to stay on the defensive was a navy that would soon be visiting Davy Jones' Locker. His navy was going to roam the seas; his navy was going to look for the enemy and hunt them down. His would be a navy eager for combat, on the move, on the offensive. "He was tough as nails," wrote one his British counterparts. "He was blunt and standoffish almost to the point of rudeness."[1] But an arrogant, self-assured brawler was precisely the sort of man Roosevelt needed to transform a sleepy, ragtag assortment of old ships into a navy ready to conduct war. On December 7, 1941, even as smoke curled up into the sky above the ships at Pearl Harbor, it was King who stepped into the void and issued the first order of the day. "Hold the Midway-Hawaii line," he said in a dispatch to his admiral on scene, Chester Nimitz, "[And] hold open the sea lanes to Australia and New Zealand."[2]

In mid-October 1943, Roosevelt invited Admiral King to the White House to discuss the upcoming war conference. Because Europe and Scandinavia were in Hitler's hands, the standard war route of travel from America to Iran was across the Atlantic Ocean to North Africa then across North Africa to Egypt and up to Iran. Roosevelt told King he was planning to meet Churchill in Cairo, but he might travel onward if the arrangements could be made with Stalin. King knew Roosevelt's distaste for flying, so he said that the best way to start the trip would be to go by sea. The German U-boat threat was real enough, but they were getting the upper hand on that, said King, and of course the Atlantic was rough in November, but a large ship like a battleship could take the seas and provide a reasonably smooth ride. Moreover, a battleship was a fort. It carried plenty of guns, had a double hull to blunt the worst effects of most torpedoes, and the newest battleships were fast enough to outrun any German U-boat. One was on the East Coast right now, King said, the USS *New Jersey*, among the newest to the fleet.

Roosevelt liked the plan but had a question. "Ernie," said the president, "when John left the White House, I told him I hoped that someday I could join him in the *Iowa*. Is the *Iowa* available? Could she do this?"

Admiral King said, "Yes."[3]

"John" was Roosevelt's former naval aid, Navy Captain John L. McCrea.

*

Navy Captain John L. McCrea was the captain of the USS *Iowa*. A tall, confident man with thick black hair, McCrea had a steady bearing to him that exuded that sort of confidence that made one feel no enemy would ever dare sink one of his ships. When he took command of the *Iowa*, he addressed the crowd that had come to celebrate her christening. He exhorted the sailors to set to their tasks with vigilance and unflagging energy and to learn their assignments until they could do them in their sleep. "When we have accomplished these things, then, and only then, will we have the sort of ship on which you and I will be proud to serve," he said to an appreciative audience. "She will then be the sort of ship that when the moment comes, the enemy will have reason to believe she is truly the largest and most powerful ship in the world."[4] He paused as the echo of his words died out and looked out over the sea of twenty thousand faces. McCrea stood rigid in his Navy whites, a 1915 graduate of the United States Naval Academy who by good fortune had started his sea career with a plum assignment that put him shoulder to shoulder with the great admirals of the day. "Our enemies are bent on destroying us," he said, his voice hushed but rising. "Our business, until this war is over, is to kill and kill and destroy and destroy!"[5] A roar of applause rose from the crowd, and through this applause walked a triumphant Admiral E.J. Marquart, the director of the Brooklyn Naval Yard, who came to the microphone and finished the formalities with the straightforward honesty of a man who had spent a life shaping vessels from raw iron. "We have given you our best," he said to the assembled crowds. "The *Iowa* is built strong and true."[6]

The *Iowa* was indeed built strong and true, but more to the point it was the single most lethal weapon of war yet to sail under the American flag. It was a big gunship, the first warship in a new class of American battleships that dwarfed anything ever built. She plowed through the seas at the breathtaking speed of 25 knots propelled by engines that generated 144,000 horsepower. She weighed 90 million pounds, was 108 feet wide, and at 887 feet was nearly the length of three football fields. "It was so long, I couldn't believe it would float," said one of her sailors when he first saw her.[7] Another sailor compared the *Iowa* to the Empire State Building rolled on its side and cut open to reveal her pipes and wiring and frames. He just shook his head. It was a mess, he thought at the time. "Pipes, scaffolding, and hoses were everywhere," he lamented. He boarded anyway, found his rack, stowed his gear, went to the mess hall to get some chow, and became so lost that it would be two days before he found his bunk again.[8]

The USS *Iowa* was built at the Brooklyn Navy Yard. When she went out to sea, she came down the East River and inched past the skyscrapers of Manhattan as slowly as an apparition. Traffic came to a standstill as office workers lined the streets to get a better look. Her engines gave off a long, deep-throated vibration that was felt blocks away; her superstructure passed under the bridges with just inches to spare.[9] When she entered Upper New York Bay, she came towards the Statue of Liberty and one of the sailors had a thought that stayed with him for the rest of his life, "The torch she's holding, when you sail towards her it's like she's holding it out—welcoming you. But when you sail away from her, it's like she handing it to you—to take where ever you go."[10]

It was perhaps an apt comment. The flame of that torch could set afire the guns that radiated out from every deck on the *Iowa*'s superstructure—in all, some hundred barrels that pointed outward—dominant among them the nine 16-inch guns hunched down low on massive iron turrets that could belch shells skyward able to sink an enemy ship or destroy a shore installation twenty-five miles away. The 16-inchers were grouped in threes and sat on barbettes that weighed 417 tons each. There were two forward turrets and one aft, each one a small building seven stories tall. Inside each, a hundred sweat-soaked men passed the powder and shells and manned the equipment necessary to fire a refrigerator-sized shell that could hit a teaspoon-sized target. In combat, the first indication that the *Iowa* was bearing down on you might be little more than faint flickers of light that at night would look like lightening on the horizon. In fact, they were the muzzles flashes of her guns. In the urgency of a sea battle, the *Iowa* became a virtual killing machine with the 16- and 5-inchers, plus .50 caliber machine guns, 20mm antiaircraft batteries, and 40mm Bofors for close in combat. Her armor plating was up to 17-inches thick, and at a distance of between 18,000 and 30,000 yards she was so well protected that she was in a theoretical zone of immunity where an armor-piercing enemy shell would hopelessly plink against her steel as if a mere BB pellet.[11]

All of this made for the ideal ship to protect a president as they raced across an Atlantic Ocean filled with German submarines in the midst of a war that was far from decided. "Those of us who had to do with the planning for this expedition were very conscious that the President was running grave personal risk in such extensive travel by sea and air, because we believed that if the enemy could learn of his whereabouts they would spare no effort to attack by air, submarine, or assassin," said Lt. Rigdon. "We had the submarine menace in the Atlantic and Mediterranean, the new destructive glider-bomb that was raising havoc against shipping in the Mediterranean, attacks by air throughout the Mediterranean while traveling in helpless transports, and the ordinary risks of air travel in proceeding anywhere beyond Cairo. Axis agents were known to be numerous in all proposed ports of call."[12] Indeed, one lucky hit from a two thousand pound glide bomb and the core of America's war making machine would be wiped out. Not to mention the president.

CHAPTER 3: LEAVING PLYMOUTH

British Prime Minister Winston Churchill was in a cranky mood, although it was not entirely his fault, he thought. He was en route to Plymouth, England, to board his battlecruiser the HMS *Renown* to begin his own trip to Tehran. He wore a double-breasted sailor's suit with a sailor's cap and had the beginnings of a bad cold, but his foul mood had less to do with his health than with the intractable, unreasonable, short-sighted Americans. "I was feeling far from well," he wrote in his memoirs, which was true, but it was the war that had him down.[1]

Churchill promptly boarded his ship and went to bed, tossing about uncomfortably disposed by his illness and his irritation with Roosevelt. This entire trip would come to no good unless the British could convince the president to abandon his ill-advised plan for a frontal attack on Germany. A landing in France would be but a five-mile pinprick against a two thousand-mile wall of guns, poured concrete, and steel and more than a million German soldiers stretched shoulder to shoulder from Denmark to Portugal. Even if they got through the daunting shore batteries and the Luftwaffe planes and made it to the shore, at least eleven combat-hardened divisions of Wehrmacht soldiers and scores of Panzer tanks waited, ready to race forward and cut them to shreds. If they were thrown back into the English Channel, what then? "The British cannot meet any further calls on our manpower, which are now fully deployed on war service," Churchill would later say to his compatriots. No, Roosevelt needed to come over to his own view of things, which was to delay D-Day, chip away at the edges, and weaken the German forces.

Of course, there was more to all this than that. England was broke, down to her last British pound. The war with Germany had bled the British Treasury dry, and Churchill had about as much negotiating power as a pauper—and nothing got in his craw more than being forced to kowtow. Yes, Britain had done what no one else had been able to do—hold back the Germans—and for that the West was in their debt. America had responded in kind by using every loophole possible to finance more ships, planes, guns, and bullets until Pearl Harbor. Fearing the Japanese attack would divert American attention from their own war against Germany, Churchill rushed over to Washington, D.C., to forge an agreement that would coordinate the global war effort through an executive agency called the Combined Chiefs of Staff. Through various written accords that followed, Churchill and Roosevelt bound themselves to agree on all combat plans and on the allocation of precious war resources until the Japanese and the Germans were defeated. "It was realized quickly that there would have to be complete integration of land, sea, and air operations of the Allies if the war was to be fought with the greatest possible efficiency," said Admiral Leahy. "Without such unity of forces, the war would be protracted or possibly lost."[2]

Four American and four British officers were appointed to the Combined Chiefs, each the senior most military commanders from their respective services, and for more than two years it had worked as hoped. Plans were proposed, disagreements were aired and hashed out, but all war plans went forward via unanimous consent. The British and the Americans successfully coordinated the defeat of the German army in North Africa, then again in Sicily, and now they were on the boot of Italy fighting up towards Rome, with the D-Day invasion of France planned as the next combat initiative against Germany. But then the British military chiefs balked. They saw opportunities to soften the Germans by attacking them in the Mediterranean, a strategy the Americans military saw as a drain on resources and a certain path to delaying D-Day. The Americans insisted the D-Day plans proceed, but the British were firmly opposed. Nearly five hundred thousand soldiers stood idle and awaited their orders. In the case of such an impasse, the issue was sent back to the president and the prime minister. "I may have indicated in this summary that the men who made up the Combined Chiefs of Staff were the men who ran the war," Admiral Leahy wrote, "That is inaccurate. There were two men at the top who really fought out and finally agreed on the major moves that led to victory. They were Franklin Roosevelt and Winston Churchill. They really ran the war."[3]

And they were both headed to Tehran.

*

The *Renown* swung her bow out to sea and got underway. The sailing plan called for them to steam out into the Atlantic Ocean away from the Luftwaffe bases on the Continent of Europe before turning south and running down the coast of Europe abeam Spain and Portugal. They would then turn east and pass through the Strait of Gibraltar then sail down the Mediterranean Sea to Oran. In Oran, Churchill would briefly meet with his Middle East generals, then take a three-day rest stop in Malta before the final leg to Alexandria for a conference in Cairo. After Cairo, he would board a plane for the flight to Tehran. All-in-all, it was complicated, lengthy, and dangerous. The *Renown* was surrounded by anti-submarine destroyers and covered above by squadrons of British fighter pilots. Across the darkening night, the seas rolled against a slight winter storm with whitecaps dotting the Atlantic all the way to the horizon.

Inside the *Renown*, Churchill chafed at the bit. The D-Day plans hung over him like the dark clouds dotting the horizon. He was bound by a previous agreement with Roosevelt to launch D-Day in France after some initial combat in Italy but now he wanted to go further up the boot, even as far as Rome. Churchill asked his advisors how he might undo these agreements lamenting the loss of victories because "battles were governed by lawyers."[4] Instead of the D-Day plan, Churchill now argued for combat in the Mediterranean. By taking the islands of Leros, Cos, and Rhodes they could "cut the German iron ring" that blocked Allied access to the Bosporus Strait and thereby rack up some "cheap gains," as his admirals and generals put it. Such thrusts would weaken the Wehrmacht in Greece, which, if followed by more combat in Yugoslavia, might even whittle the Germans down so much that a D-Day could be avoided all together. Churchill liked the idea, it grew on him, it resonated with him.[5]

But the Americans were dead set against it. The D-Day plans were already in motion. Soldiers in helmets and boots with slung rifles were pouring into England, bombers and fighter planes were already attacking Germany, softening up the Luftwaffe bases, and cutting the rail lines to Normandy. Delays just meant more time for the Germans to anticipate the invasion, more time to strengthen their defenses, and more losses for the Russians who were alone on the Eastern Front with two million Germans at their doorstep. "We were resisting constant efforts to diminish the set-up or time element for the cross-channel operation," said General George Marshall of the british. Truth be told, Marshall said, this whole thing was foul play.[6] On that point the British heartedly disagreed, but applied their own spin to the situation. "There is still a distinct cleavage of opinion between us and the Americans regarding the correct strategy in Europe," lamented British Major General Sir John Kennedy, Director of Military Operations and later Assistant Chief of the Imperial Staff. "The Americans seem to think we have acted in an almost underhanded way over the Mediterranean…this is curious because we have felt almost the same about them."[7]

Churchill propped himself up in his bed, his body aching and running a slight temperature. He called his military chiefs to his side and ranted against the Americans. If they cared not to support his plans for the Mediterranean, he said in a tirade, he would withdraw his support for the D-Day invasion, which was now called Operation Overlord.[8] "I have been fighting with my hands tied behind my back," he declared, then dismissed his generals and rolled over. There was so much to do.

CHAPTER 4: IT CAN BE DONE

In 1919, a young Assistant Secretary of the Navy, Franklin Roosevelt, was a passenger crossing the Atlantic en route to England when his ship, the USS *Dyer,* was caught in a full-fledged Atlantic storm. It was, the sort of violent, confused weather that clawed elephantine waves out of the seas and tossed ocean-going freighters around like mere driftwood, and Franklin Delano Roosevelt was in the midst of it. The small destroyer pitched and rolled so dangerously that the crockery went flying across Roosevelt's compartment and the hull nearly keeled over to the sea. To steady himself, Roosevelt wedged his body between his mattress and the back of his bunk and held himself as steady as possible. "I hope I won't lose more than all my insides," he wrote in his diary. "I still hope to retain my self-respect." Respect he did retain. Although he was exhausted by the effort, Roosevelt came through it with flying colors, perhaps with stronger sea legs than the naval officers themselves, and, to FDR, this mattered greatly.[1]

In truth, there was no place that Roosevelt felt more at home than on the uncertain decks of a ship at sea. Franklin Delano Roosevelt, 61, was born January 30, 1882, the son of a successful New York businessman whose passion was yachting and whose wealth allowed him to indulge the family in ways few could dream of. FDR's youth was idyllic and his earliest childhood memories were shaded in hues of brown and blue—the brown of the Hudson River, which the family home overlooked, and the blue of the ocean that beat against the rocky coastlines of Maine and Newfoundland where the family had summer homes. Before he was eight, Roosevelt had grasped the tiller of an ocean going yacht and brought it about, and by the age of fourteen he had crossed the Atlantic Ocean nine times. All told, he would travel on some 110 named ships during his lifetime, and each trip seemed to do him well.[2] Arthur M. Schlesinger, Jr., then a Harvard professor and friend of the president's, regarded the ocean as a special tonic for Roosevelt and said so with a certain poetic license. "The best escape of all was the sea," he wrote of Roosevelt. It helped the president "cast off weariness and irritability under the beneficence of sun and spray and salt."[3] Indeed, Roosevelt was as adept at reading a nautical chart as he was the latest polls, but it was always the sea that centered him. His Secret Service agents, Roosevelt's constant companions, saw this transforming power of the oceans first hand. "[FDR] was never so content as when he was on blue water, and the ocean was second only to Warm Springs in restoring vigor sapped by the toughest job in the world," said White House Secret Service chief Mike Reilly. FDR confided as much to his secretary Grace Tully: "If anything should happen to me while I am at sea," said Roosevelt, "I want to be buried at sea. You know, it has always seemed like home to me."[4,5]

Home indeed, but even more. The sea was also where Roosevelt had some of his best ideas. In the remove of the noise and demands of Washington, he found the space to develop some of his most important themes. It was during a shipboard vacation that he had the idea for Lend-Lease, and on an earlier transatlantic passage to Cairo he first visualized the landscape of post-war Europe. Best of all, travel by ship slowed things down, gave Roosevelt time to think, be creative, be alone.

And so it would be again. The quiet of the night was slowly replaced by the sound of a ship awakening, the smell of coffee in the air mixing with the marvelous salt water. Prettyman awakened the boss and dressed him in a tan sharkskin suit, put his sea cape over his shoulders, and handed him his brown hat, the brim bent up.[6] They had a mug of coffee, then Prettyman pushed Roosevelt out onto the aft promenade. "Thank you Arthur," said Roosevelt, and together they watched as the great battleship loomed ever closer.

For the vast majority of *Iowa*'s sailors, this was their first time ever at sea. In the aftermath of Pearl Harbor thousands of young men rushed off to their local recruiting stations. Many of the *Iowa*'s new sailors had selected the navy for no other reason than a vague sense that they were more likely to survive the war on a ship than walking into a German machine gun nest with an M1 rifle slung over their shoulder. Now they were on their first ship, pollywogs, the lowest, most inexperienced of all sailors, men who had not so much as crossed the Equator, but they were about to do one thing that none of their experienced shipmates had done. They were about to meet a president. "At fifteen minutes before nine, the tiny, white Presidential yacht *Potomac* hove into distant view," recorded McCrea in his diary, as he watched approvingly. "As she drew near the *Iowa*'s starboard side, the seal of the Chief Executive could be observed on the bridge."[7] Seaman George Dillon, 18, was on one of the ships 20mm gun mounts and said he had an excellent view as the president arrived, as did Vincent Angilletta who was on another gun. Later when Angilletta went to his battle station, he said he could "take a peek" at FDR when the president was out on the deck.[8] Seaman 1st Class James Conroy, Jr., a handsome, dark-haired sailor from New Jersey, summed it up for them all. As sailors they would see violent combat, face death, travel the world on a warship that was almost always in great peril, but above all these life experiences they would remember this cold November morning on the Chesapeake Bay. "Having the President on board was the highlight of my Navy career," he said, and that said it all.[9] "At 9:16 A.M. the President went aboard the *Iowa,* using his special brow that was rigged from the after sun deck of the *Potomac* to the main deck of the *Iowa,* just abreast of the *Iowa*'s number three turret," wrote Rigdon. "At his request, no honors were rendered as he came on board the *Iowa.*" Instead, Roosevelt extended his hand and greeted the Captain. "It's good to see you again, John," he said. McCrea responded in kind.[10]

McCrea assigned Roosevelt an escort who led the president to the captain's cabin, where he would stay for the duration of the voyage. Prettyman settled Roosevelt into his new living quarters where he changed him into his duck trousers, a fishing hat, and a heavy maroon shirt. With his trademark cigarette holder in one hand, a blanket over his legs, and a paperback in his lap, Arthur wheeled the president out on deck and pushed him next to the lifeline at the edge of the ship. "Thank you, Arthur," he said, and Prettyman withdrew. "He inserted cigarets in his famed holder and by cupping his hands and hunching his shoulders had no difficulty lighting them in the brisk breeze that whirled across the decks," said McCrea who watched from the bridge. "Admiral Leahy came up and spoke to him for a minute or two—and later Harry Hopkins had a word. But it was noticed that most of the time he was left alone."[11]

Roosevelt, who had come aboard with the same concerns that were weighing so heavily on Winston Churchill, dealt with them quite differently. Rather than rant, he was content to be alone and read. It was partly being stricken with polio and powering through the loss of his legs that gave him such a steady perspective on life and such faith in himself. "There is always a way to get through it," said FDR, speaking of the obstacles one faces, including the obstacles of war. "If you had spent two years in bed trying to wiggle your big toe, after that anything else would seem easy."[12] "It became his policy," said his Secretary of Labor Frances Perkin, "that what has to be done can be done somehow."[13]

Satisfied that all was in order, McCrea came in from the conning tower and ordered the ship underway.

The *Iowa* had an intermediate stop to make before heading out to sea and came to her refueling anchorage at 5:30 P.M. Two large oilers came alongside, the USS *Housatonic* to the starboard followed by the USS *Escalante* to the port, as two watch officers from the White House Map Room arrived with a pouch of mail for the president to review. The watch officers waited outside as Roosevelt penned a brief cable to Stalin to confirm the meetings in Tehran. The president's message crossed the wire on November 12th with a dateline of USS *Iowa*, at sea. "I am just leaving for French North Africa," Roosevelt wrote. "Warm regards."[14]

At 6:30 P.M., McCrea came down from the bridge to have dinner with the president and to outline the sailing voyage. This was partly a courtesy and partly protocol. As the senior commander on a U.S. Navy ship, McCrea was bound to review the sailing plan with the president and formally request his approval, which he did, and which Roosevelt granted. That done, they talked. "[During the dinner] the President said to me, 'Now what are your plans for tonight?'" said McCrea. "Well, I said,' Mr. President, we have high water slack at 11:00 o'clock tonight, and I would like to get underway at 11:00 o'clock and go down to buoy 2CB and go on to sea.' He said, 'John, this is a very important mission that we are starting on.' And I said, 'Yes, it is, Mr. President.' He said, 'You know that this is the Friday.' And I said, 'I know that.' He said, 'I'm just sailor enough to not to want to start anything important like this trip that we are going on, on a Friday. Now could you manage to get under way on a Saturday morning rather than Friday night?' I said, 'Yes, Mr. President, we still will have enough water to handle ourselves getting out of here."[15]

Roosevelt was being careful not to run afoul of one of the countless superstitions of the sea, that is, the belief that undefined but terrible things happened to those who started an important sea voyage on a Friday. McCrea said he could delay their departure until a few minutes past midnight, which would make it Saturday, thus rendering the gods of the seas impotent to do their evil but still leaving enough water under the *Iowa's* hull to clear the channel out to sea. This pleased the president greatly, and he broke out into a generous smile. The deal was sealed. "The sea details went to their stations at 11:45 P.M." wrote McCrea. "The anchor was brought to short stay, and on Saturday, 13 November at 0001 hours—12:01 A.M. landlubber time—orders were given to heave up."[16]

Into the darkened seas, the *Iowa* pointed her bow. Around her, three U.S. destroyers took up positions as escorts. Somewhere further out to sea were two small aircraft carriers with their fighter planes and dive bombers. Together they formed a military task force, and together they would get the president across the sub-infested Atlantic Ocean.

CHAPTER 5: BAKU

Soviet Marshal Joseph Stalin had one hand tied behind his back. His nation was at war and had been since 1941 and the fighting was costly indeed. A tidal wave of some 2.9 million German soldiers had poured into the Soviet Union with 600,000 motor vehicles, 750,000 horses, 46,000 artillery pieces, 4,000 aircraft, and 3,000 tanks. Against them stood a well-entrenched garrison force of Red Army soldiers that, while numerically superior, were poorly equipped and even more poorly organized. The Russians were swiftly and disastrously overrun. Seasoned Wehrmacht divisions advanced deep into Russia, coming to the edge of Moscow and onto the streets of Stalingrad. The combat raged through the winter of 1941 and 1942 as heavy artillery fire and hand-to-hand combat stretched across a front that was 1,800 miles long. Horse-drawn wagons slugged homeward through rain and mud from the fronts and brought back bodies stacked like cordwood as the grinding business of war took its toll.

The Germans were relentless, and Russia's survival was in peril. Stalin needed tanks guns, airplanes, rifles, food. He needed relief, and he needed it soon. "I beg you most earnestly to understand my position at this moment," cabled Stalin to Roosevelt. "Our armies are carrying on the struggle against the main forces of Hitler with the utmost strain, and then Hitler not only does not withdraw a single division from our front but on the contrary has already succeeded in transporting, and continues to transport, fresh divisions to Soviet-German front."[1]

The Allies sent airplanes, tanks, rifles, ammunition, and other war materiel but not the requested second front. Rather, Roosevelt was mired in realities. Two years earlier, the president had spoken to the nation about the Nazis and prepared the United States for the invasion to come. "These powerful and resourceful gangsters have banded together [against] the whole human race," said Roosevelt of the Hitler's Germany, but then his momentum stalled.[2] Ships destined for the Soviet Union were being sunk by German U-boats faster than they could be replaced, and the shipyards were desperately backlogged. Neither the men nor the war machines necessary for the invasion could be accumulated in Great Britain in numbers sufficient to open the second front. Churchill had traveled several times to Moscow to meet with Stalin but what could Stalin expect? "The losses we suffer at sea are very heavy, and they hamper us and delay our operations, they prevent us from coming into action at our full strength," explained Winston Churchill to an impatient Stalin. Stalin shot back, critical of the Allies, suggesting they were afraid to fight.[3] "I must tell you that the point here is not just disappointment of the Soviet Government, but the preservation of its confidence in its Allies, a confidence that is being subjected to severe stress," said Stalin.[4] And so he waited, the delays continually fraying the Allied partnership with the Russians. "If this operation does not take place it will provoke a bad feeling of being isolated," Stalin said in November, speaking of the often delayed allied dates for D-Day. The bloodshed had to be shared, and it had to be shared soon.[5] Tehran, too, was Stalin's solution. But, unlike Roosevelt and Churchill, he alone had Germans on his soil.

With Roosevelt's cable confirming the meetings in Tehran, Stalin called in Lavrenti Pavlovich Beria to discuss his travel arrangements. Short, bespectacled, and thin-lipped, Beria was head of the Soviet secret police, the NKVD, and, as such, was directly responsible for Stalin's safety. Not surprisingly, at least considering his position, Beria was as trusted and as close a friend as any Stalin had, so much so that he was a weekend fixture in the gardens at his dacha in Kuntsevo just outside of Moscow. He was also one of the most feared men in Russia. As Stalin's right hand man, he had overseen the purges of the Red Army that cost tens of thousands of lives. It was Beria as well who was responsible for the growth in population of the Soviet gulags, which were now swollen with millions of political outcasts and for the liquidation of countless "minorities" in Russia. Valentin Berezhkov, one of Stalin's translators, remembered Beria as the sort of man who worried even his closest asso- ciates. "I felt uncomfortable in Beria's presence," said Berezhkov. "I knew that at any moment he could hint to Stalin that 'I knew too much.'"[6]

Stalin outlined the trip to Tehran. He told Beria he intended to take with him Vyacheslav Molotov, his Foreign Minister and a mem- ber of the Politburo, and Kliment Voroshilov, the Minister of Defense, also a member of the Politburo, as well as his personal physician, his translator, and twelve bodyguards made up of loyalists from his home region in Georgia. It made the most sense to travel by rail from Moscow to Baku; the skies were still unsafe at best, and Stalin did not wish to fly in any event so he decided to use his private train that weighed some eighty tons, half of the weight given over to the thick steel plating and armored glass. The train would take him 1,300 miles to Baku in Azerbaijan, the point closest to Iran. That trip would take a day and a half under the best of conditions. Stalin would then fly from Baku over the Caspian Sea nestled inside a formation of twenty-seven Soviet fighters and four Russian IL-47 bombers. He would land at the Russian Gale Morghe airbase in Tehran and, from there, go to the Russian Embassy compound in the old city.

Because of the war, Beria decided that he would put three extra cars in front of Stalin's train and two in the rear, all loaded with armed NKVD soldiers. He decided to line the tracks with his soldiers the entire way, six NKVD officers per kilometer in Russian territory, ten per kilometer in Azerbaijan.[7] One company of soldiers would secure the air terminal at Baku and another at the airbase in Tehran.

The Soviet embassy, once the property of a wealthy Persian mag- nate, was both ornate and collegiate. Inside the steel gates were several small residences all interconnected by handsome sidewalks lined with lawns, shrubs, and trees. The largest residence was the official home of the Russian ambassador, while in the front stood the imposing embassy building itself, with handsome columns and broad steps leading up to its entrance.

These all would be secured. Molotov and Voroshilov would be assigned the Ambassador's residences while Stalin would be given a private residence. Beria said he would check all of the buildings for booby-traps, as well as all of the plumbing and electrical connections. Because the American Legation was some miles away and far less secure, they decided to invite the president to share the more spacious residences inside their own grounds. Beria smiled. Yes, that was a good idea, he said, and to make it even better he would place bugs inside all the rooms.[8]

Stalin nodded his approval.

But Roosevelt would decline . . . At first.

CHAPTER 6: THE JOINT CHIEFS OF STAFF

The USS *Iowa* plowed through the seas, her boilers running at full speed ahead. It was Saturday, November 13th, the first full day of their crossing. They were now two hundred miles out into the Atlantic Ocean, slow for a plane, fast for a battleship. Three destroyers flanked the great battleship with depth charges ready, and two aircraft carriers held positions to the north and south. Although there had been no signs of German U-boats, the *Iowa* was nonetheless at one-third battle stations and zigzagging at 23 knots, running blacked-out and radio silent.

No formal meetings were scheduled for today, in part because the president rarely worked on weekends, and in part because of the weather. For a few hours the *Iowa* pitched and rolled through stormy waves in explosions of white off her bow so forceful that inside the wardroom the occasional plate and chair flew about. "For a while it was necessary to keep all hands off the top side," said Rigdon, but the engines gave off a reassuringly steady hum, and the long, slow creaking sound that echoed through the hull slowly abated as the weather passed.[1]

Inside the various compartments of the ship, the war planners were at work organizing their files and unpacking their crates. The Joint Chiefs brought with them some forty senior officers from their Washington staff. They carried sensitive war information with them. They set up easel boards in their briefing rooms where they would hash out answers down to the infinite what-if questions the president or the chiefs would surely throw their way during the voyage to Oran. These responsibilities were in addition to their regular tasks on shore, so the ship's commissary kept busy supplying fresh cups of coffee and packs of cigarettes.

In truth, Roosevelt was going to Tehran without the passions of Churchill or the impatience of Stalin. In fact, he was not sure what positions he would take with the British, or what he wanted from Tehran, but he regarded the days ahead with the confidence of a pilot regarding an airplane he was about to fly. "There is, in this global war, literally no question, either militarily or politically, in which the United States is not interested," he had said on several occasions, and this trip was no exception. For the political questions, which had much to do with the post-war landscape of the Europe, Roosevelt held his own counsel, but for military matters he relied on his Joint Chiefs of Staff, the retired Admiral William Leahy, Army General George Marshall, Navy Admiral Ernest King and Army Air Forces General Hap Arnold.[2] The Joint Chiefs of Staff were entirely Roosevelt's doing, and they ran the war without any act of Congress or any presidential directive or even the shortest executive order—they were simply willed into existence by Roosevelt who had such authority under the U.S. Constitution. "The Founding Fathers," explained Harry Hopkins, Roosevelt's close friend and political advisor, "gave the President the supreme authority as Commander in Chief in peacetime as well as war."[3] The absence of any official charter helped keep the war moving without any second guessing from Congress. It was not popular with the press, this undeclared, unsupervised, unelected war cabinet of his, but it worked well. "If our functions were put down in writing in the form of a charter, there would arise, in all certainty, questions as to what the Joint Chiefs could or could not do," said Marshall.[4] What they intended to do was win the war.

The Tehran meetings would involve considerable military negotiation and none of it would be pleasant. The British wanted to delay D-Day, but the American military chiefs were impatient to launch it, to win the war in Europe, and move to the Pacific and beat the Japanese. The British plans had considerable merit, but they would extend the war. "We had to go ahead brutally fast in Europe," said Marshall. "We could not indulge in a Seven Years' War. A king can perhaps do that, but you cannot have such a protracted struggle in a democracy in the face of mounting casualties."[5] In other words, said one of the American military planners of the job ahead in Tehran, "The time has now arrived when further indecision, evasion, and undermining of agreements cannot be borne.

In plain American words, the talking stage is over and the time has arrived to 'fish or cut bait.'"[6]

By far the most commanding presence of the four men on the American Joint Chiefs of Staff belonged to United States Army Chief of Staff General George Catlett Marshall. Tall, with drooping eyelids and a shy smile, Marshall had a presence, a bearing to him that exuded confidence and trust and transcended ordinary accolades. "His figure conveyed intensity, which his voice—low, staccato, and incisive—reinforced. It compelled respect. It spread a sense of authority and calm," wrote Dean Acheson, Secretary of State under Harry Truman.[7] After first meeting George Marshall, Prime Minister Churchill leaned over to his personal physician Lord Moran and said, "I have met the noblest Roman of them all."[8] Years later President Harry Truman, evidently agreeing with this assessment of Marshall, who by now was his own Secretary of State, put it this way: "The more I see him and the more I talk to him, the more certain I am he's the great one of the age."[9]

Marshall, 63, was born in 1880 in Uniontown, Pennsylvania, of a prosperous family with a long military tradition. He attended the Virginia Military Institute from which he graduated in 1901, just in time to be commissioned into the United States Army and posted to the Philippines at the tail end of the Philippine-American War. He arrived as a green infantry platoon leader with impeccable credentials but stepped into a witch's brew of barbaric hostilities triggered by a murderous attack on a group of U.S. soldiers, butchered with long knives while walking down a remote village road. To retaliate, a group of American soldiers broke into a local cathedral, stole the silver from the chancellery, and torched the building. The soldiers threw on the priest's robes and danced around the burning church, waving the silver chalices and crosses.

Marshall was justifiably outraged by the behavior and thought the soldiers should be arrested and court martialed, but he was not for a moment surprised by the savagery nor did it offend him. His superior officer, Captain Walter Krueger, recalled a conversation with Marshall at the time: "He said to me, 'Once an army is involved in war, there is a beast in every fighting man which begins tugging at its chains, and a good officer must learn early on how to keep the beast under control, both in his men and in himself. It was a remarkable statement to come from such a youngster." Krueger quickly added that Marshall was not priggish or off-putting—he drank and laughed and was well liked by the men. "But somehow you got the feeling that he'd been though things we hadn't even experienced, not even those of us who had fought in the jungle. He had a sagacity and thoughtfulness far beyond his years."[10]

This soundness and discernment only grew with the years. During World War I, Marshall was one of the first soldiers to land in Europe and was involved in the details required to prepare the arriving troops for combat on the continent. His men worked feverishly, but it was impossible to keep up and his company was overwhelmed. During one inspection tour by General John "Black Jack" Pershing, the Chief of Staff of the United States Army, George Marshall's superior officer came under fire for his unit's utterly poor performance. Marshall thought Pershing had picked on the wrong man and said so. There was hushed silence. Pershing turned and impatiently barked, "You must appreciate the troubles we have."

"Yes, General," said Marshall, "but we have them every day, and they must be solved by night."[11] Pershing was astonished by the clarity of that statement and looked at the young officer out of the corner of his eye. He soon added Marshall to his own staff, which proved an excellent decision indeed. "The troops which maneuvered under his plans always won," wrote one of Pershing's World War I generals about the young Marshall, which was high praise indeed.[12]

All the more surprising, then, that Marshall would fall out of favor with anyone, least of all another member of the Joint Chiefs of Staff, in this case his counterpart from the United States Navy, Admiral Ernest J. King. "I had trouble with King because he was always sore at everybody," said Marshall. "He was perpetually mean."[13] At one point it looked as if they were at an impasse, so Marshall took it upon himself to walk down to King's office to ask that they try harder to work together. With a war starting, they could not afford to be seen fighting in public, said Marshall. "We just have to find a way to get along." King considered that for a moment then looked at Marshall square in the eye. "You have been very magnanimous in coming over here the way you have," he said. "We will have a go at seeing if we can't get along. And I think we can."[14] Historian Arthur Bryant wrote about these two outsized personalities and the balance they found. King was "tough and stubborn ... the old crustacean, as one of his countrymen called him—the ablest strategist on American Chiefs of Staff, though overshadowed in statesmanship and grandeur of character by the great Virginian, Marshall."[15]

On September 1, 1939, Roosevelt made George Marshall the Chief of Staff for the United States Army. That same day, Hitler invaded Poland, setting in motion World War II.

*

Whereas Marshall and King were often at odds, Marshall and Hap Arnold were the closest of friends. Tall, handsome, and blessed with eyes that crinkled into a radiant smile when he laughed, Arnold A "Hap" Arnold, Commanding General of the United States Army Air Forces, was the fourth member of the American Joint Chiefs of Staff, a tenacious, high-spirited man who confounded his critics, impressed his friends, and somehow managed to survive his own stubborn streak. Said British Air Marshall Sir John Slessor, "He was an intensely likeable person was Hap Arnold, transparently honest, terrifically energetic, given to unorthodox methods...always with something of a schoolboy naiveté to him."[16]

Perhaps, but at his core he was a military commander determined to build a war-winning air force and was no schoolboy in the ways of the world. Hap was a cradle aviator, someone who had flown since nearly birth, one of the earliest military flyers in America and the second pilot trained and certified by the Wright brothers themselves. Like Marshall, he too was from Pennsylvania, born in 1886 into a well-respected family. He graduated from West Point where he achieved little distinction (but many accolades for his pranks) and was sent to the Philippines in 1907 where he entered active service in the United States Army. There he met Lieutenant George Marshall, six years his senior, who, with the uprising now over, directed the mapping and surveying of the islands. Both men took to each other, both were industrious, and both would gravitate towards the other in their off hours. In time, though, Arnold would split off from the traditional Army and migrate to the new Air Corps where he won his wings and where his life would become a living chronology of the many milestones of early military aviation. Arnold was a young aviator in the military at the same time that Billy Mitchell famously used an airplane to bomb a ship at sea. He was there for the first aerial refueling between two planes, the first flight by an airplane on instrument navigation alone, the first flight by an airplane that flew more than 200 into the open oceans, and for the countless speed and distance records set by aviators in the four decades after Orville and Wilbur lifted off the ground at Kitty Hawk, N.C. Arnold saw it all, or flew the record setting missions himself, such was the span of his career during those years of early flight. "More than anyone I have ever known or read about," Hap once said of his life, "the Wright Brothers gave me a sense that nothing is impossible."[17] When the Army Air Corps was charged with flying the mail for the U.S. Postal Service, Arnold was one of the most determined pilots and braved one of the worst winters on record to get the mail through. Edmund William Starling, chief of the White House Secret Service Detail under President Calvin Coolidge, met Arnold when he was a junior officer and saw a comer if ever there was one. "I had met him first when, as a lieutenant, he had flown the mail to President Coolidge in the summer of 1927 when we were in the Black Hills, [South Dakota]," wrote Starling of Hap Arnold. "His smile, his friendliness, his lack of temperament, and the fact that he was always on time no matter what weather prevailed, had impressed all of us. We put him down as a young man that would go far, and he did."[18]

As he moved through the ranks, Arnold was drawn to the puzzling mathematical calculations of aeronautical engineering that to others seemed to be a foreign language. To him, however, they were second nature. He brought in the physicist Theodore von Karman for advice. Von Karman was full of ideas about aerodynamics and airflow over wings, ideas that translated into bigger bombers and faster fighter planes. In the end, though, Arnold asked him just one question: what would make a meaningful difference in the development of a superior combat aircraft—nothing trivial, mind you, Arnold insisted, something big, something major. Von Karman did not hesitate. "Build me a wind tunnel," he said, and Arnold did just that. He installed von Karman in the Pentagon, which took his friend George Marshall by surprise. "What on earth are you doing with people like that?" asked Marshall. Answered Arnold, "Using their brains."[19]

Hap and George Marshall remained the truest of friends. They paid close attention to each other's careers, and when they were in Washington together they often spent their Saturdays going on walks or to the local football games. Hap was the sort of buddy who would come over and help paint a garage, though not always artfully. To the delight of George and Katherine Marshall he did just that one weekend at their home in Leesburg, Virginia. He had arrived one Saturday afternoon, and, without saying much, he grabbed a bucket of paint, climbed a ladder, and painted. Katherine was appalled by how much paint he got on himself, but Marshall just smiled and scarcely said a thing. "They were simply two senior officers who had known each other for thirty years with mutual friendship," remembered a fellow officer. "Marshall never pulled rank. Arnold was free to announce his plans or intentions. I never heard him asking Marshall's permission."[20]

For all of Arnold's many talents, he had a tendency to say the wrong thing at the wrong time, however right he was, and in 1939 he naively crossed Roosevelt by taking a public stand against one of his military policies. A frost immediately descended on their relationship, which lasted almost a year. Although Arnold never knew how he righted his ship, he finally acquitted himself and was readmitted to the president's inner circle. The rapprochement came about a few weeks before Christmas in 1940. Hap had been invited over to the White House for cocktails and arrived a bit early, or so he presumed. As it turned out, it was just FDRs way of doing things informally and intimately. There Roosevelt waited, in coat and tie, beaming, a cocktail mixer in his hands for just the two of them. "Good evening, Hap," said FDR grinning expansively. "How about my mixing you an Old Fashioned?"

"I will enjoy this one with you tremendously," said Arnold, and there it all ended.[21]

Hap was up at his regular hour, had his coffee, and later, when the weather improved, threw on his great coat and went outside on the weather decks to walk back towards the stern of the battleship. He had a lot on his mind. For one, his air war commanders in England were not doing well against the Germans, whereas his air war commanders in North Africa had handily defeated the Germans. He liked his air war commanders tremendously, but one was a tiger and the other was an intellectual and he needed a tiger in England, not an intellectual. Thus, in addition to everything else on his plate, he knew he had to reorganize the air war in Europe against Germany and to brief the Joint Chiefs on his plans.

Arnold hunched a shoulder into the wind and walked past the three-barreled aft turret. The sailors on the *Iowa's* decks could not help but notice his rank and snapped to attention as he passed. "Walked on the big, main deck from bow to stern," he later wrote in his diary. "Never saw so many sailors and so much saluting in my life."[22]

Arnold turned around and walked back amidships, the wind-whipped Atlantic streaming past him, an invigorating breeze in his face. The time at sea would do him good, he thought; he could get this situation resolved. He looked up. The superstructure towered over him, the radar dishes spinning against the clouds, a thick black plume of smoke rushing from the smokestacks. He turned towards a hatch to go inside. "It is a big ship," wrote Arnold after his walk, a very big ship.[23]

At 6 P.M. Arnold, Marshall, and King had dinner in the officers' wardroom while the president ate in his cabin with his guests, Leahy and Hopkins. Afterwards, they all joined the president and watched *The Phantom of the Opera*, a new movie from Universal Pictures. As the lights came up, they said good night and walked through the passageways back to their own quarters. Valet Prettyman came in and dressed Roosevelt for bed as his doctor arrived to massage his crippled legs with rubbing alcohol.

George Marshall retired to his compartment and picked up a book, relishing this rare opportunity to have some quiet time. "I wanted to sit down and put on a flying coat and put on sneakers and put on what do you call—moccasins, loafers—and sit down in one chair with my feet on the other, and probably read the *Saturday Evening Post* or some such books as that," he said.[24] Rather, though, he read the speeches of William Pitt the Elder.

Marshall propped the book on his chest and lay down to read until he, like the others, was fast asleep.[25]

CHAPTER 7: TORPEDO

Sunday dawned gloriously warm, a sharp contrast to the day before, a bright sunny sky with velvety smooth seas. The president's friends called it "Roosevelt weather", a good day to go outside. Prettyman dressed the president in his duck trousers, a work shirt, and his fishing hat, and lifted Roosevelt into his wheelchair to go out onto the promenade deck. He chose a space behind the No.2 turret as a suitable nook that was sunny but sheltered from the wind. "Thank you, Arthur," said the president, then he lit a cigarette. The ocean was a deep, glorious blue—blue water operations, as the Navy called it, deep waters under the keel—while across the surface the reflections of sunlight sparkled to the horizon. Roosevelt spent his morning enjoying the weather, reading, and meeting, returning to his cabin only for lunch.

There were two official activities today, a meeting of the Joint Chiefs in the afternoon to discuss leftover business from Washington and a fire-power demonstration for the president scheduled just after lunch. The firepower demonstration was designed to simulate an air attack on the *Iowa*, which would be repulsed using the *Iowa's* considerable antiaircraft firepower and numerous deck guns. Smoke shells and balloons would be used as targets, and the three destroyer escorts would stimulate the procedures to hunt down and kill a German U- boat.

Several diaries record the incident, but on the key facts there are minor discrepancies. The *Iowa* was just off the island of Bermuda at the time of the demonstration. Hopkins and three aids lunched with Roosevelt until 1:30 P.M. As they finished, Roosevelt beckoned to Prettyman who pulled him back from the table and wheeled him outside to the starboard rail.[1] At 2:00 P.M., General Quarters sounded, and the *Iowa* turned into a beehive of activity as sailors scrambled over the decks and into their gun tubs. The targets were balloons filled with helium and sent aloft. Once they were ready to go, the demonstration was on.

"Three balloons were released—tied together—and the batteries of forties and twenties let loose when the balloons reached a proper height and distance from the ship," wrote Hopkins. The guns fired their projectiles upward in a curtain of laser-straight trajectories and hit the balloons. Next, the big five-inch guns came to life and barked their smoke shells high into the sky. Inside the adjoining mounts, the gunners elevated their barrels and trained their sights on the balls of smoke. They fired, too. All over the *Iowa* shells arced upward from every inch of the ship. "It seemed pretty good to me altho the five-inch guns made a whale of a racket in spite of the cotton balls which all of us put in our ears," wrote Hopkins in his diary.[2] One balloon somehow escaped the outpouring of lead and fell away towards the destroyers. One of the escorts—the USS *William D. Porter*—picked it off.[3]

There was a pause as the first phase was completed and the ship took a breather. "Wheel me to the other side, Arthur," said Roosevelt. Roosevelt said he was enjoying the demonstration immensely and wanted to go across the deck to see the action from the other side, the port side. Prettyman pushed his wheelchair towards the port rail again using the gap behind the No.2 turret. As he did, the guns started up again, but around him the sailors were suddenly alarmed about something and they were not pointing towards the sky. "We had just moved to the port side to see the five-inch guns fired a second time," said Hopkins. "Suddenly an officer from the bridge two decks above leaned over and yelled 'It's the real thing! It's the real thing!'" In one of those moments of terribly bad timing, the real thing was in fact a live torpedo headed directly toward the *Iowa*.

"All hell broke loose," remembered Bill Lee, a sailor who was on deck. A flurry of excited voices started yelling out commands, but FDR hardly moved a muscle. For some reason he did not comprehend what was going on. "The President doesn't hear very well," explained Hopkins, "and, with his ears stuffed with cotton he had a hard time getting the officers' words which I repeated to him several times before he understood.

I asked him whether he wanted to go inside—he said 'No—where is it?'"[4]

Hopkins pointed to the right. Etched across the surface of the ocean was the white, bubbling trail of a torpedo coming directly at them, and it all began to register. "Arthur! Arthur!" said an excited Roosevelt. "Take me over to the starboard rail. I want to watch the torpedo."[5] Prettyman hurried the president across the deck and as they did the loudspeakers came to life. It was Angelo Zangozi, the telephone talker amidships for the 20mm, 40mm and 5' guns. He too had spotted the wake and was using his phone to repeat, "This is not a drill! This is not a drill!"[6]

The first batch of news to reach the bridge was somewhat confusing. One of the American destroyers managed to get a message through and confirmed that the torpedo was one of ours, not the Germans'. McCrea was somewhat relieved of course but he was overloaded with information and still had a torpedo bearing down on him. "I rang up full speed and started to swing away to run away from the torpedo, because the torpedo would be making about 45 knots or thereabouts, and I figured that—I didn't know where it was coming from—and I thought I could run away from it."[7]

"The crew began racing to emergency stations," wrote Gregory Freeman, a sailor on board. "Those on deck soon saw the incoming torpedo as the ship leaned heavily to the left in a desperate maneuver. The list was so pronounced that Roosevelt's bodyguards had to steady his wheelchair. One of the guards even reached for his pistol with the intent of shooting the torpedo as it came closer." The Secret Service agents were now moving swiftly doing what they do best. They moved Prettyman aside, surrounded the president to shield him with their bodies, then started running him towards the elevator to take him up to the battle control station where the ship's armor was 17-inches thick. He was safer there than anywhere on the ship.[8]

Then, as one, the guns on the *Iowa* were trained down towards the ocean and starting blasting at the torpedo.

"Just as I got to the starboard side, everything fired at once at the wake of the torpedo," said Hopkins."[9]

On the bridge, Admiral King stepped up and stood behind Captain McCrea.[10] McCrea gave the admiral a running update on what was happening when suddenly there was a thundering blast that shook the entire ship. "We were just nicely in the middle of this turn, when there was this big explosion," remembered McCrea. "I said to Tom Casey, my executive, 'Tom, do you suppose we've been hit?' And he said, 'No, I don't think so, Captain. If we had been hit, I think the reaction would have been much heavier than what we experienced.' This torpedo exploded in the turbulence of our wake, that's what kicked the torpedo off."[11]

But that was hardly the end of it. Fearing a Nazi crew had taken over the *Porter,* the destroyer that accidentally fired the torpedo, McCrea ordered his gunners to train their weapons on the small ship until they proved otherwise. Over on that destroyer, however, the situation was dreadfully apparent as were the potential consequences; there was a long silence on the bridge. A seaman who saw the torpedo hit the water turned to the captain and timidly asked, "Did you give permission to fire a torpedo, sir?" The ash-white captain shook his head, but by now it did not matter: He knew, as did every man around him, that his career was over.[12]

Back on the *Iowa,* the Secret Service was now in damage control. Most of the *Iowa's* topside crew were called down to face the agents, Zangozi among them. "This never happened," the agents said to him and then abruptly dismissed him. These same orders were given to the ship's crew and for fifteen years, the incident remained secret.[13]

*

It took a while to settle things down after the torpedo incident, but in an hour or so order was restored and the ship returned to its everyday rhythm. It had been a terrible mistake—potentially a lethal one—but it was over, and it was business as usual. The Joint Chiefs gathered up their binders and papers and made their way through the passageways up to the flag plot to discuss the agenda for tomorrow's conference with FDR. Admiral Leahy, the chairman, called the meeting to order.

In the 1920s, when Roosevelt was the Assistant Secretary of the Navy, his favorite naval ship had been the *Dolphin,* which at the time was captained by a young Lieutenant named Bill Leahy. During his trips on the *Dolphin,* Roosevelt and Leahy stood at the bridge for hours, lost in their conversations about the sea and about naval history. Leahy progressed through numerous commands as he moved up through the ranks of the navy until he was appointed Chief of Naval Operations, the pinnacle of a naval career. In this position, and convinced of an impending war, he fought for appropriations and upgraded the navy's fleet to the extent his funding would allow, and for that noble effort he felt the warmth of FDRs approval. Tall, with penetrating eyes and a receding hairline, Fleet Admiral William D. Leahy retired in 1939 at the age of 64, but continued to serve the president by accepting his appointment to be the governor of Puerto Rico and, later, as ambassador to Vichy France. However, with the war spreading, FDR recalled Leahy and asked him to serve as the senior member of the American Joint Chief of Staff. It was an exceptionally good idea. "Leahy was the one that could bring this group together," said Captain Robert L. Dennison, a staff officer with the JCS. "He didn't really use any pressure, but his technique was most interesting...Marshall, for example would start discussing some plan of his, something he thought we ought to be doing next and Leahy would say: 'Well George, I'm just a simple sailor. Would you please back up and start from the beginning and make it simple, just say step one, step two, and three and so on.'"[14]

The first item on Leahy's agenda was Hap Arnold's plan to reorganize the bombing against Germany. This plan had been in the works for several weeks with preliminary versions discussed, so it was a continuation of unfinished business from ashore. Arnold reminded Leahy that the air war was the only combat against the Germans on the European continent, and it was not going well. The Eighth Air Force had been in England since 1942 and had been flying missions for more than a year, but their missions tended to be small ones with no more than a few hundred bombers in each raid. The priority was to destroy the German aircraft factories to cut the flow of new planes to the front, and their ball bearing plants to halt engine production. But after a year of attacks with thousands of bombers, German fighter production had actually increased. Worse, the bomber formations were being mauled. During the month of October 1943, said Arnold, his losses were as high as 30 percent. No combat force could long survive such attrition, thus he had halted all deep penetration missions just before he left for Tehran.

Against that bad news there was some good news, said Arnold. American fighter planes were being fitted with external fuel tanks, which would extend their range and allow them to escort the bombers all the way to Berlin and back. This would certainly cut down on the losses. In addition, hundreds of new crews and bombers were flowing into England, which meant they could mount larger raids with five or six hundred bombers per target. But, said Arnold, the problem was not simply additional bombers, tanks, or people, but rather leadership. If he was going to gain air superiority for D-Day, he needed fresh blood, he needed imagination, he needed tigers in command

Arnold passed out his proposal. First, the people. His commanders in England were not nearly as innovative as they should be, so he proposed replacing the top general there with General James D. "Jimmy" Doolittle of the Tokyo Raiders fame and, more recently—and more importantly— of the successful North African campaign. Next, he proposed to create a new American bomber command called the United States Strategic Air Forces Europe under which he would place the Eighth Air Force in England and the Fifteenth Air Force in Italy. He proposed naming General Carl A. "Tooey" Spaatz, also tested in North Africa, as the commanding general of this new entity and transferring him up from North

Africa to England. Both Doolittle and Spaatz were battle hardened, proven leaders of complex air wings, and each echoed Arnold's feelings about the need for persistent and unrelenting bombing. "Air power means the employment of airplanes in numbers large enough to secure complete destruction," said Arnold of this doctrinal approach, and that goal, he now argued, would be best accomplished by combining these two air arms into one.[15]

The Joint Chiefs nodded in agreement. They liked both Doolittle and Spaatz, each of whom had exemplary combat records, each of whom was known to be bold in their use of new air tactics, and each of whom was thoroughly experienced in the complexities of running air wings in war. They also liked the plan to consolidate the two American air forces into one overall group. Missions could be better coordinated, resources more evenly shared.

Arnold smiled and continued. There was one final piece to the puzzle, he said. The British RAF believed in nighttime bombing of German cities while Americans believed in daylight bombing of German factories and airfields. To some extent there was an overlap in the areas targeted and thus a degree of duplication but also a degree of mutual support. Some "cities" were, after all, largely factory towns and thus were targets for both forces. To wit, the Americans often bombed a target by day that the British had hit the night before, and vice versa, but it was disjointed and generally uncoordinated. The way to beat the Luftwaffe, said Arnold, was to take an even bolder step—to fold all of the British and American bomber forces under one overall commander and let them mount massive raids that could deliver knock-out blows in one strike. By way of an example, a decisive blow against the sprawling Messerschmitt complex in Regensburg, Germany, would probably take 2,000 bombers but the best Arnold had been able to muster was a 400-bomber mission, which meant the damage they did could be quickly repaired by the Germans. With the British and American air forces folded under one commander, multiple 1000-bomber raids might be flown in a matter of days, assuring a massive, fatal blow against a plant like Regensburg. No country could long withstand such attacks.

That was the ideal situation, said Arnold, but he had his doubts that it could ever happen. For one, he was all but certain that the British would never allow the Royal Air Force to operate inside a joint British-United States command. In that case, he said, he intended to create his new United States Strategic Air Forces Europe. At the least, this alone would fold two-thirds of the available bombers in Europe under one coordinated command.

Arnold turned it over to Leahy. The Joint Chiefs very much liked the plan but they agreed with Arnold's assessment that the British would never go for it.[16] The RAF transcended a mere air arm, it went to the heart and soul of what it meant to be British, and it was as nearly revered as the Crown itself. The RAF was the RAF and they had to accept that.

Arnold smiled in agreement. He knew as much.

But Arnold's other plan made complete sense, and, because it involved his own air wings, it did not require British approval. They agreed to go ahead and formally recommend the latter arrangement to the president and, if Roosevelt approved, to the Combined Chiefs. King did have one question. He agreed with the importance of a unified American air command, but it created complications with the navy's lines of command as naval aircraft were also operating in Europe, albeit from aircraft carriers in the Atlantic. Based on what he had just heard, it sounded as if those naval aircraft would fall under the new U.S. Strategic Air Forces. King said that he did not think it should be done that way and that the navy had its own air power needs, which should be excluded. "This question of air command was always snarled up because of the fact that you had all these air fellows on carriers," explained Marshall, but Arnold said he had no objection to carving out King's aircraft carriers and allowing naval flight operations to stand apart from his strategic command. King seemed satisfied with that, and the Joint Chiefs agreed to take the plan to the president.[17]

Next, they turned to the thorny issue of the overall commanders in the European and Mediterranean theaters. This was a complicated matter for several reasons. In general, the Combined Chiefs of Staff had already agreed that the nation with the most soldiers in a given theater should name the overall commander for that theater. For political reasons, however, the invasion of North Africa had been given to the Americans and General Dwight D. Eisenhower led the invasion and commanded the victorious forces there. After North Africa, the fighting had stayed in the Mediterranean and crossed over to Italy, which was now called the Mediterranean theater. As of now, Eisenhower commanded those forces, but they were largely British.

The next major operation was D-Day, and because the majority of soldiers landing in France would be American, the overall commander in that theater would again be an American. The problem was the inevitable competition between the theaters for critical combat materiel. In practice, theater commanders were by nature loath to let go of their tanks and guns for another commander, whereas a joint theater commander would be impartial and more likely to spread his planes and tanks around based on the immediate combat needs of one over the other.

The issue was how to consolidate theaters and reduce the number of competing demands for men and materiel. The first proposal was to combine the forces remaining in North Africa with the active combat soldiers in Italy under one Supreme Allied Commander for the entire Mediterranean region. If approved, the Joint Chiefs intended to give that command to the British, which, as far as they knew, would be agreeable to the idea. This wasn't just altruism. The British and Americans sought to share commands. In Europe, the Americans intended to make the top commander an American.

The next iteration of that issue was a bit more problematic: that in truth, there should be just one overall commander for Europe *and* the Mediterranean, that is, all the theaters should be folded into one giant theater and one man should command it. The arguments for the move were sound; scarce resources would be more efficiently allocated, soldiers would be better supplied, and war plans could be seamlessly integrated. But there were numerous problems with that scenario—and of course, it went back to that general agreement that the nation with the most soldiers in a given theater would be allowed to name the commander. The majority of the soldiers in North Africa and Italy were British, while the majority of soldiers landing in France would be American. But, overall, American soldiers vastly outnumbered British soldiers, so if they held to their formula the overall command would go to an American, which the British were not likely to accept. However, the arguments for the efficiency of a consolidated command were so convincing that the Americans were willing to give up their rights to the command if necessary to make it happen.

But there was another problem, more political than military in nature. It is common knowledge that a soldier fights hardest when fighting to defend his home or his nation, and a nation finds it easier to send its sons into combat when they know their sons are led by one of their own. In other words, the plan might be smart militarily, but it would be a public relations fiasco if D-Day, which would consist predominately of American soldiers hitting the beaches, were under a British general. Leahy canvassed the three chiefs and they again nodded in agreement: the consolidation offered too many advantages not to trump PR concerns. It was their job to present the best military plans, and the military advantages were too strong not to present the idea to the president. He would likely veto it, but they voted to put it on tomorrow's agenda.

Three more minor topics were covered before they adjourned. There was a general overview of the war in Europe, an overview of the war in the Pacific, and a discussion of the post-war control of the domestic and international airways. Oddly, Tehran was not on the agenda and therefore not specifically discussed, nor was D-Day, other than the general issue of command. Satisfied that they were well prepared for the meetings with Roosevelt, the meeting came to a close.

Hopkins and Leahy joined Roosevelt in his cabin for dinner. As always, Roosevelt relished his job as host and greeted his guests by first name. "We usually had an aperitif before dinner," said Leahy. Roosevelt took great pleasure in mixing the drinks and as host was always manning the bar.[18]

As he had the evening before, FDR invited the others to come over and watch a movie. The movie that night was *Princess O'Rourke* and it was enjoyed by all.

As Sunday drew to a close, they were now 1,164 miles out in the Atlantic Ocean. The seas were soft, the night skies unspeakably beautiful. "That evening, the stars glimmered, and the Atlantic moon cast a trail of silver lamé across the sea," wrote McCrea in his diary, a sailor's night if ever there was one.[19] Arnold wrote that they were in bed by 9:30 P.M., lulled to sleep by the steady hum of the *Iowa's* enormous engines.

CHAPTER 8: STRONG POINTS

Monday dawned, a breezy day with the smell of salt water heavy in the air. There was a light chop across the face of the ocean that speckled the seas with whitecaps as far as the eye could see. As planned, fresh destroyers arrived to relieve the first escorts. The USS *Hall*, USS *Macomb*, and USS *Halligan* hove into view then stood to the *Iowa* from the south while the *Cogswell, Young,* and *William D. Porter* prepared to head back to port. On the horizon was an escort carrier, and in the air were navy fighter pilots covering the maneuver. "We all said, 'Oh my God. They have got half the Navy out there," remembered General Thomas Handy, Chief of the Operations Division of the War Department and Marshall's number two. "We had a bunch of these escort carriers...we had destroyers all around us... we had a whole screen around us."[1]

And it was good thing that they did. Admiral King's intelligence staff estimated that there were 429 German submarines of all types in operation at some level of capability, of which 166 were in the Atlantic Ocean, most along the southern convoy route over which the *Iowa* was now sailing. The U-boat menace had lessened in recent months but not gone away. In fact, much of the activity had shifted towards the very passage they would soon transit. Days before, the German submarines U-732 and U-340 had attempted to sneak through the Strait of Gibraltar to the safety of the German naval bases in Marseille and Toulon, France, on the Mediterranean, but they were picked up by the anti-submarine patrols and sunk. Then on November 10th, the U-966, also headed towards the Strait, was picked up along the Spanish coast and sunk, as were U-134, and U-535, neither of the latter lasting long enough to send even the shortest of SOS signals.[2] Additionally, two of the twelve oversized German refueling U-boats were at large, and their positions were unknown.[3] "The danger of submarine attack was ever present, particularly during the last half of our voyage, and the danger increased as we neared Oran," said Leahy, and the lookouts were told to be sharp.[4]

*

The first formal meeting of the Joint Chiefs of Staff started at 9:30 A.M. Monday morning, at sea, in the ship's flag plot. Leahy, Marshall, King, Arnold, Handy, and the senior members of the planning staff arrived with their binders and steaming cups of coffee. Altogether, there were sixty-three generals and admirals on the *Iowa,* which included eleven war planners from the U.S. Army Operations Division who ran the bulk of the war, eight Army officers and five Navy officers who specialized solely in logistics, five Army officers and two Navy officers who were the nation's highest ranking specialists on the nuances of combat in their theaters of expertise, plus twenty-five admirals and generals from a specialized group that handled the integration and coordination of war plans between the Army, Air Force, Navy, and Marines, the "Joint" staff generals.[5] Taken together this group knew every secret about every combat capability and every weapon the United States had. They could tell Marshall, Arnold, King, or the president where any soldier was on any given day and where he was supposed to be next. They could not fall into enemy hands.[6]

The senior Army Operations officer was Tom Handy. Tall and with a furrowed brow, General Thomas Handy, 51, had combat experience in World War I and, like Marshall, was a graduate of the Virginia Military Institute. As Chief of the Operations Division of the War Department, Handy directed the groups that put together detailed combat plans that often ran several hundreds of pages in length. Under him were the battlefield experts, the air staff experts, and the naval experts. It fell to this group to break down a general concept into the minute details that could be handed down to a division commander and then to a company commander and then to a group and a squadron—all the way down until every soldier knew where they were supposed to be and what they were supposed to be doing. When he boarded the *Iowa,* Handy carried under his arm a heavy briefing book that never left his side. It was called the "Condensed Information Book", the top secret, statistics-laden compilation of the summaries of the war situation in each of the theaters with the latest and most recently revised plans for subsequent actions, including existing troop dispositions and pending troop movements. It contained in exacting detail every battle plan that was being formulated.

Leahy welcomed the group to the meeting and handed out the agenda. The first item was a carryover from Washington, a review of the latest war plans to defeat the Japanese. This was of utmost importance. The president assured the American people that he would defeat Hitler first, then take care of Japan, but the popular sentiment was to engage and beat the Japanese right now. Roosevelt placated the American's by sending soldiers and marines to fight the Japanese in the Central Pacific, while the Chinese Nationalists battled them in China and Burma. But all of this was a holding action until Germany fell. The next step had to be decisive and speedy. Roosevelt wanted a war plan for the Pacific that would deal the Japanese a fatal blow, and do it quickly.

Over the last several months General Handy's group had worked on several master plans to defeat Japan, but none had met the critical requirement set by the Joint Chiefs that the war in the Pacific be won within twelve months of the end of the war with Germany.[7] Today, they had a new approach. Leahy asked Handy to start the meeting. Handy rose, unfolded some maps, and laid them out for the chiefs to review. The new plan was a pincer strategy. One attacking force of Allied soldiers would continue island-hopping up through the Central Pacific to the Marianas where they would jump off to Japan itself, while a second force would come down from Alaska via the Aleutians to Hokkaido. From Hokkaido, which was Japan's second largest land mass and its northernmost prefecture, this second force would fight its way down to Tokyo and join up with the first to take the city in the final thrust. The pincer strategy was important because combat in one area would prevent the Japanese from sending reinforcements to the other area, thus diluting the Japanese strength and achieving victory in the twelve months.

It fell flat. "Army planners … concluded that the best possibility for ending the war against Japan in 1945 lay in the invasion of Hokkaido in early 1945," said Marshall of Handy's presentation. "To do this, they felt that the scale of operations in the Central and Southwest Pacific must continue at the same pace … while the offensive against Hokkaido was being launched."[8] But none of the chiefs liked it. There was no denying that the Aleutians represented a reasonably direct route to Japan, but the whole idea seemed to come out of left field. No previous plan had mentioned Hokkaido, much less the exceedingly difficult and dangerous prospect of moving armies across the bitterly cold and hostile waters of the Bering Strait.

They shook their heads; Handy's plan was rejected and sent back for further review.

The Joint Staff Planners presented an alternative. This plan called for Allied forces to battle across the Pacific Ocean to the island of Taiwan where they would launch an attack on southern flanks of the Japanese mainland. "If this proved futile," explained Marshall of this strategy, "an alternative operation against northern Sumatra in the late 1944 or early 1945 was better."

But it was becoming a kettle of fish with no more clarity than before. Hokkaido? Taiwan? Sumatra? Arnold spoke first. He suggested the planners consider a third strategy that relied on his new B-29 Super Fortress bomber. The B-29 would have an enormous bomb load and the range to strike any target in Japan from air bases in the Marianas— the islands of Tinian, Saipan and Guam. His planes could mount an intense aerial bombing campaign while at the same time dropping mines into the various Japanese harbors to prevent raw materials and reinforcements from coming in. The bombing would destroy Japan's military infrastructure to the point of ineffectiveness, while the mining would keep Japan from rebuilding. After a few months of intense bombing, Arnold said, Japan would have little left to repel a ground invasion and should fall quickly. Someone asked how soon the B-29s would be available, and Arnold said that they would be coming off the production lines in large numbers by mid-summer 1944.

Admiral King liked Arnold's plan but suggested a slightly different variation on the same theme. He asked the staff to consider a plan that called for the destruction of the Japanese naval fleet, which, like aerial intense bombardment, would leave the Japanese mainland defenseless against a major assault from the sea. If Arnold's bombers did not arrive in time, this plan would soften Japan much the same way that bombardment would.[9]

Marshall picked up on these ideas. If the B-29s were late, he asked, could the Navy's aircraft carriers be used as striking units against the mainland—that is, could they become miniature islands from which air attacks could be launched against Japan, rather than using the carriers just to protect the landing operations? He felt extensive damage could be done to the Japanese mainland without the sort of head-on invasion that had proven so costly on the other Pacific Islands. For instance, he said, there was no need to seize the heavily defended islet fortress of Truk if it could be starved of its oil through bombing and blockades. In a sense, if isolated by the navy and attacked by air, the Japanese mainland would be no better off than Truk.

They paused. There were still too many variables and too many unknowns, and, in war, admirals and generals did not make outsized bets on unknowns. Because the situation was so fluid, said Marshall, it might be best to accept that a hard and fast blueprint for the defeat of Japan could not yet be written. Everything would change, for instance, if the Japanese fleet could be brought into action and defeated at sea as in King's plan, but so far the Japanese fleet had proven to be too elusive. Equally, if the B-29s arrived in sufficient quantity, there was no doubt they could level most, if not all, of Japan's industrial complex. But what if there was a delay?

Marshall then suggested they consider a military strategy he called "opportunism." In the absence of any discernible preference or advantage, a flexible approach would allow the United States to exploit opportunistically any Japanese mistakes or weaknesses, such as exhausting their oil supply, or to leverage any military advantages gained through something like the arrival of the B-29. And even if they found no weakness, or if the new bombers did not arrive, the planners could hardly anticipate the unknown opportunities that might open up as the soldiers island-hopped up through the Central Pacific and retook Japanese islands. Marshall's idea was met with murmurs of approval. "I thought it was not possible in such a broad theater to plan so far in advance, when so much depended on the success of certain of the local operations," said Marshall. However, a strategy of "opportunism," or better yet, "aggressive alertness," and "flexibility" might work. Flexibility could guide operations for the immediate next few months after which the standing combat forces would be folded into any of the other invasion plans presented today.[10]

Not surprisingly, King concurred. They needed the Pacific islands anyway because war materials would be flowing out there in huge numbers, and they had to store them somewhere, so the island hopping strategy still made sense. Flexibility appealed even more because striking the Japanese was by nature an offense-oriented strategy, and it dovetailed perfectly with King's own point of view about winning wars. "No fighter ever won his fight by covering up—by merely fending off the other fellow's blows," King liked to say of good naval strategy. "The winner hits and keeps on hitting, even though he has to be able take some stiff blows in order to be able to keep on hitting."[11] Under Marshall's plan, Navy ships could roam the seas and hunt down the Imperial Japanese Navy, but, equally, they could strike when opportunities presented themselves and take more islands.[12]

A consensus was beginning to form. The advance through the Central Pacific had been relatively fast and was going much better than the land advance from India and China. Thus, the chiefs agreed that island hopping should remain the priority in the Pacific, and that all other operations should be subordinated to it. The end point would be the Marianas, which had natural harbors for King's ships and terrain flat enough to accommodate six to ten runways for Arnold's B-29s. From there, the new Super Fortresses could strike virtually any target in Japan and return safely, albeit at the very end of their fuel reserves.

As to a formal strategy for ending the war, the Joint Chiefs were still empty-handed so the Joint Planning Staff were given their instructions. The first was to develop a war plan that assumed that the B-29s would arrive in large numbers and that heavy bombing would result in the collapse of Japan, with no land invasion necessary. The second was to prepare a plan that assumed an early conclusion of the war against Germany with a subsequent rapid movement of forces from Europe to the Pacific. For this plan they were told to assume that the B-29s would not arrive in numbers to do any good, thus there would be a land invasion that would require intense ground combat with several million well-equipped American soldiers. The Joint Chiefs asked the planners to give them an "energetic" and aggressive assault to end the war and to include two variables: that the Soviets would throw their weight into the battle, and that they would not.[13]

Moving on Leahy turned his attention to Russia and shared some new information about Stalin. Days before their departure, the Joint Chiefs had received an urgent communiqué from Major General John R. Deane, the senior military attaché in the Moscow Embassy. On November 9th, Deane had talked with the Russians about the D-Day invasion, and the conversation had been rather unsettling. It seemed the Russians were not placing as much importance on Overlord as the Americans had thought, he said.[14] The combat along their Eastern Front was going better than expected, and the Russians were suggesting that if the Allies came in now, there was a long-shot chance at ending the war now. Instead, they noted, D-Day was scheduled for May of 1944, which was six months off. If the Allies opened a second front now instead of 1944, the Germans might be forced to withdraw divisions from the Eastern Front sufficient to allow for a Soviet breakthrough that might land the fatal blow.

Deane warned of a worrisome subtext to this. The Russians wanted action. The Allied combat in Italy, which had stalled south of Rome, had failed to draw off any German divisions from the Soviet front, and the Soviets were openly disappointed by that effort. They had been hoping for more vigorous combat, more decisive action, the sort of initiative a big nation like the United States could have undertaken that would have drawn off Germans from their own front lines. But it had not come to pass, and, as a result, the Germans continued to throw everything they had against the Russians. If the Russians were offered a choice and were forced to choose now, said Deane, they would probably align with the British in favor of immediate combat operations in Italy, the Balkans, and the Aegean Sea, and abandon Overlord altogether.[15] This report dovetailed with other diplomatic intelligence, all of which suggested that Stalin was losing his patience with Britain and the United States, both. Wrote Army historian Maurice Matloff regarding the gravity of the situation, "From London and Moscow, danger signals were being reported. They raised the serious question for General Marshall and his advisers of whether the Russians, like the British, were now willing to settle for opportunistic Mediterranean operations even at the cost of postponing the final crushing blow against Germany on the Continent."[16]

Leahy let the news sink in and then dismissed the group. They needed to have lunch before they met with Roosevelt.

The Joint Chiefs made their way through the passageways down to Roosevelt's cabin for their 2 P.M meeting with the president. The ship gave a steady ride only a hint of rolling or pitching, the *Iowa* plowed through the ocean and on toward Oran.

Roosevelt had a way of keeping things to himself. Just when one thought they knew his plan, the plans would change. It was one of the many ways he controlled the world around him, kept it centered, but it also reflected his improvisational style, a style that kept people off guard. It had nonetheless served him well. "Roosevelt's plans were never thoroughly thought out," said Roosevelt's Secretary of Labor Frances Perkins. "They were burgeoning plans; they were next steps; they were something to do next week or next year. One plan grew out of another. Gradually, they fitted together..."[17]

So it would be today. As his chiefs entered his cabin, Roosevelt welcomed them by name and began the meeting by announcing that they were indeed going to Tehran. It was likely that all present knew this by now, but they had not been formally told as much. As they absorbed that formal decision, the president brought them up to date. Over the last seven months a meeting with Stalin had been on and off, moving forward or stalling out based on the ebb and flow of the war on the Eastern Front. It was fair to say that Roosevelt had tried to arrange a meeting with Stalin ever since the start of the war, but to no avail. In fact, until the day before he left Washington he assumed that there would be no meeting. No longer. Happily, said Roosevelt, it was all confirmed. They would be meeting with Stalin in Tehran, and they could put their differences before the Russian leader and get his opinion. Stalin was bringing Vyacheslov Mikhailovich Molotov, the Soviet Commissar for Foreign Affairs, and Kliment Efremovich Voroshilov, Marshall of the Soviet Union and Stalin's chief military advisor, both well known to the chiefs. Roosevelt asked that a cable be sent to Averill Harriman, the U.S. Ambassador in Moscow, and have him meet the party in Cairo. He also asked that Harriman bring along Roosevelt's Russian translator, Charles F. Bohlen, the much-liked First Secretary of the Moscow Embassy. Marshall nodded and said it would be done.[18]

Roosevelt pushed his shoulders back, waved his cigarette, and beamed. There was a rustling in the cabin, people exchanging thoughts as the meeting continued.

Roosevelt turned to the first topic, the provisioning of guns to the French army. The current plan anticipated the participation of eleven French divisions after the D-Day landings, all to be armed and outfitted by the United States with U.S. rifles and ammunition. Roosevelt looked around the table: should they go ahead with this, or not? There were several subtleties to the question, and they all knew it. When France was overrun by the Germans in 1940, soldiers in the northern half of France had fought the Germans while the southern half of France, a part called "Vichy France" because the provisional government was headquartered in Vichy, had signed an armistice with Hitler. The Vichy were therefore neither allies nor, strictly speaking, enemies. During the invasion of North Africa, for instance, the Vichy soldiers had opposed the Allied landings, and, as a result, the Allies had been forced to face the French as potential adversaries. Ultimately, they dropped their arms but now what? Who would speak for France after the war?

There was one obvious person, French General Charles de Gaulle. De Gaulle had led the French forces that fought the losing battle against the Germans and was now exiled in England awaiting his return. His forces were called the Free French Army, but de Gaulle held no elected office in France, even though his ambitions were clear.

De Gaulle however was openly derisive of the Americans, which made him an immensely unpopular figure with the Joint Chiefs, and he was terrible at holding secrets, which made sharing military plans with him risky. "It was the way he demanded these things," agreed General Handy, as he shook his head. 'He *demanded* we furnish him with a capital ship to go to France in. [But] he went in a landing craft like the rest of us."[19]

Given all this, asked Roosevelt, when do we, or should we, arm the Free French soldiers? The answer from the chiefs was unanimous:

not now. De Gaulle might use the soldiers to feather his own political nest, said King. He might strut into France like a peacock at the head of a column of soldiers who had not done a thing to liberate their own country. Leahy agreed but had an even more forceful take on it. Not just vanity, he said, de Gaulle might go a step further and use the Free French Army to conquer France and put himself in power without true elections.

Roosevelt interrupted, not liking this line of reasoning. He reminded them that the Allies had agreed to equip these divisions and that the British were in favor of a powerful post-war France to help keep the Russians in check on the European continent. Marshall understood the point and suggested that they hold off answering the question until they talked it over with Eisenhower, who was on the planning staff for D-Day. "[Let's] not say anything about this matter until after we have an opportunity to talk with General Eisenhower," said Marshall. If Eisenhower had no need for the soldiers now, he could deliver the rifles after he moved his front forward, said Marshall, but if he needed them now, they could be armed immediately. "This would give General Eisenhower an easy out," said Marshall, "i.e., provide the French with equipment as *we* move out; in other words, not ship in any additional equipment for the French but transfer United States equipment as United States troops go out," or, do it now. In either scenario, Marshall said, the United States would be making good on its promise. FDR thought that made sense.[20]

Roosevelt moved on to the next subject: Combat in the Balkans. This was of course tied to the central issue behind the entire trip. The Balkans were a part of Europe just east of Italy between the Adriatic Sea and Turkey. The Balkan Peninsula paralleled the boot of Italy and consisted of Yugoslavia and Greece, Hungary and Bulgaria. The British wanted to open a new war front there, but, geographically, that front moved the combat away from Germany, not towards it. Moreover, because the terrain was mountainous and a difficult place to do battle, mechanized operations would be nearly impossible. Worse, a victory there would hardly matter in the grand scheme of the war, but it would certainly impact the timing of D-Day, perhaps fatally so, thus making a shift to that area dangerous.

The Joint Chiefs were unanimous in their opposition to combat in the Balkans. Leahy handed Roosevelt their position paper that explained their reasoning. It said that the Balkans should be not be any part of the Allied war plan except to the extent that they might covertly parachute supplies into the region for the Yugoslavian Partisans, or begin strategic bombing of German targets there. Other than that, there should be no U.S. presence in that area. "The implementation of our agreed strategy for the defeat of Germany will require all available military means," wrote the chiefs, meaning nothing was available for anything else. If a new front were opened, it would invariably suck in more resources than the Allies were prepared to expend. Minor commando operations were fine, they wrote, as was bombing by the B-17s, but that was all.[21]

Roosevelt peered over the top of his glasses and put the paper down. "Amen," he said, and exhorted his chiefs not to back down. "Stand on it," he said, and that was that.[22]

Papers were again shuffled, and the subject turned to Rome and whether to declare it an "open city". In the sense of the term as used, an open city was a designation used to create a no-combat zone, which was largely done to protect significant cultural and historical sites from war damage. If an area was declared open, combat would be halted and a demilitarized zone would be created. No military command posts could be in that zone, no military manufacturing could occur there, and local rule must be restored. But this was tricky. The Germans controlled Rome and the Allies, who were well south of Rome, would have to fight through it sooner or later. Of course, Roosevelt did not want to burn down Rome any more than Ike did, but war was war and Ike might need to attack the Germans in Rome or at the least use the rail lines through the city. Because of such possibilities, said Roosevelt, he did not want to tie Eisenhower's hands and suggested that the decision be left up to Ike.

Marshall agreed. If we announce our intentions to make it an open city, Marshall said, the Germans might use it to their advantage by stalling inside Rome then slipping out at night and declaring Rome an open city behind them, which would cut off Allied access to the rails precisely when we needed them the most. It was agreed: best to allow this matter to unfold on the battlefield before making any decision.

The topic of "strong points" and "free ports" came up next, two concepts that were of particular interest to Roosevelt. "Free port" was an umbrella term that Roosevelt used to describe essential transportation choke points vital to world trade and commerce, such as the Suez Canal and the Panama Canal. Keeping those passages open to shipping despite regional conflicts had precedent dating back to the Convention of Constantinople of 1888 that declared the Suez Canal a "neutral zone" and left it to the British to enforce it. The Panama Canal was the same way. The nation of Panama had been formed through a series of diplomatic maneuvers and treaties in the 1900s that also created an independent "Canal Zone," which was placed under the oversight of the United States.

Roosevelt viewed air routes much the same way as the Panama Canal. The air route between Dakar, French West Africa and Recife, Brazil, for instance, was the shortest air route across the Atlantic—the Panama Canal of the air. If they would go along with this, said the president, both Dakar and Recife should be designated free ports and placed under world rule, or, at the very least, under shared rule with the United States. For Recife, Roosevelt leaned towards fifty-fifty ownership with Brazil, but Dakar was a French colony and he felt France did not deserve to get any of her colonies back. There should be "outposts for the Americas on the continent," said FDR of Africa. Those outposts would be designated as free ports, starting with Dakar and extending out to cover most of the coast of West Africa. Dakar's ports, airfields, and armaments must be kept in the United Nations' hands, said FDR somewhat boldly, and Brazil's port city as well.[23]

"Strong points" were a different and rather radical concept involving the victorious nations policing the world in the aftermath of World War II. In the post-war landscape, FDR envisioned a network of military bases strategically located around the world with quick reaction police forces that could immediately quash any expansionism by a belligerent nation. Just as soon as any of the "victorious nations", the world's "policemen," as Roosevelt put it, picked up signs that another nation was growing hostile, these prepositioned forces would deploy from their strong points and intervene. This, according to Roosevelt, would prevent another Germany or Japan from rising again.

The Joint Chiefs asked where Roosevelt thought these strong points should be. FDR mentioned Morocco as one possibility, but also Cairo, Egypt, the Philippines, and Formosa, now called Taiwan.[24] Roosevelt said he would take up the matter with Churchill and Stalin during the upcoming conferences.[25]

The last topic was the selection of the Supreme Allied Commander for D-Day, and, while this was one of extreme importance, it was given surprisingly little prominence. In August of 1943, Roosevelt and Churchill had met in Quebec, Canada, for a war conference, and George Marshall's name was circulated as the front runner for the D-Day command. Leahy button-holed Marshall in the hallway and asked him if this was true. Marshall said it was, and, because of that, he would henceforth be silent on the topic during all deliberations of the Joint Chiefs.

That was fine with Leahy but King was instantly—and vocally—against it. "Marshall cannot be spared from his present job," said King, pleading with the president.[26] "Marshall was a 'key man' in the set-up of the United States and also of the Allied organization ... this was no time to swap horses in mid-stream."[27]

Leahy agreed and surprisingly, and somewhat awkwardly, so did Marshall's close friend, Hap Arnold. There was no denying that the D-Day command would be the crowning achievement of any military career and by all rights Marshall deserved such a thing—but the war was so vast, so complicated, it was hard to imagine who could handle the difficult and diverse military, political, and production issues as well as Marshall did. Leahy and Arnold felt the same way that King did—it wasn't ideal, it might not be fair, but Marshall should remain in Washington. "None of us, least of all me, wanted to deny Marshall what all of us felt was the thing he wanted most—to lead the victorious armies in a crushing blow, which he himself had largely planned, against the enemy," said Leahy. "On the other hand, he was a tower of strength to Roosevelt and to the high command, as embodied in the Joint Chiefs of Staff, which to now had planned the war with success but still faced many difficult problems."[28]

Unfortunately, the debate went public, and the media began reporting on it. Eventually, it reached the influential and much respected senior military officer from World War I, General of the Armies John J. Pershing. Pershing wrote to FDR and weighed in with similar reasoning, that is, no matter how enormously fond he was of Marshall, he was against the appointment. D-Day was a tactical command, said Pershing, just one part of the war and thus somewhat of a step down for Marshall. "We are engaged in a global war of which the end is still far distant and, for the wise strategical guidance of which we need our most accomplished officer as Chief of Staff," wrote the General. "I voice the consensus of informed military opinion in saying that officer is General Marshall. To transfer him to a tactical command in a limited area, no matter how seemingly important, is to deprive ourselves of the benefit of his outstanding strategical ability and experience. I know of no one at all comparable to replace him as Chief of Staff."[29]

Roosevelt wrote back saying that he agreed, but he also disagreed. Marshall was vitally important in Washington, but he also deserved to be the next Pershing and that could only happen if he commanded a victorious army on the battlefield, not strapped to a desk in Washington, D.C. Marshall, the president suggested, would command the invasion.

But then on October 30th, 1943, he equivocated. The British, despite the objections to the D-Day date, sent Roosevelt a cable urging him to name a commander so the D-Day planning could at the least begin in earnest, but Roosevelt declined to do so, fashioning the rather thin excuse that such information "would give definite notice to the Germans of our plans." Perhaps that was so, but he switched back and forth. He affirmed that he could not name Marshall but went on to discuss how General Eisenhower might be used as Marshall's replacement in Washington when he did name Marshall. Eisenhower, who was junior in rank to Marshall but had commanded the forces in the victorious North African campaign, had proven to be an excellent field commander as well as a diplomat adept at negotiating the subtleties of coalition warfare with the British. On some levels Eisenhower was an obvious choice for D-Day, but he also had the breadth of credentials to come back to Washington if Marshall received the D-Day command. It came down to one thing—for reasons known only to him, Roosevelt did not want to name a commander, not yet.[30]

In today's meeting the topic came up again, tempered now by the unwelcome news that Russians were impatient and might very well align behind Britain's Mediterranean strategy if action were not taken to open a front soon. The president spoke to the group, framing the issue in terms of a broader Allied command in Europe, not just D-Day. He said that if all of the Allied operations were folded into a single command, then that commander would have undeniable gravitas and as such the command should go to Marshall.[31] "It is my idea that General Marshall should be the commander-in-chief against Germany and command all the British, French, Italian, and U.S. troops involved in that effort," said Roosevelt to his chiefs. And then the conversation was tabled.[32]

In line with Roosevelt's sentiment that there was "in this global war, literally no question, either militarily or politically, in which the United States is not interested," some miscellaneous topics of conversation followed that had no real bearing on military issues. One such topic was a discussion of FDR's vision for the sort of financial and governmental aid that should be given to the various Pacific islands that would be liberated from Japan. FDR told the chiefs that an extensive communiqué was in the works that would call for the release of all islands acquired by Japan since the end of World War I and the removal of all Japanese nationals from the islands taken during the current war. The United States would oversee those islands through a benevolent "trusteeship" that would help them transition from the dependence of occupation to the independence of statehood without the economic shock of going it alone. The chiefs nodded in concurrence.

Roosevelt put his cigarette aside and pulled out a pouch of mail that contained a set of conference notes from the October diplomatic meetings in Moscow between the United States, Great Britain, and the Soviet Union. He asked that copies be made and distributed to everyone. That done, FDR closed the meeting by asking the Joint Chiefs to draft an agenda for the upcoming meetings in Cairo with the Chinese and an agenda for the meetings in Tehran with Stalin.

They adjourned at 3:30 P.M.

*

The shrill sound of music suddenly came over the loudspeakers as the dinner hour was announced. "Bagpipes before dinner," Arnold wrote in his diary. It was 6 P.M., a favorite hour on any ship, chow time, down time. "Drum and bugle, drum and fife, an English and British Navy custom [to] notify the gentlemen that it is dinner time, get ready for it," wrote Arnold. "Not aboard all ships but aboard the *Iowa*." The compartments emptied as sailors scrambled out to their messes. Tonight, Admiral King split off from the rest of the group to eat with the officers in the ship's wardroom. Here the officers of the *Iowa* assembled nightly for their own dinner service, eight or ten tables, fluorescent lights, columns of cigarette smoke curling above a hot cup of strong coffee.

King made his way through the passageways, entered, grabbed a napkin ring, and sat down to his dinner. He rose to speak as dessert was served. "I want you all to know that we have been taken care of very nicely in this ship,'" said King, a comment that triggered smiles and ripples of applause. "You are well aware that you are participating in an historic voyage." King then outlined the mission and the importance of the meetings ahead and offered some everyday advice that was no doubt born from his own experiences at sea. Be self-reliant, he told the officers. Keep your nautical skills honed. And be cautious about technology; it doesn't always work when you need it. Remember to be sailors, to rely on your training and your instincts. "You have a fine ship," King said, "but don't get to trusting these mechanical gadgets too much. They're good. But radar has been known to fail. Just look at it this way: these gadgets are necessary—but for your own sake, and the fighting capabilities of this ship, try not to depend on them solely."

It was of course smart advice considering that an enemy shell could take out a radar fire control station or destroy a map room or a flag plot in a fiery hot flash, As if to underscore his point at that exact moment, the mike died. King tapped the lifeless thing, and the entire wardroom broke out in an appreciative burst of laughter led by King himself. "I am wondering," said the ship's Executive Officer, who promptly seized the moment and jumped to his feet. "if the Admiral didn't arrange this himself." A second burst of laughter swelled up in the wardroom thus ending dinner and for King a pleasant evening with his men.[33]

McCrea was on the bridge as King arrived back from dinner. The officer of the deck ordered the helm to change course in accordance with the anti-submarine zigzag pattern. That surprised King. "May I see you in your cabin," he whispered to McCrea. The two men left the bridge and repaired to McCrea's sea cabin.

"It is dark and I note that *Iowa* is zigzagging, which is unusual during dark hours," said King. "Why?"

McCrea answered, "When I was in Washington recently, I discussed this trip with Rear Admiral [Francis Stuart] Low, your submarine fellow, and he informed me that the enemy had made significant developments in radar periscopes. With that in mind, he suggested I zigzag at night. The suggestion made sense to me, and that is why I am doing it."

McCrea waited. King held his eyes, and they nodded almost imperceptibly. "Thank you," he said, and that was that.[34]

*

The movie that night was a propaganda film made by the Soviets depicting the German invasion and the bloody battles that followed. Arnold, Hopkins, Leahy, Marshall, and the others watched it in the president's cabin before going to bed. They reported that it was rather graphic and unsettling. But then again, that was war.

In the days of sailing vessels and high-mast ships, long before there were reliable clocks, a ship's orderly was required to adjust the time and confirm that time with the officer of the deck. At 1 A.M. in the morning, the orderly would arrive on the bridge and report to the officer of the deck, and say, "One bell, sir." The officer of the deck would reply, "Report to the captain one bell and chronometers wound." The orderly then reported to the captain, "One bell and chronometers wound, sir," to which the captain replied, "Very well, make it so." Thus the time would then officially be 1 A.M.[35] So it was on the *Iowa*. Five times during the Atlantic crossing to Tehran, and always at 0100 in the morning, the clocks on the *Iowa* were turned forward one hour to adjust for the changing time zones, and when that happened, McCrea said to the orderly, "Very well, make it so."[36]

It was now 1:00 A.M. The lights were dimmed on the bridge, the ship running blacked out, watchful eyes peering out to the seas with only the dull shape of the bow and the twin turrets to be seen.

Behind her, the propellers beat the ocean in a frothy white foam, and then the seas closed in around her hull leaving only the faintest hint of her passing. "Only the sounds of waves washing the sides could be heard by the keepers of the night watches," wrote McCrea of his warship, and on to Oran they sailed.[37]

CHAPTER 9: RANKIN

It was Tuesday. Four short days remained to iron out the strategies and prepare for Churchill and Stalin. Inside the ship's compartments the staff planners were going over their orders from the day before. New war plans for the Pacific, agendas for Cairo and Tehran. Handy was with his Army planners in one compartment, the Joint Planning Staff was in a second, and still others held Arnold's and King's air and naval staff meetings. Coffee mugs crowded tables, binders and clipboards were stacked in piles, and green chalkboards were filled with ideas scribbled in white. Each group worked on one piece of the puzzle, each trying to see how one strategy played off the other against the realities of limited resources, great distances, and the unknowns of enemy actions. The most important part of it all was their fresh eyes on the problems. Marshall described how this worked: "I made it a rule never to give them my tentative ideas; I preferred that they work out something."[1] Each combat alternative started out with the basics of world geography, followed by a blizzard of options that eventually hit a decision tree, which branched off into endless what-ifs. But once an agreement was reached, once there was a plan, execution was a streamlined affair. "With the approval of the President, the Joint Chiefs of Staff issued the overall directives that sent millions of American men to the various battle fronts and marked the general course of the thousands of ships," said Admiral Leahy. "The policy and broad objectives were stated by the President, the provisions for transportation, allocation of equipment, and munitions were fixed by the JCS."[2]

But there were politics that were a consideration as well. In the case of the Russians, one had to be completely committed to a war strategy before bringing it to the table. The Russians were known for buying in and doing exactly what they said. "[An] agreement with Stalin was a serious thing," said Marshall. "The Russians were quite scrupulous about keeping their military agreements."[3]

The British chiefs were different. Churchill was difficult to pin down, and, because he wore a second hat as Secretary of State for War, his chiefs rarely had the sort of latitude Marshall gave his own men.[4] "It was very difficult, in dealing with the British Chiefs of Staff, to tell whether we were really dealing directly with Mr. Churchill or with their opinions," said Marshall.[5]

Roosevelt's nod to the politics of the U.S. electorate created its own wrinkles. The invasion of North Africa was ordered as much to show the American people some tangible gains in the aftermath of Pearl Harbor as it was to give him a lift in the November 1942 presidential elections. That the invasion came a few days after the election in the end turned out to be unimportant as FDR was reelected anyway, but the message was clear to the war planners. "We failed to see that the leader of a democracy has to keep the people entertained," said Marshall of the North Africa decision. "That may sound like the wrong word, but it conveys the thought. People demand action."[6]

That said, there was a lot of work to do before Tehran, and it was well underway on the *Iowa*. In some compartments they were working on the agendas for the meetings with the Chinese in Cairo, another for the Russians, others were writing a rework of the invasion plans for Japan, still another the command issues in the European theater, and in another on an emergency combat mobilization plan that would go into effect in the event of a sudden collapse of Germany. That last plan was called Rankin, and it was a curious thing indeed. Not only would the fall of Berlin be the capstone to the war but those soldiers there on the ground might determine how post-war Germany was run. At present, there was no agreement among the Allies how to handle Germany after the war, which meant that the ancient principal of occupation by the victors might be the precedent. If so, it would be a race to occupy the parts of Germany that each of the Allies wanted for themselves. Berlin topped each ally's list.

Thus the very secret, very bold plan called Rankin. Rankin assumed that at some point the German high command might suddenly surrender, or that some sort of civil disobedience might bring about the sudden fall of Hitler. What would the United States do if Germany suddenly collapsed? A lot had to do with where the U.S. soldiers were when it happened.

The "disintegration" of the German state, as this was formally called, might come about in a number of ways, and the United States had to be prepared for them all. For instance, there might be a gradual retreat of the occupation forces in Western Europe, in which case Allied soldiers would inch forward. Or, it might come about during a battle when a German line suddenly fell, and behind it there was no further resistance. It could happen on D-Day, or a month after D-Day, or it might happen on the Soviet front before any American soldiers were even on the continent. The point was to anticipate it, shift to Plan B, and get to Berlin. If American soldiers were too far behind, the Russians might simply lock out the Allies. That was the fear that propelled Rankin.

The original military plan to mobilize the soldiers in the event of a sudden collapse had been approved in May of 1943. The plan, however, had assumed that the collapse would happen before American soldiers were in England. That plan said that once Americans soldiers were over in England, they would use their ships and airplanes to get soldiers into Berlin. According to this somewhat modest plan, one division of U.S. Airborne would be parachuted into Berlin to take and occupy the government buildings while a second division would rush in overland. That would get twenty-four thousand soldiers into the city quickly, with reinforcements flowing in behind them.[7] "Every available man and every available weapon of war would be needed, and they would be drawn from every possible source including training schools, depots, and defense formations," wrote the Rankin planners. "The occupation [of Germany] could become 'the one interest, paramount in the world.' Speed in action would be all-important."[8]

But that plan was outdated. Hundreds of thousands of combat-ready, combat-equipped American soldiers were already in England so Rankin had to be rewritten. In the event of a sudden collapse, American soldiers could now get to Germany almost instantly, which meant that wherever they were when the war ended would largely define what geographic portions of Germany America would eventually control. The key question was this: what part of Germany did the president want to occupy?

Rankin was on the agenda for the next meeting with FDR.

"At five minutes before noon, the *Iowa* entered the European Theater of War," wrote McCrea in his diary.[9] The great ship steamed through the ocean as steady as a train on railroad tracks. Its engines could be felt from one end of the ship to the other. "How well I remember *Iowa* at high speed," said Arthur Lockwood, who was one of the sailors on the voyage. "Our 212 thousand horses giving life to everything! Everything you touched had a vibrancy life of its own, even the life lines. The uptakes on the stacks were literally screaming. Our flag was jet black from the oil smoke. Our wake, as observed from the fantail, was a boiling, churning mass of green-water and foam washing up nearly to the main deck."[10]

Hap Arnold walked the decks, passing the countless sailors and gunners. He looked to sea and saw an escort carrier on the horizon that he later confirmed was the *Block Island*. From above he no doubt heard the raspy engines of Navy Wildcat fighter planes as they patrolled skies.

Roosevelt spent most of his free time outside reading or napping, always accompanied by Arthur Prettyman.[11] Prettyman positioned Roosevelt's wheelchair alongside the rails where he was invigorated by the rush of fresh air and the warmth of the sun. "He really enjoyed the salt air and sitting on deck," said Secret Service agent James Griffith, who was with the president on the ship. "[He] didn't stay inside any longer than he had to."

Formality of dress was a convention Roosevelt rarely stood on, particularly at sea. On his own boats Roosevelt would wear his "oldest sweaters and dirtiest flannels, and he never shaved," remembered friend Arthur Schlesinger, and it was the same on the *Iowa*. The president did his best to relax.[12] "All goes well and a very comfortable trip so far," wrote the president in a letter to Eleanor. "Weather good and warm enough to sit with only a sweater as an extra over an old pair of trousers and a fishing shirt."[13]

Roosevelt relished this time alone, but by no means was he invisible. Meeting the sailors was one of the jobs he enjoyed most. Radar operator Myron E. Nelson, Sr. of Bassett, Virginia joined the Navy in November 1942. "No doubt the *Iowa* was the pride of the Navy and one of the greatest ships to sail," he said of his time aboard the battleship. Nelson had the sort of experiences young men at war seldom forget—combat in the Pacific Theater, for one—but what he remembered most was Roosevelt. One afternoon, FDR was wheeled to the opening of his darkened compartment as his radar swept the seas for enemy ships. Bassett explained to the president what the blips on the screen were and how the system worked. "It was an honor to have him sit with me in the radar shack and view the escort screen ships—our protectors," said Nelson. It was a moment he never forgot.[14]

James C. Crumlish Jr., also met the president. Crumlish's parents were old Democrats who thought FDR walked on water. Now the president was on his very ship. Crumlish had the morning deck watch and ran into Roosevelt during a routine inspection. He rounded the port side of the admiral's promenade and out of nowhere FDR was wheeled into his path. "He had on the cape and the old felt hat that were his trademarks," said Crumlish. "His legs were wrapped in a heavy blanket. I couldn't believe my eyes. 'Good morning, sir,' I said, saluting him."

"'Good morning, lieutenant,' he replied."

"I asked the President if he was having a good day and he said, 'Oh, I'm having a grand time, lieutenant.' Then the president talked about the

Navy and wondered if my education had been interrupted by the war. I answered as best I could and then asked to be excused. I couldn't believe that I had met my hero—my father's hero, too. The President was aboard the *Iowa* for about two weeks, but I never spoke to him again. I never saw him again until he was hoisted aboard in a boson's chair in Dakar in Africa for the return to Norfolk."[15]

As Crumlish left the deck, the president remained behind, quiet, alone, thinking.

CHAPTER 10: SOMEBODY KNEW SOMETHING

Churchill was at sea. Above the *Renown* was a continuous escort of RAF Hurricanes, Spitfires, and British night fighters while around her British anti-submarine destroyers pinged the seas for German U-boats. Adding to the defenses, the American anti-submarine (ASW) bomber forces based on the southern tip of England had stepped up their patrols over the Bay of Biscay with flights extending down as far south as Spain. From Morocco, a dozen more ASW B-24s patrolled the entrance to the Strait of Gibraltar and the Mediterranean, and from the Portuguese Azores, some fifty British-flown American ASW B-17s patrolled the mid-Atlantic. They flew 2,109 hours of anti-submarine patrols in October and 2,521 hours in November.[1]

Security was tight for the prime minister, too. Just a few months earlier the Germans had intercepted a British plane flying from Gibraltar to England and had shot it down, claiming the lives of all on board including the immensely popular British actor Leslie Howard.[2] Today nothing of the sort would be allowed to happen. Churchill's ship was well ahead of Roosevelt's. Although he remained ill and largely confined to his cabin, Churchill got up long enough to see the Rock of Gibraltar as they passed through the Strait, but, as soon as the *Renown* cleared the Pillars of Hercules, he was back in bed. The battlecruiser steamed east for another six hours until they ported in Oran. Churchill's North African commanders came aboard for half a day and then later evening the *Renown* weighed anchor using the cover of night to steam across the Mediterranean to Malta where they docked and remained between the 17th and 19th of November.[3]

Churchill remained consumed by his bitterness toward Overlord and the Americans in general. The plans in hand called for a cessation of combat in preparation for the invasion of Europe, but that would mean his soldiers would be idle between now and May of 1944. Churchill bemoaned what he considered to be American shortsightedness. A dead German was a dead German, no matter where. Why couldn't he make the Americans see that? Cutting the Germans down to size before Overlord made so more much sense than sitting on their hands. He shook his head. Instead of taking Rome, they were shipping soldiers back to England to prepare for an invasion that was still months off. This lack of imagination was giving the Germans openings they themselves should be taking. As if to underscore his point, during the stop in Malta he received the disheartening news that the British forces, which had landed on Leros some weeks earlier had fallen to the Germans who, in a decisive victory, had retaken the island for themselves. Great Britain suffered the loss of some five thousand soldiers in what now looked like a disaster. Had the Americans only agreed to give him air support, the situation would have been reversed, groused Churchill, but now he had an embarrassing defeat to explain to his people back home.[4]

Churchill called his British Chiefs of Staff to his bedside on the *Renown*. If the Americans would not support his plans for the Mediterranean, he repeated, he would withdraw his support for Overlord.[5]

It was Wednesday, November 17, midpoint on the *Iowa's* transatlantic crossing, and there were problems everywhere. In Oran, Secret Service Agent Mike Reilly had been handed a fresh batch of intelligence, which suggested that there was a new and very immediate threat to the president's ship. "The Germans were using a new weapon called the glide torpedo," remembered Reilly. "These torpedoes, when dropped into the sea, were magnetically attracted to Allied ships and at the moment were causing havoc with the shipping at the entrance to the Strait of Gibraltar which was right on the course of the USS *Iowa*, now only two days away from the Rock."[6] If a German bomber equipped with such a weapon got into range of the *Iowa*, the president would have no chance.

Reilly assessed the situation and sent an encrypted message to his agents on the battleship and one to Captain McCrea suggesting he divert the warship to Dakar, French West Africa. But no sooner had it crossed the wires than did news come that German U-boats had been spotted hugging the coastline of Africa in precisely that area. They were in a bind. "Now there was little choice," said Agent Reilly. "Dakar meant subs, Oran meant glide torpedoes. And it looked very much as if somebody knew something."[7]

Reilly's comment on glide torpedoes was actually a slight mischaracterization. The Germans had indeed developed a highly effective U-boat *torpedoe* that had magnetic detonators and these new weapons were sinking ships. But Reilly was speaking about a new generation of smart bombs called glide *bombs*. Glide bombs were rocket powered bombs carried aloft by German bombers and fired at ships from 20,000 feet. They began to appear in July of 1943 and sunk the troop carriers *Duchess of York* and the *California*. By August 1943, reports of this weapon were widespread and attacks were frequent with convoy ships being sunk and a destroyer, the USS *Savannah,* nearly so. The glide bomb was dangerous because at the moment there was no defense against it. It was rocket powered for a portion of its flight then it glided silently until it slammed into a ship.

Reilly thus had two bad choices. He could divert the *Iowa* to Dakar and risk the U-boats or he could remain on course for Oran and risk the glide bombs. The odds were about the same, but he did have one ace in the hole: Navy Rear Admiral Henry K. Hewitt. Hewitt, 56, was by far the Navy's most combat-experienced fleet commander in the Mediterranean Sea. He had successfully led the United States Navy's Western Task Force against the Germans in North Africa and then again during the invasions of Sicily and Salerno. According to Eisenhower, Hewitt outsmarted and out maneuvered the Germans with his aggressive, fluid tactics, which kept the Germans in "a state of confusion and indecision until the last moment."[8] Outside of the Secret Service, Hewitt was one of the few who knew who was actually on the *Iowa,* and he had his destroyers prepared to provide a screen through the Strait and down to Oran. Seven of his best would meet the *Iowa* outside the Strait and join the escorts, giving the *Iowa* a cocoon of some ten ships as she squeezed into the Mediterranean. With navy pilots flying air cover and Hewitt's ships screening for U-boats, Reilly believed that only a suicidal fool would try anything and even then it would take incredible luck.

Reilly made his decision. No change.[9]

But then more bad news arrived. Later that afternoon Reilly received an urgent message from the White House in Washington saying that the overall security of the trip had been compromised by a press leak. A British censor had allowed a message to be broadcast in the clear that suggested a very important meeting would soon be taking place in the Mena House Hotel near Cairo. The message did not say who would attend but the press had the scent of a forthcoming Churchill-Roosevelt summit, and it was easy to put two and two together. The news was splashed across the front page of nearly every major paper in America and Britain.

It was a fiasco, of course. How such a thing could have happened was unfathomable, but there it was. It did not take a spy network to decode it. "The President and his staff were worried," said Lt. Rigdon, with characteristic understatement. "They reasoned that the Axis surely wouldn't be likely to overlook such an opportunity."[10]

Reilly wired his agents on the ship yet again and alerted the president. FDR read the message and called Hap Arnold down to his cabin to evaluate the risk of attack by the Luftwaffe. In essence, said Arnold, they were sitting ducks. The British pilots would be providing air cover for the meetings in Cairo, and they were indeed crack pilots, but, if the Germans wanted to attack, they could fight their way through any defensive fighter screen. Essentially, said Arnold, the president of the United States was too good of a target not to expend every possible effort to hit, and, to that end, the Luftwaffe's aircraft had the range. The nearest Luftwaffe airfields were at Kalamaki, Greece and around Athens. Additionally, Rhodes, the much-discussed island east of Athens, was occupied by the Luftwaffe, as was the island of Crete, just three hundred miles north of Egypt in the central Mediterranean Sea. These were all active Luftwaffe bases and recent reconnaissance photographs had shown that the Luftwaffe base near Heraklion, Crete, was nearly wingtip-to-wingtip with German bombers. A lone wolf with a glide bomb was one thing; A coordinated attack with hundreds of Me-109s and FW-190s, not to mention Stuka diver bombers, was quite another. Although they were bombing these bases even as he talked, said Arnold, it was impossible to get them all.[11]

FDR nodded and called in the rest of his chiefs to ask them what they thought. To a man, they agreed with Arnold's assessment of the risk: They were sitting ducks. Given similar intelligence, they would go to the ends of the earth to mount an air or sea attack, and Roosevelt knew the truth in that. Based on similar intelligence, Roosevelt had approved an attack on the airplane carrying Isoroku Yamamoto, the Commander of the Imperial Japanese Navy. On April 18, 1943, eighteen U.S. pilots made the interception off Bougainville and shot him down. The Germans would apply the same logic. There was no difference.

Roosevelt decided to send a message to Churchill on his ship and to Eisenhower in North Africa. A runner was sent to the bridge, and, by signal lights, one of the escorting destroyers was told to come alongside. Rigdon entered in the president's log: "5:31 P.M. The *Ellyson* ... came under the *Iowa's* port quarter and an important and urgent dispatch was passed to her by hand. She was then directed to leave our company temporarily to effect radio transmission of the message. This procedure was followed so that the use of her radio transmitter would not possibly disclose to the enemy the location of the main body of our task group." The message was just three words. "Khartoum as destination."[12]

But Eisenhower and Churchill immediately took exception. From their perspectives the threat was better managed if they remained in Cairo. Khartoum, which was nearly a thousand miles south of Cairo in the Sudan, had almost nothing going for it militarily, save for the comfort of knowing it was too far away to be easily hit by air. Churchill considered Malta, because it was near Oran, was in British hands, and populated by enough Allied air and land forces to make it secure. But outside of the military installations, Malta still lay in ruins, so he came back to the original plan. The leak was worrisome, thought Churchill, but Cairo was already protected by Allied ships, planes, antiaircraft artillery, and soldiers. "I therefore decided we had better stick to Cairo where all the arrangements had been perfected," said the Prime Minister. "The eight squadrons of British aircraft based in Alexandria would certainly intercept and destroy any German attack. The enclave near the pyramids, which we were to occupy, was to be guarded by more than a brigade of infantry, and there were upwards of five hundred anti-aircraft guns hard by."[13] Ever pragmatic Churchill had another thing to say about it. "We had of course always thought that the news was bound to leak directly as we got there, and the fact that it has leaked a few days earlier should not therefore very much affect our plans," he wrote.[14]

Eisenhower, who had met the Germans on the battlefield and perhaps knew them better than anyone, agreed with Churchill. The land approaches to Egypt were under his control, and the sea approaches from Crete or Greece were blocked by Hewitt's ships. Cairo was impenetrable. Even if the Germans knew about the meeting, Eisenhower knew he was ready for them. "After reflection... I made a strong recommendation to the President against any change on plans," said Eisenhower. "We had made every conceivable defensive preparation including heavily guarded enclosures and anti-aircraft defenses," said Ike, "...we would only be adding to the risk by making a sudden change to a place where we could not be well prepared."[15]

Again, no change. They would port in Oran, as planned. They would have interim meetings in Cairo, as planned. They would fly on to Tehran, as planned.

*

Lavrenti Pavlovich Beria's men were out in full force. He had one team of NKVD agents walking the track between Moscow and Baku, while another was out inspecting the train cars themselves. A third team had flown down to the airfield in Baku and were securing the perimeter, interviewing the pilots, and checking out the airplanes themselves. Satisfied, they quarantined the planes in Baku and flew down to Tehran to do the same at the airfield at Gale Morghe.

Beria himself was at the Soviet embassy. The embassy building was in good shape, solid, guarded, ensconced in a walled compound with gates and an open courtyard inside of several acres. The main conference room had a table that could seat at least twenty, but they needed a second table for the smaller, plenary sessions. Stalin was informed and ordered a round table to be custom built. He selected solid oak.

The compound was a beautiful, campus-like setting with a web of buildings and residences interconnected by hallways and lengthy side-walks. Every blade of grass was looked over with a magnifying glass; every inch and every room were inspected and swept for bugs. His men found that half of the bathrooms were not connected to any plumbing, and almost all of the rooms were in need of fresh paint, so he ordered his soldiers to make the necessary improvements.

His final touches were spy craft of the highest order. Beria replaced the cooks, waiters, gardeners, and maintenance staff at the embassy with his own men, then had his spies plant microphones in lamps and furniture. He took over a small room and turned it into a listening post with headphones and tape recorders.

Beria made one more call. He ordered his son to fly down to Tehran and oversee the eavesdropping.

Tehran presented other security problems, too. Before the *Iowa* set sail, Agent Reilly had flown ahead to inspect the president's route of travel from Oran to Tunisia to Egypt. He traveled incognito lest someone recognize that the Secret Service was there, which could itself compromise the security of the trip. "I took off for Oran and Cairo about a month before the Boss left, so I found myself sneaking around both cities in October, 1943," said Agent Reilly. "It was the same old story of living in moth-eaten, flea-bag hotels, eating out of my suitcase, cajoling or arguing with local G-2 [intelligence] geniuses and military police officials, and trying to tell as few people as possible in the Army [what was going on]."[16]

He had his people infiltrate the local bars and flea markets to pick up the sort of random intelligence that comes from small talk and rumors. During an earlier meeting in Casablanca they uncovered an extensive plot to kill the Army commander in Italy, the American General Mark Clark. They hoped to hear similar rumors if such a plot were brewing in Cairo or Tehran. Out his men went. "We attempted to find out what was being said and done in native quarters," said Reilly, but nothing of note had been picked up.[17]

Next came Tehran, and there were just two ways to get there, neither particularly appealing. The military C-54 transport that Roosevelt used could fly non-stop from Cairo to Tehran, but the city was enclosed by a ring of mountains that rose some 18,000 feet. None of the transports were pressurized, which meant everyone would have to breathe oxygen.

The alternative was to fly to Basra, Iraq, and then take the train from Basra to Tehran. This was a well-traveled route used by the U.S. Persian Command to ship Lend-Lease supplies into Russia. FDR was not fond of airplanes and would have preferred the train, but the rail option posed its own problems. The track was well-traveled by American convoys so by all means it ought to have been safe, but, in fact, one train carrying supplies had been hit by the local Bedouin tribesmen who cut a section of track, forced a derailment, raided the train, and killed the MPs guarding it. Moreover, the cars that Roosevelt would use were owned by the Shah of Iran, an exuberant twenty-four- year-old, who was using his royal cars as a rolling pleasure palace. Reilly didn't like tribal bandits and wasn't sure how sanitary the cars were.[18] He would have to reconsider the C-54s.

The USS *Iowa* remained under strict radio silence, receiving messages but not sending any. She was also still running completely blacked out. She averaged twenty-five knots on a zigzagging pattern with the only hint of her passage being the trail of fluorescent burbles in her wake.

On the bridge, the ship was at battle stations, and all eyes were watchful. "Anxiety manifest itself as the battleship drew near the European continent and within range of the Nazi glide bombing Heinkels based in Bordeaux and other parts of France," wrote McCrea. "Alertness became imperative and was enforced."[19]

CHAPTER 11: OPTION A

The morning found McCrea's Task Force under dark clouds and firmly in the grip of a winter storm that had clawed combers out of the seas that were twenty feet high. The *Iowa* was steady, 880 feet and 50,000 tons of steel plowing through the waves with bursts of frothy white water exploding off her bow. One wave washed hard over the deck outside of FDRs cabin, while rain pelted the steel of the ship like tiny ball hammers. Beside her, the small escorts were having a hard time of it. Ernie Pyle, the war correspondent, wrote a short paragraph describing the fate of such destroyers in the grips of high seas. "They roll and they plunge. They buck and they twist. They shudder and they fall through space. They are in the air half the time and underwater half the time. The sailors say they should have flight pay and submarine pay, both."[1] Thursday was just such a day.

The Task Force was coming up on Madeira, the Portuguese islands some nine hundred miles off the coast of Morocco, which meant they were just two days out. Their course would take them towards the western coast of Africa where they would turn up towards the strait staying as far from the enemy air bases as they could until the last moment.

On the bridge, a tired McCrea called up the pharmacist's mate to help him relax. He was not sleeping well, which, considering the circumstances could be expected. He was the captain of a ship carrying the president of the United States transiting the Atlantic ocean through gale-force winds in an area that might be hiding a German wolfpack. On top of that he was living in his small sea cabin across the passageway from the bridge, his captain's cabin given over to the president. "During our passage across the Atlantic, I was on the bridge or within a few steps of the conning platform at all times," he said. "No matter how relaxed one may try to be, there is a certain amount of tension in going to sea, especially if one must be available, sleeping or awake, 24 hours a day."[2]

Roosevelt again had no military staff meetings scheduled that day, unusual perhaps considering that he had his entire Joint Chiefs and more than sixty generals with him. A degree of detachment was never entirely surprising with the president; collaboration was not his style nor was sharing his thoughts. After a week away at sea, Roosevelt had spent just one day in meetings with his chiefs, and, except for the movies in his cabin at the end of the day, he had no other contact with Marshall, King, or Arnold. Of course, that was the way it was in Washington. Roosevelt did not micromanage the war, and Marshall would sometimes go weeks without visiting the White House, Arnold even longer. Yet there were many issues that remained undecided, D-Day foremost among them, and meetings were important. "I think it is true that our military people were at a marked disadvantage compared with the British," said Handy, speaking of the distance Roosevelt placed between himself and his general, "You don't just casually see the President—it isn't that kind of thing. The British knew what was on Churchill's mind. We didn't know what was on the President's."[3]

Nonetheless, Roosevelt was in no hurry for the ship to get to Oran, and a good detective novel was a tonic for his soul. "Everything is very comfortable and I have with me lots of work and detective stories, and we brought a dozen good movies," said FDR in a letter to Eleanor.[4] Merriman Smith, a United Press correspondent, recalled, "Traveling with Mr. Roosevelt was an experience in leisurely luxury. He was rarely in a hurry to get anywhere and made his trips—except during campaign years—by easy stages."[5]

Although there were no meetings with Roosevelt, there was a major meeting in the morning, and the compartments were busy inside. The war planners were working on position papers for the Joint Chiefs that would eventually find their way to the president's cabin for his review before the meetings tomorrow. Typewriters clacked out page after page of drafts, and, between cups of coffee and dashes to the commissary for cigarettes, they polished Arnold's plans for the new air force command

and cleaned up the proposals on the theater command issues. The sense of it all from the Monday meeting was that the several commands could be streamlined at great profit in terms of lives saved, war material more effectively allocated, and a quicker end to the war. But the basic question was, to what extent could that be accomplished? With each Allied combat thrust the Germans responded with their own, which created a loop of thrusts and counterthrusts that pulled in resources affecting all of the theaters. "These operations are all intimately related to each other," said the Joint Chiefs in their papers. "Events in the Mediterranean area attract enemy forces and affect enemy capabilities, which, in turn, have an important bearing upon our capabilities in northwestern Europe, and vice versa."[6] The idea of one overall theater command had made the most sense, but the British were not likely to go along with it, so they wrote up two options that they simply labeled "A" and "B."

Arnold's proposal for a new structure for his air forces in Europe was a bright spot. The core men and material were already in the European theater with more planes and airmen arriving almost daily. These air forces were already mounting raids of several hundred bombers each, although Arnold felt they could do much better. All they lacked was more aggressive leadership and a unified plan of operation. If approved by Roosevelt, the new United States Strategic Air Forces Europe would have several thousand bombers and fighters under one fully integrated, focused, and centralized air command attacking Germany under the able leadership of Spaatz and Doolittle. The Eighth Air Force in England and the new Fifteenth Air Force in the south of Italy would thereafter operate as one organization with the utmost of coordination but completely independent of the RAF. This last minute reorganization was a reflection of the impatience that characterized Hap Arnold. He was pragmatic, he was determined, and he wanted to win a war. "The thing that struck me about the Air Force, they weren't satisfied with anything they had," said Handy, admiringly. "The Air Force had the best heavy bomber in the world in the B-17. The B-24 was very good. But they weren't satisfied at all. Although they had the best, and the other fellow wasn't catching us, they had a better one, and they built the B-29." And now Arnold was proposing a new way to bomb the Germans, and new people to get it done.[7] "Arnold was primarily responsible for us having the Air Force we did during the war because he did do things, and nothing stopped him," said Handy. "You've got to have men like that if you are going to get a big job done."[8]

*

The *Renown* was in the Mediterranean, leaving Malta for the port of Alexandria, Egypt, where Churchill would disembark and fly to Cairo to be part of Roosevelt's welcoming party when the president arrived. The stop in Malta had restored his energy and he was mending well. He had the bounce in his step back and felt good enough to consider new things. Last month he has asked the British Secretary of State for Foreign Affairs Anthony Eden to consider a question he had thus far avoided. "If we win, what do we do with Germany," he asked. "Is it to be divided, and if so how?" One thought was to break up Germany into several smaller states, isolating the militaristic Prussia by folding Prussia into a confederation of states along the Danube, a "a broad, peaceful, cow-like confederation" said Churchill, that included Bavaria, Austria, and Hungary. But if not that, splitting it into even more "states" and placing bans on certain types of German factories being built was discussed, anything that would prevent Germany from regaining its strength and starting another war.[9]

And what about post-war Russia? With Germany reduced to rubble, France rebuilding, and England physically and financially exhausted by the war, who was left to keep Russia in check, and where was the balance of power? "I do not want to be left alone in Europe with the bear," he told a reporter for *The Times* of London. Churchill not only wanted the United States involved in checking Russia, but he wanted a strong

France, too, even though he could hardly reconcile his feelings of disgust about the German sympathizers from Vichy.[10]

Italy was still on his mind, and he made it clear that he thought the battles there should continue. From a military standpoint, Churchill's thinking was sound. The Germans had poured ten fresh divisions into Italy to hold Rome, and new intelligence indicated that Hitler was determined to stand his ground. If that were true, it presented a perfect opportunity to engage and defeat scores of Germans and thereby whittle down their overall strength. That could be done by moving soldiers who had been sent to England for Overlord over to Italy and land them near Rome. Churchill's theory—a dead German was a dead German—was sound, but he knew the shift in emphasis to Italy would delay Overlord, triggering Stalin's ire and certainly Roosevelt's. A fixed date for Overlord had been agreed to for months, and Britain and the United States were committed to the invasion in May 1944, a decision Churchill now thought unwise. He told his staff to write up plans to take Rome, and he would argue their case in Tehran. "It should be made clear to Stalin," he wrote Eden, "that assurances given about carrying out Overlord in May could well be modified by the exigencies of battle in Italy."[11] There might be, he told Eden to tell Stalin, a "slight delay."[12]

*

The *Iowa* plowed through the confused seas of the Atlantic Ocean in foamy explosions of water off her bow. That night, a rogue wave swept the decks as high as the third level of the superstructure. The *Iowa* shuddered then steamed onward; McCrea remained fast to the bridge. Eventually, the *Iowa* made the sweeping turn north on a heading that took her abeam the coast of Western Africa towards the Strait of Gibraltar. The map room reported to the bridge that there were no German submarines in the area, nor was there any unusual activity. "The Nazis apparently were completely unaware of the prize target now within range of their planes as well as their U-boats," said a relieved Admiral Leahy. "Conceivably the course of the war might have been changed if the enemy could have broken through our protection and killed the President."[13]

Arnold's Twelfth and Fifteenth Air Forces were hard at work bombing German targets ahead of the ships. For nearly twelve hours straight, his Forts, Liberators, and Marauders attacked Luftwaffe bases across the central Mediterranean. Athens, Kalamaki on Zakynthos, and all of the airfields in Crete were up in smoke. For good measure, they came back around and bombed the German naval base at Toulon, France.[14]

CHAPTER 12: DISMEMBERING GERMANY

When a president is on board a United States Navy ship, he immediately becomes the most senior commander in the chain of command, and thus, McCrea would be bound to have Roosevelt approve his sailing plan. Accordingly, before departing, McCrea submitted to Roosevelt the plan for voyage to Oran including the ship's speed, its course, its escorts, its fuel state, and so on. "Once the President was aboard," said FDR's naval aid Rigdon, "the commanding officer requested, through the Naval Aide, the President's permission to get underway and execute those plans. Whenever it was necessary, the captain requested the President's permission to vary or alter the previously approved plans."[1]

Tonight, that was necessary. Although the records are unclear as to precisely why, at 3 A.M. Friday morning, the day before they were to dock, the officer of the deck had an unplanned change of course that had to be passed on to the senior officer on the ship, which, of course, was now the president of the United States. Daniel J. Carlin, 30, was sent down to have it approved. As the engines rumbled from deep within the hull, Carlin hurried down the brightly lit passageway to the president's cabin. "I went to his bedroom entrance and called him several times," said Carlin. "He did not respond." Carlin stepped inside and tapped FDR on his shoulder. The president awoke and, as he did, a rush of Secret Service men came up behind the unthinking sailor, who in fact was standing over the president with his .45 strapped to his hip. Carlin was quickly apprehended, but FDR stopped them and explained what was going on. He was "proud" of Carlin for carrying out his orders "without delay," as he put it, and the course change was approved.[2]

They were 2,736 miles across the Atlantic Ocean, no U-boats sighted, but they were now nearing the nine-mile-wide choke point called the Strait of Gibraltar. To beef up their security, six fresh ships from Hewitt's Western Task Force were headed towards the *Iowa's* Task Force to increase the screen to a total of nine warships.[3] At 10:30 A.M. the cruiser USS *Brooklyn* and the destroyers USS *Trippe* and USS *Edison*, hove into view, each bristling with loaded and manned guns as they came alongside and cut through the seas beside the *Iowa*. Standing from the north were three more ships, the British destroyers HMS *Trowbridge*, *Tyrian*, and *Teazer*, also at full battle stations. The current escorts, the *Ellyson*, *Rodman*, and *Emmons*, remained in the forward line and adjusted their spacing as McCrea watched approvingly from the bridge.

By 11:00 A.M. the scout lines were organized, the escorts properly spaced, and the *Iowa* securely ensconced within a perimeter of nine submarine chasers with armed guns and live torpedoes and ready depth charges. Only a fool would attempt to bring a U-boat anywhere near the great battleship. Or perhaps only a fool would pass this opportunity up. Nothing ruled out fools.

Inside the *Iowa*, the ship's compartments were thick with clouds of cigarette smoke and the clattering of typewriters as the war planners tweaked the language of position papers and memoranda for the president. The Joint Chiefs went over each page line by line. Marshall added a sentence to the proposals for the Supreme Allied commanders of the Mediterranean forces, King asked for a change in a sentence related to the Navy. Details were important—these papers would be discussed with Roosevelt as thoroughly as any war plans in his war presidency. They gulped coffee, smoked, broke up for lunch, made final checks, then sent copies to the president for review before their 2 P.M. meeting. If ever there was a fish-or-cut-bait time it was Friday, November 20, 1943, on the USS *Iowa*.

The meeting started promptly at 2 P.M. Leahy, Marshall, King, and Arnold arrived at the president's cabin and were greeted by the expansive Roosevelt smile and a friendly "Hello Ernie. Hi Hap. Hello General," as Roosevelt swept his arm towards the table. Arthur Prettyman stood in the corner.

Leahy asked the president if he had digested the papers prepared for him, and Roosevelt said he had. The first item on the agenda was the theater commands. Roosevelt had two plans, Option A and Option B. Option A was the ambitious plan, not likely to be approved by the British, but the smarter one nonetheless. It called for the merger of the theaters into one master command under which would operate three subordinate commanders—one commander for the European forces, one commander for the Mediterranean forces, and one commander for what would be called "The Strategic Air Force." The Strategic Air Force was the merger of the Royal Air Force with the United States Army Air Forces into one bombing command with one commanding general. An organization chart was attached to the president's briefing paper that depicted a streamlined, simplified, and easy to understand command structure.[4]

Militarily, it was the soundest idea, but unfortunately the British would probably reject it. Option B had a better shot. Option B eliminated the merger of the Europe and the Mediterranean war commands and eliminated the merger of the RAF with the USAAF and dealt only with the air war and the Mediterranean. Option B called for merging Italy, Greece, Albania, Yugoslavia, Bulgaria, Rumania, Hungary, Crete, the Aegean Islands, and Turkey into one combat command, which would coordinate resources with the Middle East commanders in Cairo and have no involvement in Europe on D-Day, while the second part of Option B was the air war plan which was Arnold's U.S. Strategic Air Forces Europe with Doolittle and Spaatz in command.[5]

The president said he preferred Option A, but he agreed that the British would not go along with it. He promised to take it up with the Prime Minister, but he expected "difficulty." King urged him on, noting that it "made for the best offensive command setup," but it was hard to speculate. Roosevelt asked how many men were in the American armed forces now. He was told that the United States had 3,700,000 soldiers in England and more than 11,000,000 in uniform all over the world. "Are those exact figures?" he asked. They were not. The president said he wanted the exact figures, and Marshall sent a runner for them, but, in any case, Marshall said that the United States would soon have more men in England than the British had in their entire Army, Navy, and Air Forces combined. Arnold picked up on that line and added that his air forces already had more planes and men in action than the British and that the gap would only widen. "By 1 January 1944, we will have over 12,000 operational planes," said Hap, "while the British will only have about 8,000."[6]

The president nodded, and then expressed some concern that the overall commander in Option A would have too much authority. Marshall said that he would not. As always, the Combined Chiefs of Staff would set the strategy, and the proposed commander would handle the details of its implementation, but at any time in the future, his decisions could be easily reversed by the chiefs.

Roosevelt understood and seemed satisfied with that.

The discussion then turned to the question of who, in fact, would be this "Supreme Allied Commander" of this unified command if it were approved, a British officer or an American one? Marshall said the concept of a unified command was so important that the American Joint Chiefs were unanimous on this, and, even though by numbers alone they were entitled to the command, they were willing to make the necessary sacrifice and give it over to a British officer if that was what it took to get it through. Roosevelt considered that for a moment than asked, if the British had the top job would Eisenhower take over as the Supreme Allied Commander in the Mediterranean? He was told that Ike would.

Roosevelt then switched gears for a moment and voiced his displeasure with the British military operations in Leros and Cos. He looked at his generals. "Why Leros, why Cos?" he asked. "Had anyone been briefed on these operations beforehand?" They had not, said Marshall. "[Churchill] acted, in regard to those Greek islands, without any regard to the Combined Chiefs of Staff, which was highly irregular," said Marshall.[7]

Roosevelt wondered if that had been done to force his hand, to "create a situation in which they could push our troops into Turkey and the Balkans?' There were murmurs of agreement. The British certainly wanted to fight in the Balkans, they said, and Churchill preferred combat in the Mediterranean over D-Day and now wanted to retake the island of Rhodes more than ever. This would be a major issue in Tehran.[8]

The conversation came back to the topic at hand and turned to Hap Arnold's proposal to merge the Eighth Air Force in England with its Fifteenth in Italy and operate them as one unified organization called the United States Strategic Air Force in Europe (USSAFE). Arnold told the president that if this were approved he would have his new people in place by New Year's Day, 1944, and that they would neutralize the German Luftwaffe by D-Day. Roosevelt liked the plan and approved it on the spot. He also approved the appointment of General Carl A. "Tooey" Spaatz to lead the new USSAFE and Jimmy Doolittle to lead the Eighth. Roosevelt waved his cigarette holder and nodded, meaning this matter was resolved.[9]

Roosevelt turned the papers over.

The next, and in many ways far more profound discussion, had to do with Operation Rankin. The concern voiced by Roosevelt reflected the inescapable facts of geography. The Soviets were much closer to Berlin than were the Americans, meaning the Soviets almost certainly would get to Berlin first, and, if they did, they might possibly close down the city to the Allies. That, said Roosevelt, was something he did not want. The solutions were several, but they all came down to speed of movement—to get American soldiers, wherever they happened to be, into Berlin and get them there fast. Because the D-Day landings would be in Normandy, France, the American forces would be starting the offensive 650 miles from Berlin and would have to fight through heavily reinforced troops in Occupied France and into Germany, while the Russian front was just across Poland or only 400 miles away. Depending on how fast they moved, the Russians could be in Berlin while American forces were still fighting down in Stuttgart or Munich, places well away from Berlin.

Roosevelt did not care for that at all. Roosevelt wanted Berlin, and he even wanted Hamburg and Bremerhaven, the German seaports on the North Sea, which was entirely new to the Joint Chiefs. "We found him very fixed in his position," said Marshall of the parts of Germany FDR wanted, which began a rather lengthy discussion.[10]

Marshall said there were three variations of Rankin under consideration—one that assumed that Germany would collapse before D-Day and that U.S. soldiers would still be in England; one that assumed that the D-Day invasion had started and that American soldiers would be fighting in western France when the collapse came; and one that assumed that they would be on the outskirts of Berlin. Whatever the case, each scenario essentially became a transportation plan—how to quickly transport soldiers to Berlin from those points, and how to get them into the city if the Soviets refused to cooperate. But they had not considered the northern ports of Germany, said Marshall. This was new.

The president lit a cigarette. "Yes," said Roosevelt, "this is a very important matter." Whoever occupied Berlin would control Berlin and, in turn, Germany. If the Soviets arrived and took over the city, it would be nearly impossible to push them out, and that would be no good. "There would definitely be a race for Berlin," said the president, "We may have to put the United States divisions into Berlin as soon as possible." Perhaps soldiers could come around Scotland to get into Germany faster, he offered, while adding that U.S. soldiers had to get out of France and Italy as soon as possible, too. The British and French could handle issues in Italy and France, not the U.S. "We do not want to be concerned with reconstituting France. France is a British baby," said the president. "The British should have France, Luxembourg, Belgium, Baden, Bavaria, and Wurttemberg. The United States should take northwest Germany.

We can get our ships into such ports as Bremen and Hamburg, also Norway and Denmark, and we should go as far as Berlin. The Soviets could then take the territory to the east thereof. The United States should have Berlin. The British plan is for the United States to have southern Germany, and I don't like that."[11]

The table grew silent as this last remark sunk in. As much as victory, they were clearly talking about something quite apart from war; they were talking about the post-war landscape of Germany—indeed the post-war landscape of Europe—and as such, the American chiefs needed to adjust their plans forthwith. In the absence of diplomacy, the strongest and most powerful armies control the territories a nation occupies, but armies do not turn on a dime. If Roosevelt wanted the northern German ports, the armies had to get there, and that was a major change. Military operations involved twenty-ton tanks and hundreds of thousands of soldiers, and they could not be switched back and forth the way a phrase in a diplomatic document could be rewritten or edited. "You can't treat military factors in the way you do political factors," said Marshall. "You have to be very exact, very clearly informed, and very precise in what you say in regard to military things." If Roosevelt wanted a certain part of Germany, that was fine; they just needed to figure out how to give it to him. Roosevelt was painting a very clear picture of the political endgame he wanted, which in turn was spelling out the route their Army divisions would have to take moving across Germany—and the priority of speed. "There were a great many factors connected with all these things, but we had to give special regard to the particular military factors and make certain there were no misunderstandings or failure in this respect," said Marshall.[12]

Thinking out loud, and largely off the cuff, Marshall suggested that they might divide the advancing U.S. forces into two forces, one that went directly to Berlin and one that went to the Hamburg-Hannover area and secured it. King picked up on that and said if Germany collapsed while American soldiers were advancing through Europe they could cross over the British lines. The British would be coming across Holland, and, by hopping over their lines, American soldiers could get to Berlin and the German ports. There were details that needed to be pinned down, said Marshall, but it could be done. Marshall looked at his chiefs and then at the recording secretary to whom he gave orders that would be sent to the war planners. "We must have a scheme for disengaging Overlord at any stage of development," said Marshall, "in order to comply with the political considerations of occupation as outlined by the President."[13]

The room grew quiet for a moment. Each of the generals and admirals had the same thought. This wasn't going to be easy. "In all these occupation zone matters—in the back of our heads—I say our, certainly in mine—was the prospect that we would be rather remote from Berlin at the time the Russians got there," said Marshall.[14] Someone said that they should be ready to put an airborne division into Berlin within two hours of any collapse of Germany. There were murmurs of agreement. Leahy said we should get out of France as soon as possible even if it meant extreme efforts. De Gaulle was simply too unpredictable. "Possibly there will be a civil war in France," said the former ambassador, and, if that happened, let it be a British problem, he said.

Roosevelt said he envisioned an American occupation force of about one million soldiers for about two years. The people of Europe were in bad shape, he said. Food and potable water would be urgently needed in many areas, Holland, Belgium, parts of France, to prevent disease and starvation. "Our bombers might be needed to air drop supplies," said the president. Arnold nodded. Holland would of course return to the queen, but Belgium was a difficult country to predict because it was a nation of two languages, said FDR. It might also be necessary to create a buffer state between France and Germany, for all the obvious reasons. They nodded but remained deep in thought.[15]

King steered the conversation back to Rankin. Operation Rankin had to be reworked, he said, and they needed to be specific about their new goals. They needed a plan that would get soldiers into the occupation zones proposed by the president "from any stage of Overlord," said King. Roosevelt smiled. His chiefs were on the same page.[16]

The conversation turned to the Balkans and the British insistence that the Allies widen the front in Italy, and, secondarily, open up a front in Yugoslavia and Greece. This was, of course, their alternative to D-Day, the source of the divide, and the reason for the trip. The chiefs asked the president for direction on this but, to their frustration, Roosevelt said he was undecided. He said he needed to consult with Russia before he made up his mind. The British had made a strong case for their Mediterranean plan, he said, as we had for our D-Day plan, however, if the Russians needed immediate help, what then? The British plan would force fresh German divisions to fight in Italy and Yugoslavia, which would help Stalin. Rather than commit to anything, said Roosevelt, he wanted to see what Stalin's opinion was.

Marshall cast his eyes down and sighed. Roosevelt knew he was going against the recommendations of his American chiefs. He was putting the Balkans into play again and, worse, he was deferring this issue to Tehran, which meant he was deferring to Stalin. "We were always scared to death of Mr. Roosevelt on the Balkans," said Marshall. "Apparently he was with us, but we couldn't bet on it at all."[17]

Marshall spoke up. To leave the decision to Stalin would handcuff the Joint Chiefs who had several meetings scheduled with the British before the meetings with Stalin, he said. "We must see the question of this Balkan matter settled," said Marshall to the president, his voice low but firm. "We do not believe that the Balkans are necessary. To undertake operations in this region would result in prolonging the war and also lengthening the war in the Pacific. We have now over a million tons of supplies in England for Overlord. It would be going into reverse to undertake the Balkans and it would prolong the war materially. The British might like to ditch Overlord at this time in order to under take operations in a country with practically no communications. If they insist on any such proposal, we could say that if they propose to do that, we will pull out and go into the Pacific with all our forces."[18]

The president hesitated. What if the Russians pressed for operations in the Balkans and only the Balkans? They were already near the borders of Poland, and a new front might help them? Roosevelt wondered, "The Soviets might say, 'If someone would now come up from the Adriatic to the Danube, we could readily defeat Germany forthwith.'" Marshall said, yes, that was a possibility, and, if they asked us for help, we could use our heavy bombers to give them support, but that was not the solution. The real solution was to open a second front that could be decisive, one that could end the war, and that could only be done in France. Only D-Day would create a mortal threat to Hitler.[19] The Russians needed to see it that way, said Marshall. The answer was to paint an extremely clear picture to the Russians. If they wanted the Balkans, very well, but it would cost them Overlord perhaps by as much as several months, said Marshall. Would they be willing to hold out that long for an operation that could not possibly end the war, or did they want a decisive action that would positively end it? There were one million soldiers preparing for the landings, but if Overlord was only a tentative operation, they needed to stop now.

Roosevelt understood the point and came over to Marshall's side and added some points of his own. Not only were there military considerations on this matter, but serious political ramifications as well. The American people were sacrificing nearly everything they had for the war, said Roosevelt. Everyday necessities such as gasoline and milk were already being rationed, much less the loss of so many sons and husbands. The press was talking about England and France and the Nazis in *Europe* to the point that the American people simply would not stand for action in some remote, rugged mountain range in Yugoslavia. Yes, said Roosevelt, Marshall was right. If the British would not go along with D-Day, Roosevelt said, he wanted to go ahead anyway. It should be primarily an American operation, regardless, with a "preponderance of American soldiers and with an American commander," said FDR.[20]

Marshall nodded. The president's position was much clearer, but Roosevelt tended to waver on these things so Marshall suggested that they meet again to discuss the Balkans before they met with the Russians. The president agreed.

That was the final point on the agenda but clearly something was on the president's mind, so the meeting remained in session. Roosevelt wanted to talk some more about the post-war landscape. The Allies had to prevent Germany from rising again, he said, and the best way to do that was to split it up. "Practically speaking, there should be three German states after the war, possibly five," said FDR. "We might take southern Germany, Baden, Wurttemberg, Bavaria, and everything south of the Rhine. This area forms a sort of southern state. Take everything north and west of that area, including Hamburg and Hanover, and so forth, up to and including Berlin to form a second state, and the northeastern part, that is, Prussia, Pomerania, and south, to form a third state." There were reasons for these divisions, he said. The borders of these "states" already had a cultural or historical basis. For instance, the Roman Catholics were all in the southern state, the Protestants in the north, and the Prussians in the northeast. Moreover, these new states largely conformed to the wishes of the Russians, who in fact had little or no interest in the rest of Europe but were intensely interested in Germany. In earlier conversations, Eden said that the Russians wanted to see British and American troops heavily involved in Europe so they could concentrate on their own spheres of influence, foremost of those being the countries on their own border.

"The Soviet Government will offer no objection to breaking up Germany after the war," he said to his chiefs. The issue is to break up Germany *our* way, he said, and that would have much to do with where U.S. soldiers would be when the end came.[21] Rankin.

Roosevelt turned his head and asked if anyone had a map. Rear Admiral Brown rummaged around and found a National Geographic map and a pencil, which he handed to the president. Roosevelt took the pencil and drew lines on the map. He divided Germany into his three states. He used the western part of Germany as his starting point and drew a line down the border of the Netherlands, turning inland into Germany as far as Frankfurt and Wurzburg, then up to the north along the border of Poland and ending at Szczecin on the Baltic Sea. This was the American area, he said, Germany's north and west which included Bremen, Hamburg, Hannover, and Berlin. Tapping the map as he looked around, he indicated what he wanted for the United States. He then lopped off a second state from southern Germany, which included Munich. The British would take care of this area, said Roosevelt, and then everything to the east would be for the Russians.

He passed the map across the table. The Joint Chiefs looked it over and clearly understood their orders. This crude map was the new end state for the Rankin proposals, the new end state for the war in Europe. Indeed, it was to be the new Europe. Now it was up to them to write the battle plans to achieve it.

They began to rise from the table as the meeting closed, but almost as an afterthought the president said that Berlin might be "shared." Roosevelt was looking at Marshall and said that they may have to divide up Berlin between England, Russia, and the United States. Marshall simply nodded and said, "Yes, sir."[22]

Marshall took the map with him.[23]

"I think we discussed it halfway across the South Atlantic," said Marshall, of the emphasis the president had placed on the post war landscape.[24] Indeed, Roosevelt had in mind a Germany that had not been seen for generations.

*

The moment of truth approached, as the passage through the Strait of Gibraltar neared. Arnold's reconnaissance pilots were at 30,000 feet, flying reconnaissance over the German air bases, watching for any hint of activity. There were eight destroyers and one cruiser alongside, plus a screen of British fighter planes above.[25] It was a formidable show of force, but the *Iowa* was such a prize and everyone knew there would be no room to maneuver to shake off a U-boat or a bomber once the *Iowa* was funneled into the Strait. Thankfully, there was as yet no hint of enemy activity. No more than a dozen senior officers were in on the secret and so far the fact that FDR was on the ship was contained, but they were not taking anything for granted. "Roosevelt was going into an active war zone full of Nazi spies, all of whom would be hailed as heroes if they assassinated the commander-in-chief of the U.S. fighting forces," wrote one of Roosevelt's biographers, and now they would find out if there were any heroes out there.[26]

The sun dipped below the horizon at 6 P.M., and at 6:21 P.M. the logbook reads that the last light drained from the sky. There was no sign yet of land, but ever so soon the first grey masses would loom up from the sea, and the horizon would no longer be flat. McCrea sent the entire Task Group to General Quarters and ordered flank speed. The watches felt the ship surge and the wind rush down the decks as they swept the seas with their binoculars. Ever so slowly, they could see a hint of land, a break in the horizon here and there, a peak, then two. "Soon a light was picked up off our starboard bow—Cape Spartel, the northwestern tip of the African continent," wrote McCrea. "A few minutes passed and then the European continent's Cap Tarifa [Spain] blinked ahead to port." The faint outlines of terrain mixed with the dark of the night, and at 7:49 P.M. the Task Group formally entered the channel leading into the Strait of Gibraltar, and now things started to happen faster. "The night was clear and dark, and many, many shore side lights were visible," said McCrea. "Searchlights scanned the sky and the horizon."[27] The searchlights were from the defensive shore emplacements along the coast of Spain. There was nothing out of the ordinary about them, but they silhouetted the ships and that put the ships in potential danger. Taking no chances, the destroyers quickly turned on their smoke generators and billowed clouds into which the *Iowa* disappeared.[28] Now it was a matter of sheer force, nine mighty war ships at flank speed racing into the Mediterranean Sea with guns loaded and eyes sweeping the skies. "We decided to try to bull the *Iowa* through there," said Reilly the Secret Service chief, and that they did, head-on.[29] "Tangier Point, Malabata Point, and Point Almina winked in succession to our starboard," said McCrea. "That was Africa. Europe Point Light blazed at the foot of Gibraltar. That was Europe. And more. Much more. It was difficult to perceive anything of the famous rock save a dark, high blur against the night sky."[30]

As November 19th became November 20th, the *Iowa* steamed past the ancient smugglers den, Alboran Island, in the middle of the Mediterranean Sea, and McCrea observed three more African coastal lights, Tramontana, Tres Forcas, and Los Farallones. Near dawn, the lookouts reported a white line of surf at the foot of the Cap Falcon lighthouse, and then, finally, joyfully, into the Baie des Aiguades, the western extreme of the Gulf of Oran.[31]

They were across.

CHAPTER 13: TUNIS

She was a tired ship, six hard days at sea with her boilers straining against their rivets to make flank speeds, the storms, the U-boats, the threats of leaks adding to it all. Inside the ship, last minute details were being attended to as the passengers prepared for docking. Bags were packed, uniforms were buttoned, final notes were scribbled into diaries. Arnold, Marshall, King, and Leahy had an early breakfast and were up on the deck to watch the *Iowa* come into port, as was Prettyman, who had Roosevelt on the starboard promenade. McCrea was on the bridge. "The harbor was jammed-packed," said the captain. "Oilers and freighters of the United Nations seemed to crush into one another."[1]

From the deck the arriving passengers could make out the welcoming party. On the docks stood Army Colonel Elliott Roosevelt and Navy Lieutenant Franklin D. Roosevelt, Jr., the president's two sons, with Secret Service agent Mike Reilly, Vice Admiral Hewitt, and United States Army Lt. General Dwight D. Eisenhower, commanding general of the Allied forces in North Africa and into whose hands the president's safe passage would be turned. It was a beautiful morning, crisp and slightly chilly with a bright blue sky. The streaming sunlight shone down on the dusty shoreline of North Africa and illuminated the Moorish minarets and the rows of flowers that crowned the nearby hills. Ever so slowly, the grey battleship inched back and forth inside the harbor of Mers-el-Kebir, her size dwarfing the ships around her. The snow-capped peaks of the Atlas Mountains were a glorious backdrop to the occasion, the smell of salt water thick in the air with a slight breeze coming off the sea. "We were all up early," remembered Elliott Roosevelt of his father's arrival. "It was a clear, bright, crisp day for which we all were grateful."[33]

The meetings on board the ship had been consequential, and Arnold felt they were all "better informed and prepared on this trip than any conference so far."[2] He, like the others who were disembarking, came away with possibly their best understanding yet of the president's vision for the war—and certainly the post-war period ahead. There was a sense of accomplishment and a newfound appreciation for the Roosevelt way of travel as the first leg of their trip came to a close.

Roosevelt's arrival was planned out in exacting detail, security being the foremost consideration. The docks were cordoned off by a wall of armed soldiers, and fighter planes buzzed above. The *Iowa* came to her anchorage, and the first off the boat was Roosevelt who was lowered from the davits into a waiting whaleboat that brought him ashore, bearing a cape over his shoulders, a cigarette in hand, and that radiant Roosevelt smile. "The sea voyage had done him good," said Elliott. "He looked fit."[3] Behind him came the Joint Chiefs and then their staff, and to a man it was welcome to feel Mother Earth beneath their feet.

After handshakes and smiles, the president and his sons joined Eisenhower in his staff car, which quickly left the harbor and sped up the hills towards Algeria's La Senia airport fifty miles away. There waited their transportation for the second leg of the trip, a C-54 airplane, nick-named the *Sacred Cow*, which would fly Roosevelt to Tunisia. Waiting in the plane was the president's pilot, Major Otis F. Bryan, a seasoned captain whose crew of four would stay with the president to Tehran and back. Roosevelt, Franklin, Jr., Eisenhower, Leahy, Prettyman, four secret service agents, and a few others climbed aboard and were promptly air-borne. Second to depart was George Marshall's group, followed by a third plane with Arnold, King, and their party. It was a well-orchestrated sequence that minimized their time on the ground but equally made no effort to keep the planes together as they crossed Africa. "The planes take off, each on a different course," wrote Arnold in his diary "#1 with fight-er escort via the coastline; #2 slightly inland, no escort; #3 via Biskra, Kasserine Pass to Tunis." They now had three hours in the air to sort things out, look at mail, and watch the landscape unfold below.[4]

McCrea saw the last of his passengers off and had the tug boats reposition his ship next to the sea wall to take on fuel. Two oilers came alongside, one of which had been torpedoed, survived, but were still charred from the encounter. British Admiral Sir John Cunningham, the Commander in Chief of the Allied Fleet in the Mediterranean, was on his flagship, so, while being oiled, McCrea saw to some formalities. "I went over to call on Admiral Cunningham," wrote McCrea. "... He said to me, 'Captain, what are your orders?' And I reached in my pocket, and I read [Admiral King's] orders. He said, 'I am changing those orders.'... He said, 'You came through the strait last night. The Spaniards, those alleged neutrals, know that a big unit went through the straits last night with all your escorts. Unquestionably, the information that a big unit went through last night is now in Berlin. I want you out of here by 1800 hours today." McCrea nodded, said he understood, and departed. "At 1800 hours that night, we cast off our lines, and away we went." Roosevelt had been safely delivered, and the navy's work was over. A dangerous job had been completed with exceptional grace. The *Iowa* crossed the equator, docked in Brazil, refueled, then would return three weeks later to pick up the president off the coast of Africa near Dakar.[5]

*

In the air, the three transport planes were now winging east across North Africa, overflying the scars of the recently ended military campaign to push out the Germans and retake the southern shores of the Mediterranean Sea. It had been bitter, bloody combat. General Dwight D. Eisenhower had been named the commander of Operation Torch and led his army of British and American soldiers into combat in November of 1942. They came in from the sea and landed in Casablanca, Morocco, and Oran. Facing them were hundreds of thousands of battle-hardened German soldiers and scores of Panzer and Tiger tanks under the command of German Field Marshall Erwin Rommel. "Our future was murky and foreboding," said Eisenhower as he contemplated combat against the seasoned German armies, "the Nile delta was only a few hours from

[Rommel's] advance...we had to be decisive... our forces were to clean out resistance from Morocco to Tunisia."[6]

The Allies began their advance to the east across Africa to Tunisia, but the Germans defended their lines and struck hard, drawing blood as the Allies untangled the complexities of coalition warfare. Months of combat followed with relentless shelling from heavy artillery, attacks from fighters and bombers, tank battles, and savage hand-to-hand combat. The final battles came near Tunisia, where the German line finally collapsed, forcing Rommel to evacuate to Italy. The fighting then jumped to Sicily and then to the boot of Italy.

As the three planes made their approach to Tunis, they saw the detritus of Eisenhower's campaign—burned-out German aircraft along the runways, the charred hulks of tanks, and the skeletons of personnel carriers and trucks scattered to the horizon.

Once on the ground, the president was lowered to a waiting staff car and, with Eisenhower, was rushed to Guest Villa No.1, a White House-like compound in the Carthage area of Tunis, situated on the seashore of the Gulf of Tunis with Cape Bon visible in the distance. The villa had been used by Rommel during his occupation of Tunisia and was now used by Eisenhower when he visited the area. Roosevelt did not like to fly, but his mood was good. "He was in good health and was optimistic and confident," said Eisenhower of the drive in from the airport. The days at sea had indeed rested him well.[7]

As soon as he settled in, Roosevelt summoned Rigdon to help him sort out his bulging mail pouch. There was news from home, updates from the Map Room, messages from his cabinet, but there were no legislation to be signed. Still, it took all of two hours just to get it organized.

Hap Arnold split off from the rest of the group and went over to the villa used by his North African air commander General Carl "Tooey" Spaatz. He had dinner with Spaatz and his war general, Jimmy Doolittle, both of whom brought him up to date on the North

African and Italian campaigns. He too had a bulging mail pouch waiting and after dinner spent most of the evening with it.

Marshall and King gladly accepted invitations to stay with Ike at his other villa in Tunis. It was a small villa for three, but they were more than happy to escape the restrictions that naturally went hand in glove with traveling with the president. It was here that the conversations again turned to D-Day. Although Ike was scheduled to have dinner with the president later in the evening, they were free for several hours, and, quite naturally, they talked about the war. The Germans had reinforced Italy, and Ike was well south of Rome and wouldn't take it unless he had the landing craft he needed. Marshall listened, then King filled Ike in on their own events, including the substance of the talks with Roosevelt on the voyage across. Numerous conversations had taken place as to the commander of the D-Day invasion, said King. There had been alternative proposals as to the command structure and the number of theaters and so on, but they were not likely to be approved, so it was back to D-Day and who would get the prized command. By seniority, said King, Eisenhower's boss, Marshall should get it, but in fact no decision had been formally announced.

As the three sat in the small living area, King continued. "I told Eisenhower how I thought about who should be the 'top' commanders in France and Germany. First, I said it must be an American general and his deputy should be a British general, or perhaps a British air marshal. Eisenhower and I argued some points. Then I said that the time had come for FDR and the Allies to decide who was to be the man. I told Eisenhower, 'You, Eisenhower, are the proper man to become 'supreme commander' for the Allies on the European continent, especially in France and Germany.'"[8]

King went on to say that Roosevelt had already told him he was going to select Marshall for the D-Day invasion but that he, King, had disagreed and said so to the president. The Joint Chiefs needed Marshall, and breaking up a winning combination in Washington made no sense. King told Eisenhower that he intended to raise the issue again with the president and tell him what he had said before, that is, that Eisenhower should get the command of Overlord and the Joint Chiefs should remain unchanged.[9]

Marshall said nothing. He was never one to discuss personal matters with a junior officer—and Eisenhower was his junior—nor would he ever talk about a decision that affected his own fortunes one way or the other, particularly regarding the D-Day command. It was awkward, to say the least, to have King tell Eisenhower that Marshall was not going to get his vote.[10] "During the admiral's explanation, General Marshall remained completely silent," said Eisenhower. "He seemed embarrassed." King went on to explain that Roosevelt's tentative plans were to bring Eisenhower back from the field and install him as acting Chief of Staff in Marshall's absence. Again, King said he disagreed with that, there being no point in breaking up the winning combination of Marshall, Arnold, King, and Leahy.[11]

Eisenhower was aware of precisely none of this. As a field commander, his sole focus had been on his advance against the Germans across North Africa and now in Italy, and, while he had seen Churchill on numerous occasions during the fighting, his conversations with the Prime Minister had been purely military. Since coming to the theater, Ike said he had no contact with Roosevelt until he met the president at the docks.

King understood as much. King and Eisenhower knew each other well from the days when Eisenhower was Marshall's number two man in the War Department in Washington D.C. Ike was then the Army Chief of Operations and was the usual go-between for Marshall and King, and he and King had a similar humorless approach to things. In July of 1942, Eisenhower was promoted and sent to London to assume the role as the Commanding General for European Operations, but he was far from forgotten. During a meeting of the Joint Chiefs in

London it was King who recommended Eisenhower for the command of the North African invasion, which sealed the deal. Eisenhower was given the first American combat command against Hitler and had completed his mission victoriously.

King was well aware that Roosevelt had not yet made a decision about D-Day, but here in a war zone it was painfully obvious that Eisenhower was an excellent candidate. Irrespective of the row with the British over the invasion, at some point it would happen, and Eisenhower had experience in every aspect of an invasion. The D-Day plan was similar to the North African plan in that it was an invasion by sea that would be supported from the sea. The plan was to land 150,000 soldiers in five coastal zones of Normandy, France, using LST and Higgins boats in May of 1944. The ships would come ashore, landing soldiers who then would battle through the German coastal defenses and push inland to secure a toehold behind which would flow nearly one million more soldiers. It was bold and expansive and envisioned coalition combat on a scale that was unprecedented in world history. Soldiers from the United States, Great Britain, Canada, Australia, Belgium, Czechoslovakia, France, Greece, the Netherlands, New Zealand, Norway, and Poland were to be in the first waves. The plans took into account meteorology, weapons procurement, the construction of specialized landing ships, the manufacture and shipment of countless supplies, the laying of a gasoline pipeline across the English Channel, the movement of battleships and escort carriers across several thousand miles of open seas, a one thousand-page plan for the air support alone that detailed the take-off times, and rendezvous points and missions for more than fourteen thousand B-17s, B-24s and fighter aircraft like the P-51s, P-47s and P-38s.

An elaborate deception plan was already underway with a fake invasion force, fake airfields, fake army bases, fake tanks, and even a fake commander, George Patton, broadcasting fake messages to his fake soldiers over unsecured radio transmissions. To enhance the deception, the fake base occasionally ran out of everyday essentials such as soap or towels and would say so in radio calls. The gates were manned and there were trucks coming and going, but, had any spy been allowed in, he would have seen that they were empty. For the final touch, soldiers were driving cars around at night so their headlights could be seen by German spies peering through the hedgerows.

Even Arnold's bombers were playing their part. In addition to the regular missions against real targets, the RAF and the USAAF were relentlessly bombing the coastal defense in the Pas de Calais area of France in an effort to pin down several German divisions by creating the false perception that the invasion would take place there, two hundred miles away from the real thing.

Reconnaissance flights numbering in the hundreds of missions were being flown by fighter pilots in fast planes, most of which were armed only with cameras and rolls of film. These dicing-with-the-devil pilots were gambling their lives to get down to treetop levels so they could bring back high-quality, detailed photographs of highways, rail tracks, bridges, defensive armaments, obstacles, and other details from the coastal areas of France and the landing zones for the airborne soldiers. It was vital for intelligence, but it was an unforgiving business. Some pilots came back with branches of trees imbedded in the wings of their planes; many simply did not come back at all.

The average American infantryman had gone through eighteen months of hard training before coming overseas, and once in England, they were trained some more. They had the very finest, most reliable rifle in the M1, they had submachine guns slung across their chest, mortars and howitzers and bullets and shells by the hundreds of millions of rounds. Nothing was better for a soldier's morale than the feel of a weapon in his fists and the Army gave them the best.

The 'X' factor in war is a soldier's fighting spirit, and Marshall personally saw to that. Combat troops fight hardest for those things closest to them, for their wives, their children, their homes, but how did one instill that into a nineteen-year-old from Nebraska or Alabama who was going to be shipped off to a war that was four thousand miles away? Said Marshall, "A man's fighting quality, his stamina, his relentless purpose, comes most strongly from the association with his home and his family. The fighting of men far from home could seldom reach the effectiveness of that close to their homes—close to the issues—close to the realization of what it was all about. That was one of the reasons I thought it was so vitally important to have the Army educated as to what we were fighting about."[12] To do that, Marshall commissioned Hollywood's Frank Capra to produce the now famous series of educational films aptly titled *Why We Fight*. It was more motivational than informational—perhaps erring on the side of propaganda —but it got the message across. When tested on the battlefield in North Africa, the resolve of the U.S. soldier came through time and again during the four months of intense combat in Morocco, Algeria, and Tunisia. "It was a magnificent army when it reached its full development," said Marshall. "They displayed magnificent fighting characteristics."[13] In all, they were ready to go, hundreds of thousands of soldiers in England and fifty divisions more in the States.

That was the magnitude of the D-Day—an undertaking unique in military history, a command that would crown any military career—and King was keenly aware that Ike's success in North Africa gave him credentials no other American general had.[14]

King finished his drink, left the room and went to bed, leaving his sentiments hanging heavy in the air as Marshall and Eisenhower stayed behind. "We talked until about 10 P.M. and since I had been up since about 5 A.M., I said I thought I would go to bed," King wrote in his diary. "I don't know how long the others kept talking, but I was up at 6:30 A.M. since all hands had to be ready for a full day ahead."[15]

*

An early morning departure for Cairo was scheduled for the next day, Sunday, but Roosevelt was told that the air force pilots preferred to fly the rim of North Africa by night. The German Luftwaffe pilots were excellent daytime combat fighters, but they did not have any instrument training so they did not fly at night. "The night flight eliminated the need for fighter escort and was considered safer and more comfortable for the President," said Arnold, and Roosevelt agreed. The plan was changed. They would spend the day in Tunis, visit the battlegrounds, and then fly overnight to Cairo. In hindsight, it was a fateful decision.

Just as Lincoln had toured the battlefields with Ulysses S. Grant and, by doing so, had seen a new and very appealing side to his Army general, so it would be with Roosevelt and Eisenhower. A heavily armed convoy was organized to take Roosevelt out to see the Tunisian battlefields where the German front finally disintegrated. At 11 A.M. Roosevelt left his villa and got into a car with Eisenhower. In the lead was a truck packed with military police, while bringing up the rear were two more. To clear the traffic, eight motorcycle MPs went ahead.

The motorcade drove along the Bay of Tunis past the Roman aqueduct, which neatly divided it down the center. They passed burnt docks, saw bomb craters, and in the main harbor saw battle-damaged ships, some on their sides, some sunk with only their funnels visible, others burnt and at awkward angles low to the water. The Germans had fought tenaciously to defend their ground, but the Allies had overwhelmed them, in part because of the accurate bombing which now, weeks later, was sharply illustrated by the proximity of a bombed-out building just fifty yards from a perfectly good one.

The convoy sped into the desert leaving behind billowing clouds of dust. They passed French military convoys and Red Cross trucks as well as numerous shepherds and farmers and men in traditional turbans shuffling through the dirt. Rigdon looked out and saw the rusted skeletons of war piled up like so much trash in dumps that towered fifteen feet above him. He recorded what he saw. "Burned-out tanks (American and German) and other vehicles, still on battlefield where they were destroyed," he wrote. "Tank traps and tank barriers still on battlefields. Blown-up German ammunition dumps. Uncleared mine fields that had been marked and roped-off. Hill 609, the scene of perhaps the heaviest concentration of artillery fire in this war to date. Vast supplies of our ammunition and bombs stored along the highways and in the fields stacked in intervals to minimize loss and damage in case of an enemy raid. A large salvage dump filled with burned-out tanks and other vehicles."[16]

Ike gave Roosevelt a running commentary of the battles and described the bitter combat at Medjez el Bab, at Tebourba, at Bizerte, and the eventual Allied breakthrough, which brought about the collapse of the German front. He described the genius of Patton and Bradley and the final push over Hill 609 in May that routed the Germans. More than two hundred and fifty thousand Axis soldiers surrendered, three hundred thousand more were dead or wounded; of the 70,000 Allied causalities, the Americans had more than 2,700 dead and another 14,000 wounded or missing.

Roosevelt could scarcely speak, such was the enormity of it all, but he could see in Eisenhower a cold, detached familiarity with war that only a man who knew combat could have, and Roosevelt respected that very much.

At 1:25 P.M. they pulled over for lunch. Eisenhower stepped out of the car and walked out into the desert to inspect some burnt-out foxholes and bullet-riddled tanks. Roosevelt watched his general deciphering the sequence of events, the exchange of shells, the twisted metal, the gaping holes. A noise suddenly welled up. It was the raspy sound of engines from a flight of bombers that were coming in to land. Roosevelt looked up and noticed that several of the "V" formations were missing one or two of their planes. Someone counted fifty-one bombers in total and another person said they were returning from a mission over the European continent.

War.

In truth, Roosevelt did not know Eisenhower particularly well; he had never had a lengthy conversation with him until now but had liked what he saw, so he felt compelled to level with him. "Ike," said the president, as he waved Eisenhower back to the car. Ike came back, opened the door, and sat down.[17] "Ike, you and I know who was the Chief of Staff during the last years of the Civil War but practically no one else knows, although the names of field generals—Grant, and of course Lee and Jackson, Sherman, Sheridan, and the others—every schoolboys knows them," said the president. "I hate to think that fifty years from now practically no one will know who George Marshall was. That's one of the reasons I want George to have the big command—he is entitled to his place in history as a great General." Because the Americans would have the D-Day command in Europe, said Roosevelt, it was only fair to return the Mediterranean to a British general, which would leave an opening for Ike in Washington. Roosevelt said he had in mind giving Eisenhower the job as Acting Chief of Staff.[18] Eisenhower, no doubt crest fallen, nonetheless said he would do as he was ordered, whatever that may be.[19] But then FDR said one more thing that threw it all back up in the air: "...but it *is* dangerous to monkey with a winning team," said Roosevelt, and with that both men pulled on their cigarettes in thoughtful repose.[20]

*

The C-54 was one of the newest, most sophisticated multiengine aircraft in the military, a rugged transport with four 1,450 horsepower engines and the most recent instrumentation in the cockpit. It was a third generation aircraft, a sturdy marvel of aeronautical engineering from the genius of the Douglas Aircraft Company, originally destined for the commercial carrier Eastern Air Lines to fly the wealthiest of travelers up and down the eastern seaboard. It carried fifty jammed-packed soldiers or twenty-six comfortably seated passengers, and it sped along at 190 miles per hour. It was just the sort of plane you would want for a president

This C-54 had been extensively modified for Roosevelt's use. It had a self-contained lift that raised him in and out of the plane, two private cabins for sleeping, and specially built windows that had been lowered to allow FDR a good view of the countryside below. Ever cautious, all of the modifications were disguised. From the outside, Roosevelt's plane looked like any other C-54, plain, simple, drab.[21] Although it was not yet so christened, and it would be many months before a C-54 arrived with a name painted on its nose, even now, the C-54 that FDR flew was dubbed the *Sacred Cow*.[22]

Lunch over, the convoy reformed and headed back towards Tunis. The cars arrived at 4 P.M. leaving little time for anything more other than dinner and packing. The next leg of the trip would be a very long one, nearly half the distance of the Atlantic Ocean crossing, ten hours by air from Tunis to Cairo, some 1,860 miles over a very large continent.

Eisenhower, Marshall, King, and Arnold gathered their belongings and went to the airport to fly ahead. Roosevelt and his party had dinner, then boarded their own planes at 10:30 P.M. FDR had a sleeping berth on the *Sacred Cow* and turned in for the night while the rest of the president's party made do. "Sleeping in a chair of a transport is not restful," wrote Admiral Leahy of the flight, which seemed to say it all.[23]

Major Bryan pushed up the throttles to full power, and the *Sacred Cow* roared down the runway and into the night sky. In minutes, the twinkling lights of Tunis were left behind, and a sea of ink-black emptiness cocooned the planes as they flew towards the Levant, the place where the sun—and Man—rose in the east.

Fig. 1   The British wanted combat in the Mediterranean. The Americans wanted D-Day.
          The divide was so deep President Franklin D. Roosevelt, left, and British Prime
          Minister Winston Churchill took the question to Soviet Premier Joseph Stalin.
          Stalin would be the tie breaker.

(Courtesy of the National Archives)

Fig. 2   The American Joint Chiefs of Staff meeting in Washington DC.
From the left, Chief of Naval Operations Admiral Ernest J. King,
Army Chief of Staff General George C. Marshall, Admiral William
D. Leahy, Air Force Chief of Staff General Henry A. "Hap" Arnold.
They would travel with Roosevelt to meet with Stalin in Tehran.

(Courtesy of the National Archives)

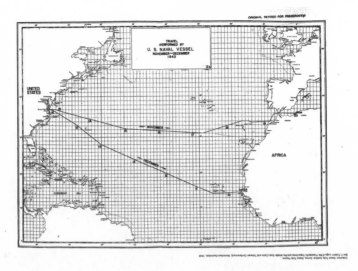

Fig. 3   Map showing the Atlantic Ocean routes to be taken by FDR

(top)   and staff on the USS *Iowa* to and from the Tehran Conference.

(Courtesy of the Franklin D. Roosevelt Library)

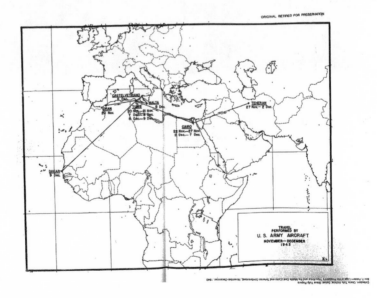

Fig. 4   Second map showing FDR's air travel from Oran to Tunis to Cairo

(bottom)   to Tehran, then back to Cairo to Malta and Italy, and then on to

Dakar where he would reboard the *Iowa* for the return trip home.

(Courtesy of the Franklin D. Roosevelt Library)

Fig. 5   The USS *Iowa* seen just before her departure for Oran.
           This is one of only two known photographs that show
           the external elevators installed for the President. See the
           thin vertical shaft just below the main stack, forward.

           (Courtesy of the National Archives)

November 12, 1943.

At about nine-thirty last night the President's party left the White House and proceeded in a motor car cavalcade to Quantico where we boarded the U.S.S. POTOMAC and sailed at once for the mouth of the Potomac River. The party consisted of the President, Mr. Harry Hopkins, Rear Admiral Wilson Brown, U. S. Navy, Major General E. M. Watson, U. S. Army, Rear Admiral Ross McIntire, Surgeon General, and myself.

At nine-thirty this morning we boarded the U.S.S. Battleship IOWA, Captain John McCrea, Commanding, and sailed at once for Hampton Roads.

We found already on board the IOWA, General Marshall, Admiral King, General Arnold, Lieutenant General Somervell, and about fifty American Staff officers of subordinate rank and position in the Joint Staff Organization. - PASSENGERS ON USS IOWA

RANK	NAME	TITLE
	The President	
	Hopkins, Harry L.	C. of S. to the President
Admiral	Leahy, W. D.	Chief of Staff
General	Marshall, G. C.	Cominch
Admiral	King, E. J.	CG, AAF
General	Arnold, H. H.	CG, ASF
Lt. Gen.	Somervell, B. B.	Naval Aide
R. Adm.	Brown, W.	Surgeon General
R. Adm.	McIntire, R. T.	Military Aide
Maj. Gen.	Watson, E. M.	DepCos-Cominch
R. Adm.	Cooke, C. M. Jr.	Planner (Navy)
R. Adm.	Bieri, B. H.	Asst. VCNO
R. Adm.	Badger, O. C.	Asst. CofS CPD
Maj. Gen.	Handy, T. T.	Asst CofAS-Plans
Brig. Gen.	Kuter, L. S.	AAF Planner
Brig. Gen.	Hansell, H.S. Jr.	JWPC
Captain	Burrough, E. W.	U. S. Secretary
Captain	Royal, F. B.	AAF, JWPC
Colonel	Smith, J.	Adv. Council AAF
Colonel	O'Donnell, E.	OP Membr, JWPC
Colonel	Hessell, V. E.	Planner (Navy)
Captain	Doyle, A. K.	Planner - CPD
Colonel	Roberts, F. N.	Aide to Adm. Leahy
Captain	Freeman, W. L.	Aide to Cominch
Comdr.	Long, V. D.	Secty, JWPC
Major	Miller, C. E.	Asst to DepSecy
Major	Chapman, W. W.	Asst to Surgeon General
Lt. Comdr.	Fox, G. A.	

Fig. 6 (above)   A page from Leahy's diary showing the names of the passengers on the transatlantic crossing. Highly risky to begin with, this was the only time in U.S. history that such a concentration of key military advisors would be in the same place at the same time.

(Courtesy of the National Archives)

Fig. 7 (right)   Captain John L. McCrea, captain of the *Iowa*. McCrea slept next to the bridge during the entire crossing.

(Courtesy of the National Archives)

Fig. 8   General Marshall speaks with Harry Hopkins, a close friend and
             advisor to FDR. Hopkins accompanied the President on this trip.

             (Courtesy of the National Archives)

Fig. 9   Admiral Ernest J. King

(Courtesy of the National Archives)

Fig. 10   General Henry A. "Hap" Arnold at his desk surrounded
            by models of some of his creations. Most biographies say
            "Hap" was short for Happy, as in Hap's sunny disposition.

            (Courtesy of the National Archives)

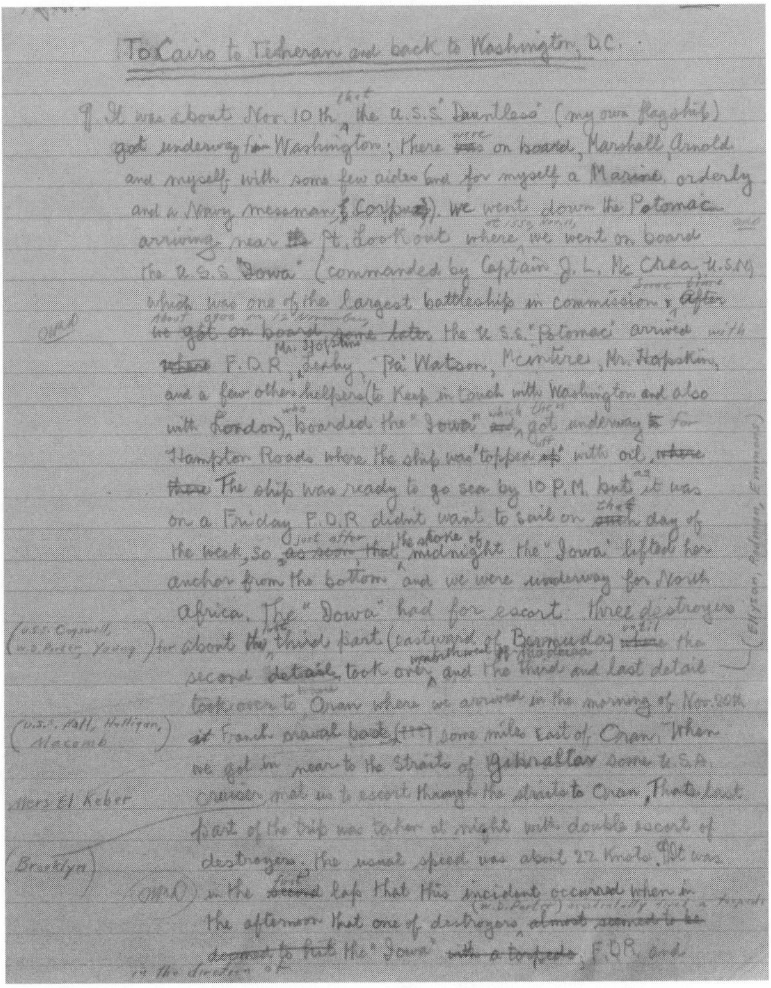
To Cairo to Teheran and back to Washington, D.C.

It was about Nov. 10th that the U.S.S. "Dauntless" (my own flagship) got underway from Washington; there were on board, Marshall, Arnold and myself with some few aides and for myself a Marine orderly and a Navy messman (Corpus). We went down the Potomac arriving near Pt. Lookout where we went on board the U.S.S. "Iowa" (commanded by Captain J. L. McCrea, U.S.N.) which was one of the largest battleship in commission. Some time after the U.S.S. "Potomac" arrived with F.D.R., Leahy, "Pa" Watson, McIntire, Mr. Hopkins, and a few other helpers (to keep in touch with Washington and also with London) who boarded the "Iowa" which then got underway for Hampton Roads where the ship was "topped off" with oil. The ship was ready to go sea by 10 P.M. but as it was on a Friday F.D.R. didn't want to sail on that day of the week, so just after the stroke of midnight the "Iowa" lifted her anchor from the bottom and we were underway for North Africa. The "Iowa" had for escort three destroyers for about the first third part (eastward of Bermuda) until the second took over and the third and last detail took over to Oran where we arrived in the morning of Nov. 20th at French naval base some miles east of Oran. When we got in near to the Straits of Gibraltar some U.S.A. cruisers met us to escort through the straits to Oran. That last part of the trip was taken at night with double escort of destroyers. The usual speed was about 22 knots. It was in the first lap that this incident occurred when in the afternoon that one of destroyers (W.D. Porter) accidentally fired a torpedo in the direction of the "Iowa". F.D.R. and

Fig. 11 Admiral Kings handwritten notes from his Trip Log recording his experiences during the voyage and the ensuing conferences.

(Courtesy of the Library of Congress)

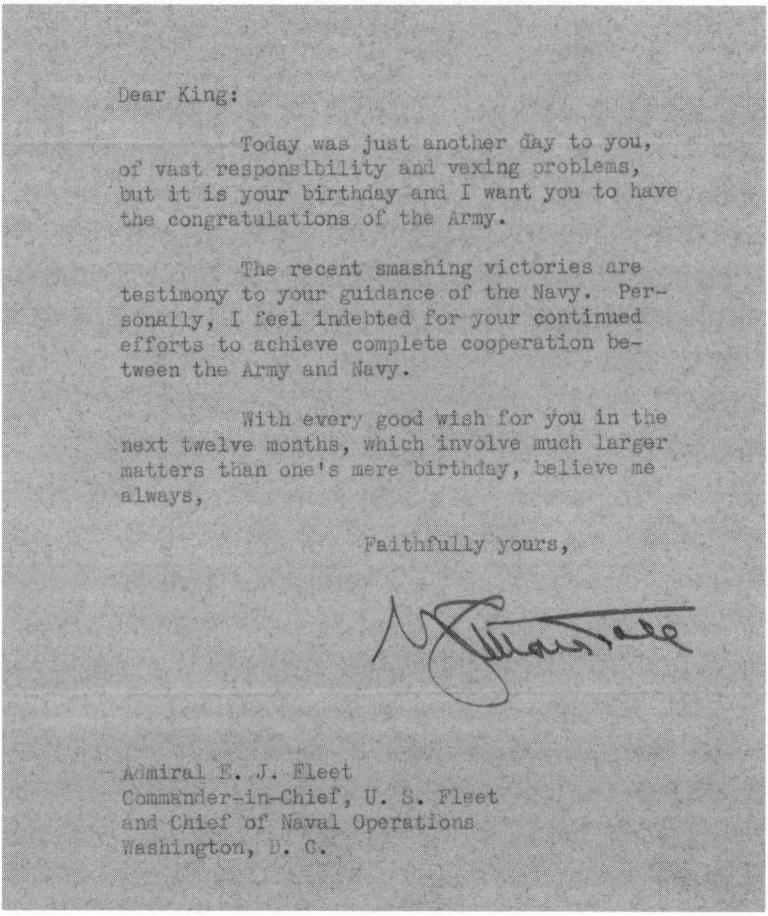

Dear King:

Today was just another day to you, of vast responsibility and vexing problems, but it is your birthday and I want you to have the congratulations of the Army.

The recent smashing victories are testimony to your guidance of the Navy. Personally, I feel indebted for your continued efforts to achieve complete cooperation between the Army and Navy.

With every good wish for you in the next twelve months, which involve much larger matters than one's mere birthday, believe me always,

Faithfully yours,

Admiral E. J. Fleet
Commander-in-Chief, U. S. Fleet
and Chief of Naval Operations
Washington, D. C.

Fig. 12 Marshall penned this note to Admiral King on the occasion of his birthday. The two members of the Joint Chiefs got off to a rocky start but notes like these helped smooth things over in their relationship.

(Courtesy of the Library of Congress)

Fig. 13   The main harbor at Oran, Algiers as seen from the deck of the *Iowa*.
           This is one of the few photographs taken during the entire voyage.
           No cameras were carried by any of the passengers and no photographs
           were allowed while the President was on board.

           (Courtesy of the National Archives)

Fig. 14   Chiang Kai-shek, FDR, and Winston Churchill, Cairo, November 25, 1943.
           The interim meetings regarding the China theater were largely unproductive.

           (Courtesy of the National Archives)

Fig. 15   Landing Ship, Tank (LSTs) such as this were one of the issues
causing friction between the Americans and the British.
Marshall once commented that with a few dozen extra
LSTs he could have ended the war six months sooner.
Seen in the Aleutians delivering tractors.

(Courtesy of the National Archives)

Fig. 16   General Dwight D. Eisenhower meets with George Marshall in Tunisia enroute to Tehran.

(Courtesy of the National Archives)

Fig. 17   Roosevelt's C-54 transport dubbed The Sacred Cow
           during one leg of the trip. FDR was no fan of travel
           by air. He had his own sleeping cabin on the plane.

(Courtesy of the National Archives)

Fig .18   Inside the Sacred Cow while traveling across North Africa during an
           earlier conference although with much the same traveling companions
           (excepting McCrea). Roosevelt is talking with Harry Hopkins. Seated behind
           him are Navy Lt. George Fox and Admiral Ross McIntire FDR's personal
           physicians. Across the aisle, with his back to the camera, is a secret Service
           agent, facing forward is John McCrea. Behind them are, left to right, Valet
           Arthur Prettyman, Charles Fredericks (with hands folded), Hipsley and
           Deckard, two secret Service agents, and the pilot of The Sacred Cow,
           Captain Otis Bryan. Unidentified man in rear of plane.

           (Courtesy of the National Archives)

Fig. 19   The conference room in the Mena House Hotel in Egypt enroute to Tehran.
(top)   (L to R) General Arnold, General Marshall, Captain Royal, Admiral Leahy,
             Admiral King. The British are on the opposite side of the table.

             (Courtesy of the National Archives)

Fig. 20   The gravity of the situation reads on the faces of the British Chiefs of Staff.
(bottom)   From left, Sir Hastings Ismay, Sir Alan Brooke, Sir John Dill,
             Sir Andrew Cunningham, and aides.

             (Courtesy of the National Archives)

Fig. 21   Hap Arnold reviews papers during a meeting of
           the Combined Chiefs of Staff at the Mena House.
           Sir John Dill is in the foreground.

(Courtesy of the National Archives)

Fig. 22   General Carl A. "Tooey" Spaatz looks at aerial reconnaissance photos of
German air bases along the Mediterranean. These bases were bombed to
secure the route of FDR's travel across North Africa. Spaatz was part of Arnold
plan to consolidate his air forces under a central command based in England.

(Courtesy of the National Archives)

Fig. 23   A truck makes it way along an unimproved
           dirt road heading into Tehran.

           (Courtesy of the National Archives)

Fig .24   Cameo of Stalin walking briskly past
           Arnold and Churchill (who has his back
           to the camera). Tehran.

           (Courtesy of the National Archives)

Fig. 25
(above)

Churchill addresses Stalin during the presentation of the sword commemorating the
Battle of Stalingrad. FDR's Secret Service men noted how tall and physical Stalin's
security men were, one of whom is about to accept the sword and hand it over to Stalin.
Inside the Soviet Embassy, Tehran.

(Courtesy of the National Archives)

Fig. 26
(right)

British Foreign Secretary
Anthony Eden, in dark
suit, is just behind Churchill.
Flanking Stalin are Voroshilov
to his right, and Molotov.
During presentation of the
sword to commemorate the
Battle of Stalingrad.

(Courtesy of the National Archives)

Fig. 27   Voroshilov shows Roosevelt the ceremonial sword. Stalin is at the extreme left.
Elliott Roosevelt stands behind the President. Tehran.

(Courtesy of the National Archives)

Fig. 28   The Big Three seen on the front portico of the Soviet Embassy
in Tehran. FDR shakes hands with Churchill's daughter, Sarah.
Behind the heads of state are Hopkins, Molotov, Averill Harriman
Ambassador to Russia, and Anthony Eden (sporting the mustache).

(Courtesy of the National Archives)

Fig. 29   One of the iconic images of World War II,
            the Big Three on the portico of the Soviet Embassy, Tehran.

            (Courtesy of the National Archives)

Fig. 30   Behind the scenes of the official portrait session at the Tehran Conference.
In the background, on the left, are Marshall, King, and Arnold.
On the right side are Leahy, Voroshilov, (Harriman?), Molotov, and Eden.

(Courtesy of the National Archives)

Fig .31 (right) From Leahy's diary, the seating chart for the dinner celebrating Churchill's 69th birthday. This event was held at the British Legation in Tehran.

(Courtesy of the Library of Congress)

Fig .32 (above) Found at the Library of Congress, a poor quality but priceless image from Churchill's birthday celebration. Churchill sits with Roosevelt and Stalin on either side. Bohlen is to FDR's right. This was when Stalin gave his well-received "machines" toast.

(Courtesy of the Library of Congress)

Fig. 33   FDR spent his last night in Tehran with the American soldiers at nearby Camp Amirabad.
(above)   His jeep has just been driven up the small wooden platform built for the occasion of his
            short speech before the assembled soldiers.

            (Courtesy of the Library of Congress)

Fig. 34   FDR reviews the troops at Camp Amirabad in Tehran. Note his cape and fedora hat—Roosevelt
            trademarks—and the beautiful Alborz Mountains in the background.

            (Courtesy of the National Archives)

Fig. 35   Roosevelt stopped by the hospital at Camp Amirabad. Amirabad had about 2,500 U.S.
(above)   soldiers based there as part of the U.S. forces in Iran.

(Courtesy of the National Archives)

Fig. 36   Safely home from a long journey, FDR thanks the men of the *Iowa*
(below)   and says goodbye. This is the only known photograph of FDR while
           on the *Iowa*. Taken moments before he departed to board his own
           vessel the Potomac for the final leg up the Potomac River to Washington, D.C.

(Courtesy of the National Archives)

Fig. 37   D-Day was the crux of the issue that forced the meetings with Stalin.
           It was resolved in favor of the American plan. Here Marshall meets
           with Eisenhower on the Normandy Beaches 15 days after the successful
           D-Day invasion. Marshall wanted the D-Day command but did the
           President's bidding. It was given to Eisenhower.

           (Courtesy of the National Archives)

Fig .38   It was over. General Marshall, Admiral Leahy, and Admiral King,
during a Victory in Europe Day radio address (VE Day).
The last minute decisions made in Tehran led to this moment.

(Courtesy of the National Archives)

CHAPTER 14: THE PSYCHOLOGICAL MOMENT

It was November 22, 1943, almost twelve full days since they left Washington, D.C. It had been a long trip, 3,800 miles across the ocean, and another 630 miles by air to Tunis, followed by a red-eye flight of some 1,800 miles to Cairo. The plane carrying Arnold, Marshall and King had arrived in the middle of the night with plenty of time for them to get to their villas near the Mena House Hotel, a luxury resort in the shadows of the Great Pyramids of Giza and the site of their first meetings with Churchill.

The plan was to meet at 11 A.M. with the U.S. ambassadors to Britain and Russia to get up to speed on the world situation prior to meeting with Churchill and Stalin. This would take place at the Mena House, which, for all practical purposes, was now the most heavily guarded hotel in the world. The security measures taken by Mike Reilly would become legend in Secret Service circles and would rank Roosevelt as one of the most thoroughly protected presidents in history. First, every room in the Mena House had been rented by the White House, and every villa near the hotel had been inspected and secured. Next, the hotel employees were removed and replaced by men vetted by Reilly. FDR's own Filipino cooks took over the main kitchen.

The Army Corps of Engineers then brought in the bulldozers and scraped a sterile perimeter around the hotel and enclosed it with heavy barbed wire. Gate houses were built for passage in and out of the grounds, and a full battalion of soldiers armed with pistols and rifles patrolled the area day and night. The soldiers were reinforced with heavy machine gun nests that were strategically placed at vital choke points, and antiaircraft artillery for enemy airplanes. Reilly later proudly recounted his precautionary measures, "Mine detectors checked the entire area, buildings were searched for listening devices or bombs, and the residences of the President and the Prime Minister were tested for any radioactive substances by Geiger counter. Heavy antiaircraft batteries were deployed around the area. [American] Fighter planes based at nearby airfields reinforced radar-equipped British night fighters. The Navy set up special surface patrols in the nearby Atlantic."[1] And of course, Arnold was also bombing German air bases, another security measure.

The next step was to control telecommunications. The Mena House was put behind a wall of electronic silence. No outgoing message traffic was allowed over any electronic device, no reporters could file stories. "Long distance telephones were arbitrarily put out of service, censorship was ironclad, and certain forms of communication to the outside world were stopped altogether." As Reilly put it, a wall of "dead silence" rose between the locations where the president would be and the rest of the world.[2] To secure their own radio transmissions, the Secret Service gave the senior members of the president's party code names. Marshall was Peach, Arnold was Cherry, King was Apple, Leahy was Tarpon. FDR's code name changed frequently to prevent people from guessing it. He was variously called Maple, Spruce, Beech, Redwood, Zephyr, and Citadel. Mike Reilly was Dandy.[3]

*

Leahy, who was on the president's plane, was running late. While in the air, FDR had asked his pilot to turn south and take the *Sacred Cow* down the Nile River to Luxor and the Valley of the Kings so he could see the Sphinx and the pyramids from the air. Roosevelt, who had a bit of the truculent schoolboy in him, no doubt smiled at the thought that he had lost his mother hens. The detour took a good deal of time and threw off the fighter escorts who were supposed to rendezvous with the president's plane, but never found it.

Marshall decided to go ahead with the morning meetings without Leahy.

The conference room at the Mena House was a richly appointed room with walls draped in luxurious Egyptian cotton hangings, stuffed chairs, and a well-polished conference room table with silver trays of biscuits, crystal goblets of water, and room to comfortably seat twenty dignitaries. The room was crowded this morning, even though this was a private meeting for only American staff. There were a total of thirty-one war planners and state department officials most of whom took chairs along the walls.

General Marshall called the meeting to order. "There is no formal agenda for this meeting, which has been called principally for the purpose of hearing the views of Ambassador Winant, Ambassador Harriman, and the representatives of the various theaters present as to the current situation in their particular areas," said Marshall. There was, however, one business matter to attend to. "The British Chiefs of Staff have proposed a meeting of the Combined Chiefs at 1500 hours in order to consider the matter of the procedure to be pursued during the conference," said Marshall. This was par for the course; the meetings of the Combined Chiefs were always formal affairs with tightly regulated agendas and exacting protocol including specific agendas and rules of order. Marshall asked if there were any objections on the part of the U.S. chiefs to this proposal. There were none. That decided, he turned to Ambassador Winant.

John Gilbert Winant was a former WWI fighter pilot and Princeton graduate, twice governor of New Hampshire, and, since 1941, Roosevelt's ambassador to England. Tall, thin, and handsome with dark hair, he was well known by the generals in attendance and well liked as a diplomat. Said Marshall, as he smiled towards the ambassador, the U.S. Joint Chiefs would like to know what the British were thinking about the various D-Day proposals and the upcoming meetings with Stalin, to discern "the state of mind of the British with respect to the current situation." Would he care to start? Winant nodded and stood.

The news from England was not good, he said as he began. The British were not pleased with the American Joint Chiefs. According to them, the American chiefs were far too wed to their own plans and much too unwilling to consider other ideas. This attitude, in their opinion, was costing the Allies opportunities for easy gains against the Germans. "The British feel the position of the United Nations is not sufficiently fluid to take advantage of the victories gained in Italy," said Winant, calling the Allied nations by the term often used during the war. "This applies to the German-occupied islands east of Athens in the Mediterranean which had been there for the taking had plans been coordinated with the American air forces, which they were not." Marshall grumbled at the suggestion that the U.S. was the problem. No one authorized any such operations against the German-occupied islands of Leros or Cos and the whole thing had been foolish, but he said nothing.

As to the American plans for D-Day and the Far East, Winant said the British were opposed a fixed date for Overlord and had no interest in sending resources to the Far East to assist the Chinese Nationalists in the fight against the Japanese, nor to divert resources for combat in Burma. He advised the Joint Chiefs to expect vigorous opposition on these points.

With reference to Overlord, Winant thought that the British had no desire to abandon the operation altogether, but they were opposed to a fixed date. The Americans were inflexible on that point, the British were complaining, and they thought that attitude was dead wrong. Rather, it was the British point of view that it was completely impossible to "fix far in advance the precise psychological moment for launching an attack on the Continent," as Winant recalled it. It was an odd choice of words, Winant said, and he had no explanation for how the British defined a "psychological moment" except that to say that they had used that specific expression, and when the British used a word or an expression, they did so on purpose.

Winant went on to say that the British were upset and wanted to undo what they had previously done, which was to sign a flawed contract with the Americans in regards to the agreement for a May 1944 date for Overlord. They felt this agreement should be changed. This "contract," as they put it, stated that Overlord took precedence over everything else including subsequent changes in the military situation, and that was a mistaken concept, said the British, and it needed to be recognized as a mistake and corrected at this conference. Winant said that they would mount a stiff fight to win this point, and they would take it to Tehran if needed. There should be no fixed date, said the British, at least not until matters in the current theaters of combat were clearer. Moreover, the British will argue that opportunities for easy wins should not be ignored even if they delay Overlord. This was their state of mind on D-Day: Winant felt the British were genuine in their desire to continue the build-up for Overlord but that the principal difference was timing.

Winant continued. He said that Churchill was of the opinion that Stalin was chiefly interested in immediate combat initiatives that would stretch German resources thin and give him some immediate relief. The D-Day invasion, therefore, was not nearly as important to Stalin as it had been. Rather, the British point of view was that Stalin very much wanted vigorous combat action against the Germans now, anywhere, and that the Soviet leader was not concerned about *where* it was brought to bear, only that it was.[4]

Marshall had something to say. If the British wanted to undo the date for Overlord they would have a fight on their hands, he said, but if the Russians needed immediate relief, a fixed date for Overlord would be another matter. As a soldier, he would feel compelled to bring immediate assistance to another soldier, but unless he heard that from Stalin, and he hadn't, he failed to see the British point of view against a fixed date. One could not prepare for a major invasion without a fixed date. One did not turn a nation on its head to build up the tanks and planes and soldiers for an invasion if that invasion was just a "maybe."

Winant took a drink of water and continued. Yes, he said, he knew that, but the Prime Minister had been considerably upset by his defeat on Leros and Cos, and although his own military staff thought his reaction was considerably out of perspective on that point, Churchill would not stop complaining about the lack of American support. But that was not the only consequence of the Leros debacle. Winant said the setback had added to Churchill's negative views of D-Day. Now more than ever, Churchill seemed to fear the German soldier. The Prime Minister went so far as to say that "the British were supreme on the sea, and that the British and the U.S. were supreme in the air, but that the Germans were still superior to both nations on the ground" and that fact bode poorly for the soldiers landing in Normandy, a bias, said Winant, that was only magnified by the defeats on Leros and Cos.

And that led into the next point. Referring to the cross-Channel operations, Winant said the British were disturbed now, not so much by the difficulties of the landings per se, but by what they thought they would face on the continent afterwards, during the first sixty days of combat. The Germans were excellent soldiers and ferocious in combat. They had ample resources and had been reinforcing Europe for years including the development of mobile reserves that could move forward and be concentrated in full force against the arriving soldiers. Churchill was convinced that the roads and rail lines that ran from east to west across France were impossible to cut by Allied bombing and that the Germans would quickly and successfully bring up their reserves and a defeat was very possible. The success of the invasion, Churchill had said on more than one occasion, was now "gravely in doubt."

Arnold took exception to that. His bombers were just beginning to do their job, he said, but already they were showing good results. They were bombing railroad stations, marshalling yards, rail lines, bridges and major roads, and German airfields, and this pounding would only intensify. For instance, said Arnold, in the thirty days immediately before the invasion, they would be doubling their efforts by dropping tens of thousands of tons of bombs on every possible road and rail line leading to Normandy—the lines of communication, in Army parlance—including all of the bridges across the Seine River south of Paris. Quite to the contrary, Arnold's bombers would not only cut the roads, rail lines, and bridges leading to the invasion beaches they would create a 130-mile-wide arc of destruction around the D-Day beaches themselves that would be so thoroughly cratered and leveled by bombs that it would make Sherman's March through Georgia look like child's play. On top of that, during the landings, some thirteen thousand fighters and bombers would be in the sky patrolling, bombing, and intercepting the forward movement of troops and tanks. Anything that moved would be met by strafing and bombing. Arnold had no intention of conducting an invasion that for even a moment would be in "grave doubt."

There was a pause. Marshall asked Winant if there was anything more to add and Winant said there was not. Marshall thanked Winant and praised both his insights and how valuable they were. It was troubling news for sure, said Marshall, but better to be forewarned and forearmed. Marshall then looked around the table and told the group that the second briefing had to be delayed because the U.S. Ambassador to Russia, Averill Harriman, had been delayed by unexpected engine problems en route from Moscow to Cairo. His presentation would have to be rescheduled for the day after tomorrow, November 24th. Tomorrow, Marshall reminded everyone, was set aside to discuss the Pacific theater with the British.

Their business now over, Marshall thanked the planners and asked everyone to continue with their preparations and proposed that they adjourn the meeting until the day after tomorrow.

As the meetings adjourned, Roosevelt and Leahy arrived. Bryan brought the president's plane down at the Royal Air Force base near Cairo, and Roosevelt was driven to the residence of Ambassador Alexander Kirk. Kirk's villa itself was beautifully decorated, and best of all it had a sunny patio in the back with a lovely flower garden where the president could spend his free time. Leahy, Hopkins, and Prettyman were housed with the president.

A considerable volume of mail had again arrived, and FDR spent most of the morning going through it. He received twenty-nine bills passed by Congress of which he signed twenty-seven and vetoed two. In another room, Leahy showered and changed and prepared for the afternoon session with the British. He anticipated an uneventful meeting.[5]

The afternoon session of the Combined Chiefs was indeed uneventful, and short. In total, twenty-nine generals and admirals filed into the conference room, more than half of them from the American side. Leahy, Marshall, King, and Arnold and the British chiefs, British Army General Sir Alan Brooke, Air Marshall Charles F.A. Portal, and Admiral of the Fleet Sir Andrew B. Cunningham, along with the Prime Minister's representative in the United States, the well-liked Field Marshall Sir John Dill, and Churchill's aide, Lt. General Sir Hastings Ismay, all arrived resplendent in their military uniforms. This entire group arrived the night before on the *Renown,* and they were well rested. Brooke, Portal, and Cunningham were the permanent representatives with Dill and Ismay as adjuncts.

Leahy opened the session. He welcomed everyone and announced that this session was entirely procedural, to establish the rules of the conferences ahead. He wished to propose the first rule, which was greeted with smiles and wide approval: These meetings would be chaired by General Sir Alan Brooke. A brief discussion ensued related to a request made by both the Russians and the Chinese to be made members of the sitting Combined Chiefs of Staff, which, for a variety of reasons, including the impossible logistics of it all, was unanimously voted down. However, the Chinese and Soviet representatives would be invited to attend meetings of the Combined Chiefs here in Cairo when matters concerning their fronts were to be discussed.

The rest of the items were parliamentary in nature and took about an hour. Then the meeting was adjourned.[6]

*

"Roosevelt weather" continued on into Egypt although it was much warmer here than in Algeria and for some of the generals their winter uniforms were a bit heavy. The sun was bright and the air dry, and the fertile Nile River delta was resplendent with color, the pyramids just a half-mile away, silent yet ever so majestic against the blue sky. There were no plenary sessions scheduled that day so Churchill came over to Roosevelt's villa for dinner. They were joined by Admiral Lord Louis Mountbatten, the Supreme Allied Commander of the Southeast Asia Command. The group renewed acquaintances and had a lively conversation about Southeast Asia while enjoying the spectacular views and the pleasant company. They accomplished little in the nature of substantive military or diplomatic decisions.

At 9 P.M. there was a cocktail reception for all of the military staffs, which was attended by some nineteen admirals and generals, including Hopkins, Leahy, Marshall, King, and Arnold, the British Chiefs of Staff, as well as Churchill and Roosevelt. Again, nothing of a substantive nature was discussed.

Secret Service Agent Reilly had a brief meeting with the president to finalize the travel to Tehran. FDR could fly his C-54 from Cairo, but his plane would have to negotiate the high ranges of the Alborz Mountains that ringed the city. That meant they would have to fly at altitudes above nineteen thousand feet, but the *Sacred Cow* was not pressurized, meaning that the president would have to use supplemental oxygen, itself somewhat risky.

More importantly, Reilly had picked up intelligence that Germans paratroopers had been dropped into the area and were on the ground around Tehran. It was his understanding that they were there to further sabotage the rail lines to cut off the flow of supplies to Russia.[7] "I wanted no part of four hundred miles of railroad lines winding through mountains heavily inhabited by characters who could be persuaded to assist the well-heeled Nazi jumpers in one or more sabotage efforts," said Reilly, and he so briefed the president. FDR told him to plan the trip by air.[8]

Lavrenti Beria and the Soviets also busied themselves in preparations for the conference. He had his NKVD agents sweeping the Soviet embassy for bugs as well as walking the grounds and checking all of the buildings. His men went through the painstaking process of reopening rooms, some of which had been sealed for several years and were in need of painting and general repairs. Beria had his agents fitted into staff uniforms so they could take on the disguises of groundskeepers and maintenance workers, albeit with guns bulging beneath their shirts. Then he sent in a special detail of technicians from the clandestine directorate. They began the slow but exacting process of planting microphones and transmitters in the guest rooms and testing the feeds that were sent to a room where conversations would be monitored and taped.

CHAPTER 15: THE BRITISH REBELLION

The next day, November 23, 1943, was spent in lengthy, combative meetings of the Combined Chiefs of Staff on the topic of the Pacific theater that neither resolved any issues nor advanced any war plans. Roosevelt wanted to show some support for the Chinese Nationalists who at the moment were engaged in combat with the Japanese, but the British demurred. On their part, the Chinese, who had flown in to attend these meetings, came to complain that the Americans were not doing enough for them. This struck a nerve with Marshall who knew the great burden placed on the resources of Arnold's pilots who were flying in military supplies. He said there was little to apologize for—supplies were flowing over the Hump, soldiers were in place. The same could not be said of the armies of the Chinese Nationalists who had done little to show for themselves.

Still, their point was hard to ignore. America had gone to war because of the attack on Pearl Harbor, yet progress in the Pacific had been held up while Germany was defeated. That could not go on much longer. Roosevelt wanted to lend support to the Chinese Nationalists but even after hours of lengthy talks interrupted by tiring translations, resolution was not reached today.

That evening, the American chiefs joined the British Chiefs of Staff for a dinner at the British compound while General Marshall had a private dinner with Churchill. Marshall and Churchill enjoyed each other's company, but in the end it was cloakroom politics, with Churchill usually being the one trying to soften Marshall's opposition to this or that, in this case, his Mediterranean strategy. Tonight was no exception, except that both came with agendas and neither did the other much good. They went out into the garden behind the Prime Minister's villa and admired the distant pyramids and the spectacularly clear sky. Their conversations continued over dinner and drinks, lasting until

2:00 A.M. Each offered their positions on the war in Europe and the Far East and, each time they did, they stalemated on their differences. There were light moments. Marshall told Churchill that he had been reading William Pitt the Elder on the transatlantic voyage, which greatly amused the Prime Minister. Pitt, a British diplomat and a military commander from the 1700s, served his nation without any official title and thus was known to his countrymen as The Great Commoner. During the Revolutionary War, Pitt had argued quite passionately for peace with the U.S. colonies and, because he excelled at public speaking, delivered magnificent speeches that were well known to every British schoolboy. Churchill stood up before Marshall and briskly paced the room as he enthusiastically recited lengthy passages from memory.[1]

But there were trying moments, too, and they set the stage for the day to follow. Churchill voiced concerns about the fighting expertise of the American soldier and unfairly compared them to the Germans, which provoked a sharp response from Marshall. Marshall prided himself of the quality of the American soldier and had frequently taken the British down to see their training bases in the United States. Churchill quickly backed down but his theme nonetheless emerged, one Winant had warned of, that the British were convinced that an invasion would be the beginning of a defeat because of the superiority of the German soldier and his infrastructure in western France.[2]

So it was that in that fashion the first day of British-American conferences came and went, both sides unpleasantly bogged down with discussions on the Pacific. The cold night air, though, did everyone good and being together meant that they were one step closer to resolution in Europe, whatever that might be.

The next morning, November 24th, started with the receipt of a cable from Stalin to the president saying he would be arriving in Tehran on November 28th or 29th, which was a day or two earlier than Roosevelt had expected. Roosevelt quickly asked Rigdon to work out the travel details and to report back to him just as soon as possible. Rigdon met with Agent Reilly who went off with the president's pilot to check the flight through the mountains.[3]

Two major meetings were scheduled for the day. The first was a closed door session for the American staff with Ambassador Averill Harriman on the Russian frame of mind, while the second was a roundtable discussion on the war in Europe with Churchill and Roosevelt present. The meeting with Harriman had been rescheduled because his plane had developed an engine problem coming down from Moscow. Harriman, Deane, and translator Chip Bohlen had left together on November 18, 1943 on Harriman's converted B-24 for the flight from Moscow to Cairo to brief the Joint Chiefs, but the mechanical issue had forced them to divert to Stalingrad for an emergency landing. They were driven into the city to wait the repairs, but they may as well have been on another planet. "We were taken over a frozen, shell-torn road along both sides of which, for the entire length, were strewn disabled German and Russian tanks, trucks, and guns," said Deane. "As we neared the city we could see only one building had survived the destruction. The city can only be described as a mass of rubble and ruin from which but a single building escaped."[4]

Stalingrad had been ground down by German and Finnish artillery with intense bombing by the German Luftwaffe. The German thrust went all the way into the city center, and the fighting had been door-to-door. The Red Army fought back using a pincer strategy and encircled the German army, resulting in one of the bloodiest sieges of WWII. Six thousand tanks, nearly three thousand airplanes, and some twenty-one thousand artillery pieces on both sides were destroyed. The Germans had some eight hundred thousand causalities, the Soviets more than million. The battle was won in February 1943, and the German army "ragged, dejected, unshaven, in filthy greatcoats," as Stalin put it, "ceased to exist."[5] Today, it was cinders and charred tanks.

The Harriman meeting began at 9:30 A.M. in a packed conference room. Leahy, Marshall, King, and Arnold were seated at the table and were surrounded by twenty-three others, most from the planning staffs. Leahy called the meeting to order then asked Ambassador Harriman to brief the group on his conversations with his Russian counterparts regarding the war. Harriman's remarks echoed those expressed earlier by Winant. He thanked Leahy and stood up. "The immediate Soviet interest is focused on the reduction of the German forces that oppose them," said Harriman. The German soldiers fight with vengeance, and the combat has been bitter with heavy Russian losses along the 1,800-mile front, he said. The Soviet people were under the strong impression that a second front was coming and Stalin had said as much in radio messages to his people, which were certainly based on Allied promises to him. The Soviet leadership was under tremendous pressure to end the war quickly.[6]

Harriman went on to say, however, that in his last meeting with the Russians the American military attachés had presented Operation Overlord for the first time and it had been extremely well received. The Soviets were told about the scale of the landings, the size of the Allied forces, the number of ships, planes, and tanks involved, the million-plus soldiers that would sweep into France, and so on. The presentation had an extremely satisfactory effect. The Soviets asked a great many questions, but their questions were not critical or negative. They in fact reflected a degree of pleasant surprise. Clearly they had no previous knowledge of what was intended to take place on D-Day, and they were very happy with what they heard. Harriman pointed out that no promises had been made except that the Soviets would be kept informed of their progress as the buildup continued in Great Britain. Harriman repeated that the Russians seemed very happy with what they had heard and that the Joint Chiefs should expect a similar response in Tehran.

As to the current combat in Italy, the Russians were puzzled why nations as strong as England and the United States had been unable to draw soldiers away from their own lines. The invasion of Italy had done almost nothing to relieve the pressure on the Soviet fronts, which made the Russians feel as if the fighting had been largely ineffective.

There was some truth to this, of course. The Allies entered Italy with extremely limited objectives. The plan had been to secure a toehold in southern Italy, open new air bases there for Arnold's bombers, fight up the boot of Italy as far north as Naples, then withdraw soldiers and send them back to England for the D-Day invasion. This had been accomplished, and soldiers were already en route to the UK.

Harriman looked over towards Major General John Deane, the well-regarded American military attaché to Moscow, and asked if that fairly summed up the Soviets. Deane said it had and that he agreed with Harriman's assessments, particularly with respect to Overlord and the good reaction the Soviets had to it. But Deane thought the Soviets viewed Overlord more in the nature of desirable insurance than an immediate solution. As he saw it, the Russians were very focused on any assistance they could get immediately rather than waiting for the second front in May of 1944.[7] Harriman interrupted Deane to say that this was an important point. The Soviets were very impressed with Overlord, but in Tehran they may emphasize immediate help in lieu of Overlord. However, said Harriman, if Overlord was to be abandoned, it had to be replaced with a military assault of equal intensity.

Arnold asked what the Soviet attitude was towards the Aegean Sea. Were they interested in the British plans to fight in that area, to invade Rhodes? Harriman said no, the Soviets had made no such proposals on this. They only wanted immediate relief from the Germans; the details were up to us. Of course, said Harriman, they will always be very interested in the reasons underlying our actions—they always wanted to know what we saw in an operation and why we thought it was important or why we thought it would be successful—but the choices were ours. They were blunt people, Harriman warned, and they would ask blunt questions.

Admiral Leahy asked if Harriman could clearly express an opinion about their preference between immediate action now, and Overlord, which was six months off. Harriman said it was his impression that the

Soviets would demand action now. Deane agreed but said he did not believe the Russians would propose any specific action. He added that the Soviets were just now appreciating the effect the Allied bombing was having on Germany, which had not been the case before. Marshal Stalin had mentioned it to him twice, as had others. The Allied bombing was impacting the German citizenry and blasting apart their factories at tremendous loss of life, and the Soviets, now seeing the benefits of this on their fronts, were appreciating what the bombing was doing to ease their own pains. The negative effects had been confirmed by reports from German prisoners of war, they told Deane. Those prisoners were saying that the Allied bombs were demoralizing the average Germans.

Harriman added that the Soviet government was telling its people that they had strong allies in the Americans and the British, who were already fighting hard to alleviate the Russian fronts. They were trying to impress on the average Soviet citizen that the war had progressed to a favorable point and a successful completion was nearing. But they wanted help, and the Soviet people were restless.

Harriman had a final word about the meetings in Tehran. For those who had never dealt with the Russians, he cautioned them that they were direct people and they understood and appreciated bluntness in return. He said he had no fear for any basic misunderstanding or any break with them in Tehran; they wanted to work with us, not break away from us. They were impressed by our military might, and he was sure we had their confidence.[8]

The Harriman briefing came to an end in time to get the room cleared for the first session with Roosevelt and Churchill and the war against Germany. Although it was initially designed to be a level-setting meeting, tempers quickly flared.

The president opened the meeting by saying that this was a preliminary session designed to lay the groundwork for continued discussions on military operations in the European theater, including the Mediterranean. Final decisions would depend on the way things went with Marshal Stalin, he said.

To that point, the president shared his own perceptions of the Soviet leader and where Russia stood on the choices now facing the Allies, that is, the choice between the invasion of France or additional combat in the Mediterranean. There were some reports that Marshal Stalin had no thoughts beyond Overlord, said Roosevelt. According to that view, Stalin attached the highest importance to the cross-Channel invasion and saw it as the only operation worth considering. In other quarters, said Roosevelt, it was held that Stalin was anxious that the Germans be given no respite throughout the winter, and that there should be no idle hands between now and Overlord. The issue centered on whether the Allies could retain Overlord in all its integrity and, at the same time, keep the Mediterranean ablaze with this new fighting. In his view, said FDR, Premier Stalin would be almost certain to demand both the continuation of action in the Mediterranean, and the Overlord invasion.

As regards the eastern Mediterranean, and the islands of Cos, Leros, and Rhodes, Roosevelt expressed his doubts about the military value of combat in that area to either the Allies or the Germans. "Where will the Germans go from the Dodecanese?" he asked, rhetorically. The answer was "nowhere," he said, meaning there was nothing of value out there. If the same question were applied to us, said Roosevelt, the answer seemed to depend on the action of Turkey. The entry of Turkey into the war would put quite a different complexion on the matter. But, if no Turkey, what then? Where would we go from there? The answer was the same. "Nowhere," he said. The Aegean Sea led to nothing. It was too far away to be important. Rather than debate this point, said Roosevelt, this should be held over for the meeting with Premier Stalin. This was closer to the Russian's own geographic sphere of influence; perhaps he could shed light on something we cannot see.

The president smiled, concluded, and thanked the group, then looked over to Churchill.[9] Churchill smiled in return, but in an instant everyone knew that the British prime minister disagreed with Roosevelt's comments. The idea that the Mediterranean led to "nowhere" was an affront, and Churchill was prepared to say so.

He took the floor and began a lengthy, slow rebuttal of almost everything the president had just said. This was followed by his own plans. Churchill began by saying that he was in accord with the president's views, in general. "We had had a year of unbroken success in North Africa and the Mediterranean, in Russia, and in the Pacific," said the prime minister. The North African campaigns, "paved the way for the extermination of large German forces in Tunisia. This was followed by the highly successful Sicily operation, and subsequently by the daring amphibious landing at Salerno and the capture of Naples. Then came Mussolini's fall, the collapse of Italy, and the capitulation of the Italian Fleet. In the whole history of warfare there had never been such a long period of joint Allied success, nor such a high degree of cooperation and comradeship extending from the High Command down to the troops in the field between two allies."

Churchill paused to let his words sink in, then turned each of those points against the Americans. "We should, however, be unworthy of these accomplishments and of the tasks lying ahead if we did not test our organization to see whether improvements could be made. That is the purpose of these periodical meetings," he said. "As a contrast to the almost unbroken successes of the past year, the last two months had produced a series of disappointments. In Italy the campaign has flagged. We have not had a sufficient margin of superiority to give us the power to force the enemy back. The weather has been bad. The departure from the Mediterranean of certain units and landing craft has had, it seems, a rather depressing effect on the soldiers remaining to fight the battle. The build-up of strategic air forces may also have contributed to the slow progress."

But it wasn't too late, said Churchill, ignoring the growing tension in the room; there was a way to turn things around, to right the wrongs: "The main objective [now] should be Rome, for whoever holds Rome holds the title deeds of Italy. With Rome in our possession, the Italian government would hold up its head. Moreover, we should then be in a position to seize the landing grounds to the northward." Churchill lamented the fact that two crack British divisions had been withdrawn from Italy in preparation for Overlord, a decision that had been made by the Combined Chiefs and to which he had previously agreed, but that he now saw as a mistake. Moreover, said Churchill, virtually no supplies had been sent to the 220,000 Yugoslavians patriots who were engaged in guerilla warfare against the Germans, supplies that could have been used to good effect.

Point by point Churchill went on, admonishing the Americans seated before him, talking to them as if they were schoolboys. When Italy falls, said Churchill, cheap prizes would be open to the Allies, he said, although he admitted that he had some difficulty last month. "Although we had not been able to seize Rhodes, we had occupied Cos, Leros, Samos, and others of the smaller islands in the Aegean," said Churchill. "I had hoped to capture Rhodes in October, but the German enemy reacted strongly to our initial moves. He ejected us one by one from the islands, ending up with the recapture of Leros where we lost 5,000 first-class troops, with four cruisers and seven destroyers either sunk or damaged. Nevertheless, taking into account the German soldiers drowned and those killed by air attack and in the battle, neither side could claim any large superiority in battle casualties. The Germans, however, were now re-established in the Aegean. As stated by the president, the attitude of Turkey would have a profound effect on future events in this area. With Rhodes once more in our possession and the Turkish airfields at our disposal, the other islands would become untenable for the enemy. Thus the sequence would be, first Rome, then Rhodes."

Churchill paused to let his words linger, but Marshall, who had been through this with Churchill the night before and heard it all previously, was angry. There was no military significance to that area, said Marshall, and Overlord had to come first. The British invasion of those islands had not been authorized by the Combined Chiefs, nor would it have been. The whole affair had been behind their backs and in the end, they were pointless losses.

Churchill heard Marshall out but was undaunted and continued his attack on the American strategy. Having soldiers not engaged in combat was unacceptable, he said, speaking of the buildup leading to Overlord. Rather than wait until Overlord, the allies should continue up the boot of Italy and seize Rome, invade Rhodes in the Greek isles, and send support to the Partisans in Yugoslavia. "No regular formations would be sent to Yugoslavia," he said. "All that is needed there is a generous packet of supplies, air support and, possibly, a few commandos. This stepping-up of our help to the Patriots would not involve us in a large additional commitment. Finally, when we reach our objectives in Italy, the time would come to decide would we move to the left or the right."

Marshall again spoke up and voiced his strenuous disagreement with all of this, but the British pounced right back right at him. "All the British were against me," he later wrote. "It got hotter and hotter." Tempers flared and Churchill could finally contain himself not more. He rose from the table, grabbed the lapels of his suit, and raised a finger in Marshall's direction. "His Majesty's government cannot have troops standing idle," said the Prime Minister, his voice rising. "Muskets must flame!"[10]

Marshall looked at the prime minister. He spoke in low even terms. Rhodes made no sense, said Marshall; it was a pointless island in a meaningless area of the Aegean Sea far from Germany. Combat there would mean nothing, results there—even victories—would be trivial compared to Overlord. This was not where they should wage war. "God forbid if I should try to dictate," said Marshall, "but not one American soldier is going to die on that goddamn beach."[11]

Marshall's words echoed through a hushed room. Churchill was visibly shaken. "Everyone was throwing their cards on the table," said Hap Arnold.[12] Churchill then excused himself and left the room.

A few minutes passed before Churchill returned, his composure regained. The debater that he was, he simply continued. He reaffirmed his support for Overlord but warned that the Germans might redeploy more soldiers to the Normandy region than they could contend with. "I have in no way relaxed my zeal for this operation," he said. "We have profited very considerably in our experiences of amphibious operations and our landing appliances have improved out of that knowledge. There will be an anxious period during the build-up, when the Germans might be able to concentrate more quickly than we could. Nevertheless, the 16 British divisions will be ready when called upon." Churchill said that in the minds of the British staff, the timing of Overlord should depend on "the state of the Germans, and not necessarily on the preparations by the Allies."

He then repeated that Great Britain had exhausted itself of able-bodied men to put into uniform. Churchill said the sixteen British divisions committed to Overlord were the limit of their contribution to the invasion. "The British cannot meet any further calls on our manpower, which are now fully deployed on war service," he said. In a word, this was it.

Summing it up, Churchill ranked the future European military operations as follows. "Overlord remains top of the bill, but this operation should not be such a tyrant as to rule out every other activity in the Mediterranean; for example, a little flexibility in the employment of landing craft ought to be conceded," he said, a direct reference to the taking of Rhodes. Churchill waved off the American contention that further combat in the Mediterranean would strip Overlord of resources and cause it to be delayed. "The resources which are at issue between the American and British Staffs would probably be found to amount to no more than 10 percent of the whole," said Churchill. Nevertheless, he said, he wished to remove any idea that the British had weakened, cooled, or were trying to get out of Overlord. "We are in it up to the hilt," he said. "To sum up—Rome in January, Rhodes in February, supplies to the Yugoslavs, a settlement of the Command arrangements, the opening of the Aegean subject to the outcome of an approach to Turkey, and then all preparations for Overlord to go ahead full steam within the framework of the foregoing policy for the Mediterranean."[13]

Churchill looked up and down the table, then sat down. Cigar and cigarette smoke mixed in the air as silence filled the room. His speech had gone for almost an hour, the points were old ones, and the American chiefs were stone cold and unmoved. "The Prime Minister made a long, unconvincing talk about the advantage of operations in the Aegean Sea and against the island of Rhodes," said Leahy, adding with a hint of relief that "no decisions were reached."[14]

The meeting was adjourned at 12:40 P.M.

The next meeting was with the Combined Chiefs of Staff and it started at 2:30 P.M. This meeting focused on the China-Burma-India theater and in attendance were the Chinese, including their leader Generalissimo Chiang Kai-shek. Back in the United States, the American people very much wanted combat in the Pacific, and Roosevelt wanted them to have it, but, until the war in Europe ended, there were far too few resources to go around. Rather, the war against Japan was being fought on a limited basis on two fronts, the first being led by the Marines who were island hopping up the Central Pacific, and the second on the Asian mainland by the Chinese Nationalists. It was therefore both a military and a political necessity for Roosevelt to show Chang Kai-shek some support and, to that end, he instructed Marshall and his chiefs to grant significant concession to the generalissimo and his army. This included an increase in the supplies airlifted over the Hump and a naval plan to support the Chinese ground forces.

The bargaining went through the afternoon, and the tensions were high for several reasons, including a Chinese demand for even more American supplies against a British objection to entry into any naval campaign at all.

The day thus ended with no decisions from this interim stop on the way to Tehran. Marshall had a taxing day, particularly with the Chinese in the afternoon session. He had borne the brunt of the criticism directed towards the United States by the Chinese who felt they deserved more supplies and also by the British who wanted nothing to do with the proposed naval operations in the China Sea. At one point, he lashed out at the Chinese who were suggesting that the U.S. had not done enough for them. He tersely reminded them that American soldiers and American supplies were fueling their war. On another occasion he felt as if he was being browbeaten by the British, and he dug in hard and realigned them to the needs of the Pacific.

Arnold was introspective as he thought about the meetings. The war was truly global, the nations so needy, the resources so precious, he wrote in his diary. Little was actually accomplished, yes, but largely because everyone had their own perspectives on the best ways to continue the campaigns against the Japanese and Germans. "Chinese, Russian, British, and American, have so many different ideas as to methods of doing things and their effect upon the future of their different countries," he wrote.

But Arnold had another observation, and it had to do with the conversations behind the scenes and in the hallways. "Marshall gets increased stature in comparison with his fellows as the days pass; the President, Prime Minister, and Generalissimo all want his counsel and advice at the conference."[15]

Roosevelt had a small group over to his villa for dinner—Harriman, Hopkins, Leahy, and his physician, among them. He hosted the bar and mixed drinks then served a delicious meal prepared by his Filipino mess men.

The weather was good, the air was clear, and the temperatures cool so, after dinner, they repaired to the back patio and admired the towering pyramids. Some guests played cards until 12:30 A.M., the talk was lively, and it was a welcome time to unwind. Others opted for a quieter evening. Arnold, Marshall, and King had dinner in their own villa, then watched Cary Grant in *Mr. Lucky.*

CHAPTER 16: THANKSGIVING

It was Thursday, November 25, 1943. Thanksgiving Day in America. The president slept late and remained in his villa most of the day. He received numerous visitors U.S. Assistant Secretary of War John J. McCloy; Lord Frederick James Leathers, British Minister of War Transport; and Sir Alexander Cadogan, British Under Secretary of State for Foreign Affairs, to list but a few.

A second group came in to discuss the trip to Tehran, including Major General Douglas H. Connolly, Commanding General of the Persian Services Command, who was based in Tehran and had several thousand soldiers there. With him were Agent Reilly and the *Sacred Cow* pilot Major Otis Bryan. The news was reassuring—the mountain passes through the Alborz Mountains were flyable, the weather forecasts for the next several days were good, and the facilities at the American Legation were set up and secured for the president's arrival. Per Stalin's cable they could easily leave a day early and start the conference a day early. They would just need to leave Cairo first thing on November 27th, and fly a route that would take them across the Sinai Peninsula, over Jerusalem, then to Baghdad and through the mountain passes into Tehran. The flight was about 1,300 miles and would take six and a half hours. FDR agreed to the plans, and a departure time was set for 6:00 A.M. Tehran was a go.

Although Thanksgiving, it was no holiday. At 7:00 A.M. Eisenhower arrived from Tunisia and sat down with the American Joint Chiefs for an informal meeting to discuss his war situation. Eisenhower went over his positions in North Africa and Italy and made the salient point that while he disagreed with the British in general, he understood their complaint and was sympathetic to, if not in favor of, their new proposal. "There was something to be said for closing down large scale activity in the Mediterranean....and saving everything for the main operation in northwest Europe," said Eisenhower, speaking of Overlord. "[But] against this were weighty considerations. To cease heavy attacks would eliminate all threat to the Germans on the southern front and would allow the enemy great freedom of action. In Europe, Allied ground forces would be completely unengaged from the summer of 1943 to early summer 1944." This was, of course, Churchill's point and the source of his angst with the Americans.[1]

Italy was an alternative to this, said Ike, and, if resources could be spared, he would like to continue the advance up the peninsula as far as the Po Valley. Again, this was in line with Churchill's solution to avoid any down time during the winter—to keep fighting through and take Rome, which was on the way to the line in the Po Valley. Otherwise the forces in Italy would have to stop where they were and hold a defensive line, only conduct harassing raids until after Overlord.[2]

The Joint Chiefs understood. Churchill's plan was not a bad one; in fact, it made perfect sense if one did not have the grandest, most taxing invasion in the history to deal with in just five months. And that was the problem.

*

A second meeting on Overlord was scheduled for just after lunch. This was an entirely military meeting attended by the Combined Chiefs of Staff and their aides. In attendance were Leahy, Marshall, King, and Arnold, as well as Brooke, Porter, Dill, and Cunningham. At 2:30 P.M., Sir Alan Brooke called it to order and everyone took a seat around the conference table. Two secretaries took minutes.

Brooke opened by reminding everyone that there was a Thanksgiving service tonight at the cathedral in Cairo at 6 P.M., then he asked for a motion to approve the minutes from the previous meeting. That done, he turned to D-Day. The British opened the discussion with the presentation of a legalistic document titled "Overlord and the Mediterranean," which was a point by point dismantling of the American arguments for Operation Overlord in a direct affront to the standing agreements signed by Churchill and President Roosevelt.

"Our British colleagues presented a most alarming proposal to delay the cross-Channel in order to exert more effort in the Aegean Sea and in Turkey," recorded Admiral Leahy dryly in his diary.[3] This was their unpleasant "bulldog tenacity," as Leahy described Brooke's action, and he did not mean that admiringly. It was a trick move, not on the agenda.[4] Despite the obvious reactions around the table, Brooke acted like a lawyer submitting evidence at a trial and had copies of the paper passed around.

The gist of it was not hard to comprehend. "For some time past it has been clear to us, and doubtless also to the United States Chiefs of Staff, that disagreement exists between us as to what we should do in the Mediterranean, with particular reference to the effect future actions there who have on Overlord," said the British, haughtily. "This issue is clouding the whole of our future resolve and must be decided here at [the conference]." And so it went, yet another long-winded, piece-by-piece dismantling of the accords to launch D-Day in May 1944. The current plan was "illusory," and would "paralyze action in other theaters ..."

Said Brooke. "The surest way to win the war in the shortest time is to attack [the Germans] remorselessly and continuously in any and every area." He argued for combat wherever the Germans could be found and even suggested that Turkey should be brought to the war next. "If the above measures necessitate putting back the [date for Overlord]," said Brooke, "this should be accepted ..."[5]

George Marshall was floored. What had come of the prior discussions, the prior months of debates, the agreements that fixed Overlord? Why build up forces, why waste the time and effort and training? Was it not military doctrine that one attacked the enemy with a superior, overwhelming force? What he had just heard violated every tenet of winning wars. The Allies had overwhelming force, and it was building by the day, he said. The dark clouds on the horizon were not those of a stronger Germany threatening England but of a stronger America threatening Hitler.

Marshall would have none of this and he promptly—and angrily—ordered the room cleared. "Sometimes when it got down to the real nitty-gritty, if that's the right word, they put all of us out of there," wrote Handy of Marshall's action. It was now down to the "nitty-gritty".[6]

"I was furious," said Marshall.[7]

But so too were the British, and the meeting went into a closed session.

The tension in the room was palpable. Brooke spoke first, and his manner was aggressive and pointed. He explained their actions. In their minds Overlord had become the altar before which everything else had to be sacrificed. Their point was, to what degree did this despised "sanctity of Overlord" have to be preserved, particularly in light of new developments? He argued that since agreeing to a fixed date for Overlord back in May of 1943, much had changed. The Russians had decisively turned around a losing situation, Italy had collapsed, and Turkey might be joining the war effort. "In these changed conditions, we feel that consideration of adjustments to, if not actual departures from, the decisions taken, are not only fully justified but positively essential," said Brooke. The British did not want to "recoil" from or "sidetrack" the cross-Channel invasion, he added, it simply meant that they didn't want everything else to be forced to yield to a fixed date for Overlord.[8] "We should stretch the German forces to the utmost by threatening as many of their vital interests and areas as possible, and, holding them thus, we should attack wherever we can do so in superior force ... In actual fact, the German strength in France next spring may, at one end of the scale, be something which makes Overlord completely impossible and, at the other end, something which makes Rankin not only practicable, but essential," he said.[9]

It was nonsense, said the Americans. It was the opposite of strategy, it was *no* strategy: aimless, a series of "maybes," and "what-ifs."

Not true, said the British. Rather than concentrating their forces as outlined for Overlord, combat should be scattered across several regions until the time was right to launch the invasion. "We firmly believe that Overlord (perhaps in the form of Rankin) will take place next summer," said the British. "We do not, however, attach vital importance to any particular date." The British allowed that it was of course valuable to have a target date toward which they all might work, but they were firmly opposed to allowing this date to become an absolute. Instead, they proposed a strategy of opportunistic combat, going where the enemy was vulnerable, attacking where there were weaknesses. "The offensive in Italy should be nourished and maintained until we have secured the Pisa-Rimini line," said the British. The Partisans in Yugoslavia and Greece should be supported militarily, Turkey should be brought into the war, the Bosporus Strait should be opened as soon as possible, and action should be taken in the eastern European countries of the Balkans. And, if these measures necessitate pushing back Overlord, so be it. "Our policy," said the British, "would be to fight the Germans as hard as possible through the winter and spring of 1943/1944, to build up forces as best we can in lieu of this, and invade Europe as soon as the war situation gives us a good prospect of success."

To a military mind like Marshall's, this sounded as if the British were willing to allow the Germans to dictate strategy rather than imposing the Allies' will on the Germans, that is, to wait for some magical moment when they were beatable rather than taking the fight to them. The British sidestepped the obvious flaw in this position. Rather, they talked about the weather conditions and future windows of opportunity to launch Overlord and even brought documents prepared by their weather services showing a great number of good days for an invasion *after* May 1944. There were ample "quiet periods" of weather through October 1944, as well as the "suitable weather" days for an invasion, they said, thus making the May 1944 date moot and a fixed-date strategy of little consequence. There were plenty of days to launch an invasion, said the British; there was nothing magical about May 1944.

"Dirty baseball," said Secretary of War Stimson when he heard of the presentation. "[Churchill is going to] stick a knife in the back of Overlord and I feel more bitterly about it than I have ever done before."[10]

Recognizing the deadlock for what it was, and not wishing to reduce the meeting to shouting matches, Marshall drew on his reserve of diplomatic polish and said they would take the plan to Churchill, Roosevelt, and Stalin and allow their commanders in chief to make the decision, as the American chiefs had nothing further to add. That said, he asked that the meeting be promptly adjourned, which it was.

Quite remarkably, the military chiefs and their staffs were able to put their feelings aside, and together they attended the evening church service in Cairo. The rector welcomed the generals and admirals, each in their uniforms, each resplendent with medals and braids. They tucked their hats under their arms and sat down in the pews. The music swelled, the rector's message was bold. *I have fought the good fight, I have finished the race, I have kept the faith.*

After the Cathedral, they returned to the compound for a Thanksgiving dinner hosted by Marshall that was entirely amicable, a "merry party," as Marshall put it.[11] Outside the villa from the patio, Arnold watched the Egyptians in the distance as they moved about. "Camels and caravans, little ones and big ones, all heading either toward the Pyramids or away from them; donkeys and sheep and goats, Arabs and more Arabs."[12] After dinner they watched a Ginger Rogers movie then retired early.

Roosevelt hosted his own Thanksgiving dinner, a formal affair for the diplomatic corps and their family and friends. FDR's guests included his son Elliott, his son-in-law, Major John Boettiger, Churchill's daughter, Sarah Hopkins, Ambassadors Harriman and Winant, British Foreign Secretary Eden, and his aides—about twenty people in all. "For a couple of hours we cast care aside," said the prime minister. "I have never seen the president more gay."

FDR opened the evening with a toast. Thanksgiving is a tradition as old as America itself, said Roosevelt. "This old custom is now being spread by American soldiers all over the world, and I am delighted that this year I can celebrate this in the company of my good friend, the Prime Minister. Thanksgiving is traditionally a family festival, and this year Britain and America have formed one family which is more united than ever before."[13]

FDR carved the turkey and, despite their differences, Churchill gave himself over to the especially warm feeling of the evening, as did the rest of the diplomats and friends. Always attentive to detail, Churchill watched as the turkeys slowly disappeared under the generous knife of FDR. Would FDR have enough left to serve himself? Of course, as anyone who had been head of a Thanksgiving table as often as Roosevelt had would be careful to ensure, the president had just the right amount left for his own plate.[14]

Music and dance followed. Churchill's daughter Sarah was in great demand, but a shortage of partners didn't bother Roosevelt's Army aide General Pa Watson. He and the Churchill did a cakewalk together as a couple. FDR took the microphone and gave a well-received rendition of the Marine Corps hymn. Churchill commented after it was over, "This jolly evening and the spectacle of the President carving up the turkeys stand out in my mind among the most agreeable features of the halt at Cairo."[15]

Yes, but it was the calm before the storm.

CHAPTER 17: WALKING HOME

A new day dawned, the final day in Egypt, but the impasse had only deepened. Churchill remained passionate about Leros, Cos, and Rhodes and wanted to keep British soldiers fighting through the winter and even up to and during the planned date for Overlord. "I think it is an awful thing that in April, May, and June not a single American or British soldier will be killing a single German or Italian soldier while the Russians are chasing 185 [German] divisions around," he groused.[1] More to the point was the sentiment expressed by one of the British staff officers. "The American are shortsighted," he wrote, perhaps the "stupidest strategy team ever."[2]

Roosevelt though had reasons to stand firm on a fixed date. A delay in Europe would necessarily cause a delay in the Pacific theater and victory over Japan, and that was unacceptable. Roosevelt had to maintain pressure on Japan, and the agreement with the British to lend naval and air support to the soldiers of Nationalist China was integral to that, at least until victory in Europe. This agreement in question was called Operation Buccaneer, which was a naval campaign to support the China-Burma-India theater and draw off the Japanese. Unfortunately, there simply were not enough resources to go around for all three—Buccaneer in the Far East, D-Day in Europe, and the British plan in the Mediterranean. Something had to give.

Churchill had every reason to stand firm, too. In truth, his plans to fight the Germans in Italy made complete sense and ultimately would whittle down their strength, thereby reducing the difficulty of coming ashore whenever D-Day was launched. The true weakness in his plan, however, was the relatively small number of German divisions that they could tie down. Even if Hitler swarmed Italy with soldiers—not just ten divisions but twice that—he had over 240 divisions left, if not more.

The conference room at the Mena House Hotel was packed, the air heavy with anticipation. Some fifty American and British generals and admirals were gathered around the conference room table with four secretaries taking minutes. It was the 131st meeting of the Combined Chiefs of Staff; it would be long, tiresome, and, in the end, feel like a tribunal. Said historian Buell, King's biographer, "In a way, the CCS resembled a group of lawyers negotiating a contract, but the contract was deadly serious. It affected the lives of millions of men."[3]

Brooke opened the meeting. He quickly went through a few formalities then introduced the first speaker, General Dwight David Eisenhower, Commander in Chief, Allied Forces, Northwest Africa. Ike had been flown in to brief the chiefs on the situation in Italy and to express his views on the next steps in the war. Eisenhower thanked Brooke and rose to speak.

The situation in Italy was promising, said Eisenhower. The present combat was slow, but the toehold was firm and with the right resources, he could press his position up the boot of Italy, take Rome, and advance as far north as the Po Valley—but it would be impossible to do all that before the middle of January, and he would need landing craft to get it done. Nonetheless, he was engaging a significant German force and destroying German divisions that would have otherwise threatened future operations, such as D-Day, and this was one of the main benefits of combat in Italy, he said. If the Combined Chiefs approved additional combat through the winter, he was certain his soldiers could destroy entire German divisions there, commanders and foot soldiers alike. That simply was not possible anywhere else, not in the Aegean Sea, not on Rhodes, and not in Yugoslavia. "In no other area could we so well threaten the whole German structure including France, the Balkans, and the Reich itself," said Eisenhower.[4] Italy was an excellent place to eliminate significantly weakened Germans, said Eisenhower. Churchill no doubt smiled; this was precisely the point he was trying to make.

However, said Eisenhower, seven Army divisions earmarked for Overlord had already left for England, which was according to the D-Day plan. To conduct such winter operations in Italy, he would need to keep his current supply of landing craft and receive a few more. Plus, his advance would require a continuous build-up of forces behind the advance. They had a toehold, he said, but the fighting was bitter and causalities were high, and it would be necessary to keep rotating in fresh infantry divisions to the front lines to counter the exhaustion and to maintain morale.[5]

If it was not possible to keep his landing craft or to build up his forces, said Eisenhower, and if additional combat operations were limited in scope, he said he could still take Rome and advance as far as the Pisa-Rimini line that evenly bisects the boot of Italy. At that point, resources could be sent back for Overlord, and he would be able to maintain a strategic defensive posture with limited, localized offensive thrusts. U.S. heavy bombers would then be used through the winter to cut the major roads and rail lines leading into Italy from Europe, thereby boxing in the Germans, whom he could later attack and destroy. Eisenhower repeated this main point. If there was to be additional combat before Overlord, in no other part of Europe could he completely eliminate the Wehrmacht as certainly as he could in Italy.[6]

As to other areas of operations, he was in favor of lending support to the Yugoslavians but not landing there. To that end he had already equipped one division of Partisans using confiscated Italian guns and was equipping a second division now. If he was unable to advance as far north as the Po, Greece and the islands in the Aegean Sea were also good targets, but the British combat on Leros and Cos had proven how badly the Germans wanted to keep them. Now that they were aroused, any efforts to retake them would require Turkey, and it was certainly not a foregone conclusion that Turkey would even enter the war. That said, he would not go into the Aegean Sea until after the advance to the Po, in the first example, or to the Pisa-Rimini line, in the second.

Eisenhower made two more points. If he advanced to the north he would need Arnold's bombers to support his advance. That meant the bombers would have to be diverted from their current raids on Germany, which, of course, might further delay Overlord. And, he warned, if he were authorized for further combat, the shift of forces from one theater to another inevitably would take time and would result in delays while new bases were established. Far better, he said, to keep things concentrated within the one theater, Italy, which would make more efficient and expedient use of his soldiers, his landing craft, and Arnold's bombers.

British General Sir Henry Maitland Wilson, Commander in Chief of Allied Forces in the Middle East and the man who led the abortive attacks on Leros and Cos, spoke next. As expected, he supported the British position and said that the taking of the Greek islands would "cut the German iron ring" that blockaded Allied access to the Bosporus. This meant not only taking Rhodes, but Crete and southern Greece as well. A small diversion of landing craft and soldiers pulled from the D-Day build-up would set things in motion. Turkey would then come into the war and mop up the numerous smaller islands around the mouth of the Bosporus. After that, the idled British and American forces now based in the Middle East would be shifted to Greece to finish things off, all of which could be done without interfering with Overlord, assuming, as stated before, that Turkey came into the war.

Eisenhower and Maitland then took questions, after which there was a short break. Cigarette smoke rose from around the table as the generals stretched their legs. The one-hour mark had now passed.

When the meeting resumed, Brooke called for summary comments. Admiral Leahy asked if he could speak. Brooke nodded. Much to the surprise of the British, Leahy announced that the American Joint Chiefs had discussed this, and they had in fact decided that they were willing to present the British proposal to the Russians. While the Americans disagreed with the strategy, it nonetheless deserved a fair hearing and they would not prevent that. However, said Leahy, there was one proviso. Under no circumstance would the United States Joint Chiefs allow this to proceed without a similar understanding from the British that any new Mediterranean strategy would not jeopardize Operation Buccaneer. This was of vital importance to the president, said Leahy. America came into the war because of Pearl Harbor, and the American people wanted action against the Japanese. Buccaneer would be just that.

As reasonable as it sounded, Brooke flatly rejected the compromise and bluntly said that Buccaneer would not go ahead unless Overlord was pushed back.

One could hear a pin drop. The Americans had just announced their willingness to make a major concession, and the British had dismissed it out of hand. Moreover, the British had rudely dismissed Roosevelt's own proposal.

Marshall spoke up. The meetings in Cairo were coming to a close and tomorrow they were going to Tehran, he said. The United States Chiefs of Staff had just made a great concession here and were tentatively accepting the British proposals with which they disagreed, so they could be presented to the Soviets for discussion. As he saw it, said Marshall, there were four elements to the plan as proposed by the British. First, to advance to the Pisa-Rimini line; second, to capture Rhodes; third, to divert sixty-eight LSTs scheduled for D-Day to support the operations in the Aegean Sea; and fourth, to launch Operation Buccaneer so that the Japanese are attacked while Hitler is being defeated. These four actions supported the objectives of Prime Minister Churchill and those of President Roosevelt—British soldiers would stay fighting, the U.S. people would see progress against Japan, and Buccaneer would stay on schedule. Marshall looked at Brooke and asked if this was correct. Brooke repeated what he had said. Buccaneer would proceed only if Overlord was pushed back.

All eyes turned to Marshall. Yes, said Marshall, he quite understood the point but the forces for Buccaneer were ready, the operation was acceptable to the Chinese, the operations were of vital importance to the Pacific, and for political reasons it could not be interfered with.

Portal and Brooke both shot back. Not only did they disagree with Marshall's statement, but it might be necessary to consider putting off Buccaneer entirely since, by so doing, the full weight of the Allied military resources could be brought to bear on the Germans and the war could be ended even faster.

Again, there was silence.

Portal spoke. Look at it differently, he said. Instead of delaying Overlord, what if the Russians agreed with the British plan and also wanted Overlord as soon as possible. "In that case," said Portal, "we must surely consider the possibility of putting off Operation Buccaneer. It's not essential to the operation in Burma."

Admiral King took immediate exception to that. The land campaign in Burma was not complete without the naval support proposed in Operation Buccaneer, he said. British and American ships would flank the sea approaches thus preventing the Japanese from coming in behind the Chinese Nationalists. Without ships covering their backs, the land campaign would be a disaster. If the land campaign was halted, the Japanese would gather strength while the Allies fought in Europe, thus making it even harder to defeat them when the war returned to the Pacific. "Our object is to make use of China and her manpower [against the Japanese]," said King. "The delay of a year in achieving this objective would most certainly delay the end of the war as a whole."

Marshall was put off by the British attitude, but he was steady and measured his words carefully. America had entered the war because of Pearl Harbor, not Adolf Hitler, he said. The American people wanted a war against Japan, not just Germany. But when America came into the war, Britain was in bad shape and so, despite withering criticism in the press, the president had successfully crafted a Germany first strategy. That was all for the British people.

Now, said Marshall, the U.S. people were living on rations, the U.S. had converted its factories to a wartime economy, and the entire political structure of the Roosevelt administration was focused on fighting Hitler despite public sentiment to fight Japan first. All for Britain.

And this was gratitude?

Marshall looked around the table.

Even today, at this very conference, he said, the United States Chiefs of Staff had bent over backwards to accommodate the British views on Rhodes and Yugoslavia and the whole Mediterranean proposal with which they strenuously disagreed but were nonetheless willing to present to the Russians—and in return this?

The postponement of Buccaneer they could not accept, said Marshall. This was simply too important to the morale of the American people and essential to the eventual victory in the Pacific.

Again, there was silence.

The taciturn Leahy spoke. "I want it clearly understood that the United States Chiefs of Staff are not in a position to agree to the abandonment of Operation Buccaneer," he said. "We will not recede from our present planned operations without orders from the President."[7]

The room erupted into a flurry of discussions and it prompted yet another closed session, but even that did not last long. The British and American chiefs broke into small groups to huddle, and, when the meeting resumed, the Americans again repeated their position that they would allow the British proposals to be discussed with the Russians in Tehran, but they could do nothing about Buccaneer. They suggested it be referred back to the president and the prime minister. The British agreed and took it one step further by proposing that the entire matter of the war against Germany be turned over to the Russians. Because there was really no other choice, the meeting came to an end. "The afternoon session of the Combined Conference was...acrimonious at times," said Leahy, carefully parsing his words, and that was as far as the old diplomat would take it.[8]

Meanwhile, Stalin was in motion. At first light, Stalin left his dacha in Kuntsevo and boarded his train for the overnight ride from Moscow to the airdrome at Baku where twenty-seven Soviet fighters and four Russian IL-47 bombers waited to take him down to Tehran. He was dressed to travel, in a great coat, his cap, and his boots, and had, as traveling companions, Molotov, his foreign Minister, and Voroshilov, his Minister of Defense. Also with him were his personal physician, his translator, and his bodyguards from his home region in Georgia. And, of course, Beria.[9]

The train traveled through the night and arrived in Baku at 8:00 A.M. the next morning. Stalin walked across the tarmac to the waiting bombers but, ever distrustful, switched and took the plane designated for Beria.[10]

Although Stalin had never flown before and was nervous about the flight, the trip was uneventful. Stalin and his entourage landed in Tehran Saturday in the afternoon and were driven to the Soviet Embassy. Here again, security was tight: uniformed soldiers lined the perimeter of the embassy and were stationed inside the grounds. Stalin's own bodyguards accompanied him fore and aft. Beria swapped out the ordinary embassy staff for his own men, as planned, and had them dressed as gardeners, maids, busboys, and groundskeepers. All of the buildings had been checked and double-checked for booby-traps, all of the plumbing and electrical connections were operational, and every room in every building used by anyone connected with the conference was bugged. Stalin would receive daily transcripts and briefings each morning on the conversations around him.[11]

As he arrived, a glorious autumn sun cast a splendid orange hue across the grounds. Molotov and Voroshilov were assigned to the

Ambassador's residences; Stalin was given a private residence. Once inside the walls, Beria got into his Buick and began driving the grounds, his eyes in constant motion.

*

Back in Cairo, the meetings came to a close, and everyone left the Mena House for the final time. Marshall and Arnold needed a little fresh air, so they decided to walk back to their villa. The meetings with the British had ended in a stalemate, but it was a much different stalemate than any before. They had agreed to seek resolution in Tehran, and who knew where that would lead. So off they went, Marshall and Arnold, two friends, past the sentries, through the command post and the barbed wire, ribbons on their chests, heading down the road on foot. Dodging camels and trucks, they were coated in dust, two of the most powerful military commanders in the world, casually strolling as if they were on a back road in Leesburg, Virginia. Was the Mediterranean the right strategy? Would fewer lives be lost in a war of incrementalism versus a head on assault on the Normandy beaches? And what of Stalin?

Hap wrote that they burned off some energy and got some exercise, which they both needed. Their villa was four miles away on foot, which both commanders thought should be just about right.[12]

CHAPTER 18: CAIRO TO TEHRAN

One by one they left Cairo and winged their way north to Tehran, a city, as poor as any they had seen, that stood in sharp contrast to Cairo and their Mena House Hotel. Churchill arrived first, then Roosevelt, followed by Marshall, King, and Arnold. Small buses and horse-drawn wagons clogged streets crowded with people and trailed plumes of dust and dirt. The Iranians bathed with, drank from, and flushed their sewage down the same conduits of water that led into open ditches. Food was scarce, fresh vegetables were nearly non-existent, and a sack of flour on the black market could fetch a year's wages. "This is a very dirty place," Roosevelt wrote in his diary, "Great poverty."[1] Said FDR's son Elliott, "There was the capital, and then there was the surrounding country—a grazing ground for the herds of nomadic tribes who knew nothing but abject poverty."[2] Wrote journalist Sydney Morrell about Tehran, "Ten months in Iran gave you the feeling of complete isolation from the world. No other capital city was so completely cut off from the war, except perhaps Lhasa in Tibet."[3]

The president's flight to Tehran had gone smoothly. The nearest Luftwaffe base was some 1,400 miles away across the Black Sea in Bucharest, Rumania, and well beyond the range of any German plane, even with extra fuel. The main risk had been the mountains. Major Bryan had discussed the trip with FDR's physician, Admiral McIntire, who wanted to keep the plane below 8,000 feet to reduce the stress on the President's cardiovascular system. "[The pilot] had to snake though an awful lot of mountain passes," said Mike Reilly, looking back on the trip, but it could be done.[4]

The president's plane departed at 7 A.M. and flew over the Suez Canal, then across the Sinai Peninsula before turning up north over the Levant. Bryan turned inland and circled Jerusalem, and then crossed over the dry deserts for several hours before the landscape turned a rich green as they came on the Tigris and Euphrates River valleys. It was a beautiful day, another "Roosevelt day", bright and cheery and as perfect as any day yet, with perfectly clear air and nearly unlimited visibility. They flew over Baghdad and on to Basra, the port city of Iraq, where, as luck would have it, they spotted a train moving on the tracks below, yet another load of Lend-Lease supplies headed for Russia. Roosevelt craned his neck to see it all. Over 3,000 airplanes, 2,400 tanks, 109,000 submachine guns, 16,000 jeeps, 80,000 trucks, 7,000 motorcycles, 136,000 field telephones, and 75,000 tons of explosives had taken this railroad to the Soviet Union. Eggs, wheat, boots, and even the uniforms worn by half of the Red Army were coming through Lend-Lease. Now one more train was on its way.[5]

Major Bryan weaved his plane through the mountain passes and followed the valleys until he popped out on the other side, and Tehran spread out before them. Bryan turned the C-54 towards the Russian airfield and lowered the landing gear as he let down and landed. As they taxied, they went past dozens of American fighter aircraft lined alongside the runway, each waiting for a Russian pilot to fly them on into Russia. They recoiled a bit, however. Although clearly American planes, they all had the red star of the Soviet Union painted on their tails.

The plane came to a halt, and FDR was lowered down to the runway and helped into an armed Army staff car, which promptly sped him into the city some five miles away. The president's entourage went directly to the American Legation, a somewhat small compound three miles outside of the old city. "Streets were swarming with Iranian, American, and Soviet troops," said Army General John Deane, the military attaché to Moscow, who was frequently caught in the dusty gridlock. "Unless one was properly documented, to say nothing of the elaborate identification required of cars and chauffeurs, it was impossible to arrive anywhere on time."[6]

Like Roosevelt, Churchill had flown up in a military transport, one that Stalin said looked rather "comfortable" inside.[7] After landing,

Churchill's motorcade had sped away from the airport, but the pace was slowed considerably by the crowds. "As we approached the city, the roads were lined by Persian cavalrymen every fifty yards for at least three miles," wrote Churchill. "It was clearly shown to any evil people that someone of consequence was coming." Churchill's car made its way in towards the British Legation, but the streets narrowed and the throngs of people grew to alarming proportions. Churchill worried about his own safety. "The pace was slow," he said. "As far as I could see there were few if any foot police. Towards the center of Tehran, the crowds were four or five deep. The people were friendly but non-committal. They pressed to within a few feet of the car. There would be no kind of defense at all against two or three determined men with pistols or a bomb."[8] Finally Churchill's convoy made it safely, if slowly, to the British Legation, which was reassuringly surrounded by a squadron of well-armed Ghurkas.

FDR settled in and promptly sent a message to Stalin inviting him over to dinner, but the Soviet leader, who had arrived earlier that day from Baku, was tired and declined. Stalin had traveled through the night twenty-seven hours from Moscow to Azerbaijan, then boarded his plane in Baku for the four-hour, five hundred-mile flight across the Caspian Sea to Tehran. Like Roosevelt, Stalin disliked flying. Also, as with Roosevelt, it was sometimes a necessity. He rested.

Averill Harriman and John Winant had also arrived in Tehran and called on FDR in the late afternoon. Roosevelt invited his ambassadors to stay for dinner. The three had a splendid evening that ran late and ended at 11:30 P.M. and so the day came to an end, 7,000 long, tiring miles from home on a dirty, hardscrabble patch of Earth in the shadow of a mountain range few had ever heard of, just a hundred miles from a sea that most had never seen. But it was Tehran, and that meant they were finally one step closer to deciding how World War II would end.

CHAPTER 19: MEETING UNCLE JOE

It was Roosevelt weather again, sunny and warm, a new day, on Sunday, November 28th. Marshall, Arnold, and King, along with their planners, were staying at Camp Amirabad, the U.S. Army base just outside of Tehran that, in truth, was little more than a wind-blown cluster of simple barracks. They had a base hospital, a commissary, an officer's club, some administrative buildings, and, at the center of it all, an assembly area of dirt and grass where the American flag snapped from a forty-foot flagpole. Arnold, Marshall, and King were given small guest houses while the rest of the planners were in the Bachelor Officers' Quarters. They woke up to a striking panorama of snowcapped mountains under a spectacular blue sky with clear, dry air. They had coffee and breakfast, and attended to the official papers in their mail pouches.

Roosevelt was up too, and had breakfast by himself before going through a new mail pouch that had arrived the night before. With his big mug of coffee in hand, he worked for over an hour. There was no legislation, but there were letters and memoranda that needed his attention.

For a trip that had been so well organized, November 28th was anything but. Marshall and Arnold would miss one of the most important meetings of the conference, while Agent Reilly would find his well-laid plans in Tehran dashed by a brazen Nazi plot.

The first meeting of the day was a preparatory session with the president that started at 11:30 A.M. in the American Legation. Leahy, Marshall, Arnold, and King were in attendance, as was a secretary, who took minutes. After the usual pleasantries, FDR called the meeting to order and asked what they should do next in light of the contentious meeting in Cairo. FDR fired off questions. Eisenhower had made sense in Cairo, so if it goes that way, should we advance up the boot of Italy? And if so, how far? And if then, what next? Leahy and Marshall thought the advance could go as far north as Rome, but anything further than that, such as the Po Valley, would delay Overlord by at least a month, perhaps much more. But Leahy had a more strategic take on the meetings. He said that Italy represented something larger. The choice was between Overlord or a combination of Italy and Rhodes, and, if the decision was made in favor of Italy and Rhodes, Overlord would then revert to the category of an "operation of opportunity," meaning, a military operation executed only if the circumstances presented themselves, something like Rankin. That was not what anyone wanted, said Leahy. They had to come down in favor of one strategy or another. They were in an "either/or" situation, he said: either keep Overlord on track or go after Rhodes.

Marshall said he agreed with that assessment and added to it. If the British strategy were adopted it might involve more than a mere delay in Overlord; it might cost them Buccaneer. The British proposal to undertake operations against Rhodes was specifically in lieu of any plan to support the Chinese, said Marshall. This was very important to understand. Because of conflicting goals and the uncertainties of combat, if we allow Rhodes, said Marshall, it might be a considerable amount of time before anything will be done to support the Chinese. As Eisenhower had suggested, the mere shift from Italy to the Aegean Sea involved a complex set of unknowns over which they would have little control. "In order to undertake operations in the Aegean, a change of base will be required," said Marshall, "and it always takes considerable time to shift from one base to another."[1] Roosevelt understood the point.

"Suppose we can get the Turks in, what then?" asked Roosevelt. The chiefs shook their heads. That was one of the problems. According to the British plan, the Turks *had* to come in. If they didn't, Rhodes was off. If they did, then Bulgaria was next door and would be forced to take sides. Because of their leanings toward the Axis, they would almost certainly go to war against the Allies, and no one knew how hard they would fight. They might fall easily, or it might be a major land battle. It was impossible to foresee. And then after all of that, they would *still* have to get to Berlin.

What they did know was that the Mediterranean had no value: The war could not be decided there. It was too far away from Germany, and it served no strategic purpose. On the other hand, Overlord was the exact opposite—it was strategic, it was on the continent, it put soldiers where they needed to be, and it was the fatal blow they needed to strike. Already the Germans could see that Allied forces were being massed in England and that an invasion was coming. That was no secret. But any delay would only give the Germans more time to build up their Atlantic wall and more time to prepare for the invasion, which was going to be bloody enough as it was. Right now, the Germans had their hands full with the Russians, but in another month or two? It was entirely possible that they could concede small portions of the Russian front, and shift their soldiers to France to oppose the landings. If they did that, our own losses would soar. No, the timing was right. The invasion should go ahead in May while the Germans were bogged down in combat with the Russians.

Roosevelt posed the question differently. If the war is going far worse than we imagine, what should we do if the Russians asked for immediate relief? Go in through Yugoslavia after all?

That was tricky, said Marshall. If the Soviets wanted immediate help, we would have to come to their aid. One way we could accomplish that, said Marshall, would be to increase the pressure in Italy by expediting General Eisenhower's advance through Rome and thus tie down more German divisions there. Alternatively, he said, the U.S. Army could blast its way into the Balkans by landing soldiers in some Yugoslavian ports and moving inland up towards Germany. This too would tie down German soldiers who might otherwise be on the Soviet front. It would, however, be hard and costly combat across difficult, rugged, mountainous terrain to fight through Yugoslavia, but it could be done, he said. Both strategies would give them immediate help, albeit leaving our own forces facing the Alps, which was not the case for Overlord.

Roosevelt switched topics. If there were enough ships to go around, he asked, could we handle the demands in all theaters?

It wasn't just ships, said Marshall; it was a matter of overall resources. More land vehicles were needed to open the Burma Road while more LSTs were needed for Overlord and the Mediterranean.[2] Ships were tight, and in particular landing craft, because all of the invasions had to come in over beaches. Operating across three fronts, the Far East, the Mediterranean, and Normandy, at the same time was just not possible.

Roosevelt let that sink in then said that he did not have the heart to bring Turkey into the war, and he didn't like operations in the Aegean Sea in any event. "The British will probably say after Rhodes was taken, 'Now we have to take Greece.'" Roosevelt shook his head and waved his cigarette dismissively. No, he preferred to operate up through Yugoslavia if he was forced to delay Overlord.[3]

Marshall listened but wanted to make it clear that the landings in Yugoslavia were not a recommendation, just a possibility. Combat operations in Yugoslavia would require an enormous diversion of scarce men and materiel. By contrast, they had tens of thousands of well-trained Allied soldiers sitting in North Africa without adequate equipment because they simply did not have the shipping necessary to get the equipment to them. Worse, King added, some of the LSTs planned for Overlord would most certainly be destroyed or damaged in any such Yugoslavian operation, and that would further hamper supply across the region.

The point was, equipment was needed in every theater, and equipment was more or less the deciding factor in military matters. Marshall suggested they turn the question back to the Soviets. Let the Soviets spell out what they mean when they say "immediate help." Turkey? Rhodes? Greece? Italy? Yugoslavia? They were all options, they all required different equipment, but they all affected Overlord. Let the Soviets define what they mean then let the Joint Chiefs determine what it would take.

Roosevelt liked that and played it out. "We could mount commando group operations, on a small scale, say 2,000 men to a group," he said. Marshall nodded yes: Commando operations were very doable and possibly the best solution.

Roosevelt thought for a moment then said, "[I'm] afraid that Marshal Stalin will ask just how many German divisions could be taken off the Soviet Eastern Front immediately."[4]

Yes, said Marshall, they were all afraid of that.

Roosevelt lit another cigarette and leaned back. If Stalin asked for help he needed to tell his Allies where he wanted force applied; Roosevelt liked that approach.

As the meeting came to an end, Marshall and Arnold asked the president if they would be needed that afternoon. Roosevelt said there were no meetings that afternoon, and they were free to do as they pleased. Marshall and Arnold planned on touring Tehran and asked King if he would like to come, but the Admiral declined explaining he had papers to attend to. That said, they all rose to leave with the president's good wishes.

FDR had decided to stay at the American Legation, which was a well-guarded compound, but it was three miles outside the city gates. To attend the plenary sessions, Roosevelt had to be driven to and from the various embassies through the congested streets of Tehran. Stalin had earlier delivered an invitation to stay at the Russian embassy, but the president had declined because he did not want to sacrifice the independence he would naturally lose as a guest.

That decision no longer seemed like a good idea. While Roosevelt had been in Cairo, Agent Reilly had traveled to Tehran to meet his Soviet counterparts in the NKVD who updated him on the status of the German paratroopers that had been dropped in behind the lines. It turns out the Germans were there not to sabotage the rail lines, but rather to attempt an assassination. The Russians, he was told, had undertaken a massive search and ferreted out a well-known German spy living in Tehran who, after some "painful persuasion," as the Soviets put it, confessed to the plot. After that, the NKVD swept in with additional forces and, using elaborate schemes and spy craft, they were able to ensnare and capture thirty-eight of the forty-four assassins. "Are you sure it was thirty-eight?" asked Reilly. "Very sure," answered the Soviet secret police, who were not amused by the question. "We examined the men we caught most thoroughly." The Soviets said they extracted information that indicated six well-armed German soldiers were still on the loose.[5]

All of this did not come as a complete surprise to Reilly. The FBI had passed along their information that Nazi assassins were in Tehran. These assassins would be dressed in American uniforms, said the FBI intelligence, and they planned a commando-style raid on one, if not all three, of the leaders gathered there. Reilly felt this information, corroborated as it was by the Russian agents, constituted a credible threat to the president. He decided to move Roosevelt's residence.[6]

Reilly met with Roosevelt and laid it out. He explained the Russian intelligence, the thirty-eight Germans, the corroborative intelligence from the FBI, and the risk of an attack along the three-mile drive from the American Legation to the British and Soviet embassies. "I pointed out that Stalin and Churchill would be subjected to unnecessary dangers when they came out to visit him. FDR was not only risking his life but theirs by living outside town." The British embassy was next door to the Russian embassy, and both were walled and guarded. "Do you care which Embassy I move to?" asked FDR.

"Not much difference sir," answered Reilly.

"All right. It's the Russian then. When do we move?"[7]

Reilly laid out his plan. A motorcade going through Tehran would attract plenty of attention, so he decided to use it as a decoy to draw any potential fire while behind the scenes he would send FDR down the back roads in a second car. "I had no stomach at all for sending him through the crowded streets of Tehran. It was a tough enough job normally, but with six Nazi paratroopers around somewhere it was a real headache. We could line his entire route with soldiers but half a dozen fanatics with the courage to jump from aero planes could probably figure out some way to get in a shot."

To make this work, the fake motorcade had to look completely real, which meant a stand-in for Roosevelt would be in the car, and the car had to be surrounded by plenty of guards. "We lined the entire route with soldiers. Shoulder-to-shoulder," said Reilly. "We set up for the standard cavalcade with the gun-laden jeeps fore and aft, and it traveled slowly along the streets guarded by the soldiers." Agent Bob Holmes had the unenviable job of being the president's double. They made it so he was visible through the windows dressed in FDR's cape and holding a cigarette in a long cigarette holder, albeit obscured just enough by a hazy curtain.

The real car would take off with Roosevelt, Leahy, and Hopkins once the motorcade had pulled out.[8] "As soon as the cavalcade left the American Legation we bundled the President into another car, put a jeep in front of him, and went tearing through the ancient side streets of Tehran, while the dummy cavalcade winded its way slowly through the main streets with agent Bob Holmes accepting the cheers of the citizens and, I hope, the curses of the few bewildered parachute jumpers from Germany."[9]

At 3:20 P.M. Roosevelt's car sped through the gates of the Soviet Embassy with agents on the running boards. They passed uniformed Soviet police who were positioned every few yards on the outside, while inside they went past a line of hardened NKVD soldiers who watched with their usual suspicions. Among those observing was Beria, who, with only the greatest of reluctance, had allowed the Secret Service to remain inside the embassy to guard the president.[10]

In hindsight, the decision to move Roosevelt proved to be exceedingly prudent. "The six German paratroopers who escaped the roundup were captured three months later," said Reilly. "They were executed by the Russians."[11]

*

The Soviet Embassy was a handsome, three-story stone building with tall glass windows and stately columns that sat inside a walled compound some four blocks in size. The residences given over to the president consisted of a suite of six rooms including a master bedroom and bath, a large reception area with sofa and chairs, a dining room, four smaller guest bedrooms, and a large kitchen facility one floor down. A decided advantage of the residence was the mobility it offered Roosevelt. The suite adjoined the main conference room where the meetings with the Soviets and the British would take place.[12]

Prettyman wheeled FDR into his residence followed by Hopkins and Leahy who would stay there, too. Just minutes later, the phone rang. It was Stalin's translator asking if the Marshal might come over for a visit. Roosevelt was utterly delighted and immediately had Prettyman wheel him back into the sitting room and lift him into the large wing chair that was next to the sofa. To his right was a handsome vase on an end table, and behind him was a portrait of Stalin holding a pipe. It was a warm, comfortable room, an ideal place for the first meeting between two of the world's most powerful leaders.[13] Chip Bohlen, his translator, arrived minutes later.

Joseph Vissarionovich Djugashvili, 65, was born in 1878, the son of an alcoholic shoemaker and an impoverished mother who did laundry by hand for rubles. He joined the Communist Party as a teenager and rose through the ranks during the Bolshevik Revolution of 1917. He played key roles under Vladimir Lenin and was made the party's Secretary in 1924. A skilled negotiator, Stalin was viewed as one of the smart ones:

ruthless, determined, and direct. "Stalin was of course distinguished by his rudeness," said Molotov, his Foreign Secretary. "He was a very blunt person."[14] The British Foreign Secretary Anthony Eden agreed. "If I had to pick a negotiating team, Stain would be my first choice."[15]

By title, Stalin was now Chairman of the Council of Ministers and Secretary of the Central Committee, but, by rule, he was the undisputed dictator of a nation of one hundred and eighty million people and the head of the Red Army. "He was a worthy supreme commander," said Marshal Georgi Zhukov, the much-respected commander who had stopped the Germans at Stalingrad.[16] But he was also cold-blooded and responsible for the deaths of millions of his own people, including numerous purges of his military. He was not well traveled but was worldly in a different way. He was profoundly aware of how the press viewed him in America and Great Britain and, equally, what Churchill and Roosevelt had said about him in their speeches.

FDR would later say to his Secretary of Labor Francis Perkins, that Stalin had "an elegance of manner none of the rest of us had."[17] George Marshall had a favorable impression of him too. Said Marshall, "He had a dry wit. He was agreeable, and in regards to me, he made a sort of semi-affectionate gesture. When we were in opposition, he would stand with his hands on my shoulders."[18] "We could tell when Stalin was coming," Rigdon later wrote. The guards who lined the grounds of the embassy would "literally leap to attention as he approached and stand like iron men as he passed expressionless, muscles taut."[19] Stalin was accompanied by his translator, Vladimir Pavlov, and surrounded by body guards, ten NKVD men in front and ten in back. It was a glorious autumn afternoon as he began his walk across the compound; the chrysanthemums and roses were in bloom, and the air was warm with a full sun and clear skies. He wore a great camel-hair coat and was in a dark blue uniform with no ribbons or ornamentation save a single medal on his chest—the Hero of the Soviet Union.[20] He arrived at Roosevelt's door at 3:15 P.M., accompanied by a young U.S. Army officer.[21] "He walked into the room, well-guarded I might add, with the most engaging grin on his face," said Agent Reilly. "He had a twinkle in his eye," remembered Rigdon, "a small man, only about five-foot-six, but stocky."[22] Stalin came into the sitting room and saw the president, then broke into a generous smile. "[He] sort of ambled across the room towards Roosevelt grinning, and reached down to shake FDR's hand for the first time," said Reilly. "As they shook, the Boss grinned too and said, 'It's good to see you, Marshal,' and the Marshal burst into a very gay laugh.'"[23]

Stalin took a seat on the sofa next to FDR, and their translators listened carefully. Charles Bohlen, FDR's translator, was in the chair next to Roosevelt; Pavlov was standing. Roosevelt was dressed in a blue business suit with a pocket square and looked every bit like the man who was about to address a session of Congress, but the two beamed at each other like long lost brothers. "I think the Boss liked him on sight, and I also feel that the happy first impression was completely mutual," said Reilly.[24]

Roosevelt asked Stalin how the battles were faring on his fronts, and Stalin painted a picture that was somewhat bleaker than American intelligence had provided. The Soviets had recently lost two cities to the Nazis, including an important rail center, and the Germans had recently moved in new divisions along the Soviet front, he said. Roosevelt asked if the initiative remained with the Soviet forces, and Stalin said that with the exception of the losses he had just referred to, the initiative still remained with the Soviet armies, but that the situation was so bad that only in the Ukraine was it possible to take offensive operations.

Roosevelt said that he wished that it were within his power to bring about the removal of thirty or forty German divisions from the Eastern front. Stalin smiled and said it would be of great value if such a transfer of German divisions could be brought about.

Roosevelt nodded and lit a cigarette. At the end of the war, the American-British merchant fleet would be far larger than either nation could possibly use, said Roosevelt. He would like to make some of these ships available to the Soviet Union. Stalin replied that an adequate merchant fleet would be of great value, not only to the Soviet Union, but to the development of positive and lasting relations between the Soviet Union and the United States, which he hoped would be greatly expanded after the war. Stalin said that if such equipment were sent to the Soviet Union from the United States, a plentiful supply of the raw materials from the Soviet Union could be made available to the United States in return.[25]

Both men no doubt smiled. Like two old traders on the ancient Silk Road, they had met, they had commiserated, and they had negotiated a show of goodwill, an interchange of sorts. And they seemed to be getting along famously.

The conversation turned to the Far East. Roosevelt informed Stalin that the United States was equipping thirty Chinese divisions to fight the Japanese, but Roosevelt waved off any undue importance to that by saying the Chinese did not fight very well, something he blamed on their leader Chiang Kai-shek. Stalin nodded, then asked about a problem in Lebanon. Roosevelt said that the recent difficulties in Lebanon had been caused by Charles de Gaulle. Stalin smiled a knowing smile. Stalin said he did not know de Gaulle personally, but he thought the French leader was "unreal" in his political acumen. He said de Gaulle represented the soul of France perhaps, but the real France, the actual people of France, were helping the Germans by giving them ports for their submarines, material and machines for their soldiers, and so on. He said the trouble with de Gaulle was that he had no real connection with the physical France, which, in his opinion, should be punished for aligning with Nazi Germany, for helping Hitler. "De Gaulle acts as though he were the head of a great state," said Stalin, "whereas, in fact, he actually commands little power. The French must pay for their criminal collaboration with Germany."[26]

Roosevelt agreed. He said that after the war, no Frenchman over forty, and particularly no Frenchman who had ever taken part in the present French Government should be allowed to return to any political office. Stalin went a step further and said that in view of their past record of collaboration with Germany, no one in government and no one in the French ruling class should be entitled to share in any of the benefits of the peace. To give but one example, Stalin said that he did not intend for the Allies to shed blood in Indochina only to give that area back to the French. Roosevelt said he agreed completely. "After 100 years of French rule in Indochina, the inhabitants are worse off than they had been before," said FDR. He said that Chiang Kai-shek had told him that China had no designs on Indochina and, with economic support from the major powers, the people of Indochina could develop into a self-sustaining country. Stalin nodded in agreement.

And so it went. France. Indochina. India. A conversation occurring between two men that drifted about, from one topic to another, as they felt each other out, a prelude to the greater issues that lay ahead. At one point Roosevelt looked over to Stalin and, breaking into his expansive smile, said that an additional reason that he was so glad to be staying in the Soviet embassy was that they would now have the opportunity to visit each other more frequently in completely informal circumstances. Stalin felt the same. "It seemed Stalin was as eager to get acquainted with the President as the President was to know him," said Rigdon. "Several times when I was working with the President in his private quarters Stalin would come in, unannounced, ask if we had everything we needed, explain Russian knick-knacks on the desk FDR was using, comment on the weather, and generally engage in small talk, all the while smiling and showing great deference to his guest."[27]

Of course, Stalin had another reason to smile. Roosevelt's quarters were thoroughly bugged and the last minute reshuffling of quarters meant no one on the American side knew it.[28]

Although the meeting was fueled by a desire to get along, and it seemed to be working, such was not the case with the security forces. Driving ever so slowly about the grounds was a Buick automobile with dark-tinted windows inside of which was Lavrenti Beria. "The collar of his overcoat was turned up, and his felt hat was pulled down over his eyes," said Valentin Berezhkov, one of Stalin's other translators.[29] There were guard shacks and Russian security every few yards. "They were NKVD boys of course," said Reilly. "In fact, there were about three thousand of them on hand for the meeting. We were slightly outnumbered about a hundred to one. The Scotland Yard men with Churchill were similarly outweighed."[30]

The Russians treated the Americans as if they were the enemy, and the American agents responded in kind. "While the two biggest men in the world talked of the destinies of millions, their personal body guards played a very silly game of trying to stare each other down," said Reilly. "It resulted in a draw."[31]

As they ended their visit, Stalin looked over to Roosevelt and asked why not call their staffs and get started with their real meetings? It was impromptu, entirely unscripted, but Roosevelt thought that was a splendid idea. He sent word to gather up his Joint Chiefs. Churchill, too, was reached and he readily agreed. In all, nineteen American, Russian and British admirals and generals were eventually brought over to the Soviet embassy although Marshall and Arnold, who had earlier announced plans to explore Tehran earlier, were off and unreachable.

Thus, inside, in the Soviet embassy, the first plenary session with Roosevelt, Churchill, and Stalin began as an unscheduled event on a whim, without an agenda, just minutes after 4 P.M. on November 28, 1943. Roosevelt had with him Leahy, King, and Major Deane, along with a secretary to take minutes, plus his friend and political advisor Hopkins, and Bohlen, his translator. "Getting into the main gate was a job," King later wrote. Although he was in uniform, he had to sign in with his name and rank and then wait for an escort to enter. "Inside the compound the Soviet secret police were guarding at about every few yards," he said, not counting Stalin's personal bodyguards who in their own uniforms were standing both inside and out of the buildings.[32]

After getting through the main gate, they had to pass through a security room manned by Stalin's NKVD before being admitted into the embassy itself. There they found themselves in a large hall, off of which were several rooms including the main conference room. King remembered his first impression as he walked in. Stalin, Churchill, and Roosevelt were already seated with their aids and military chiefs next to them. "There was a large round table and about it were, first, the Russians, Stalin flanked by his top general at the right hand and to the left his 'top' man about foreign affairs, Molotov, also behind was he Russian interpreter," remembered King. "To the right was [Winston Churchill] flanked by Mr. Eden and by the British major interpreter, then by the British [Chiefs]."[33] The conference room table was the one that Stalin had built for the conference, round so no one had to feel diminished by virtue of where they sat. On it were silver ashtrays and cut-crystal water goblets spaced at perfect intervals with a green baize runner down the center. Around it were ornate chairs with striped silk cushions.[34] The windows were closed off by curtains, and long tapestries hung from the walls.[35] Roosevelt was seated with Leahy on one side and Bohlen on the other.

Through his translator, Roosevelt asked Stalin who should preside and, with a small wave of his hand and a slight smile, Stalin said that the president should. Roosevelt said he would be delighted and opened the session. As the youngest member of the Big Three, he said, he welcomed his seniors. There were polite smiles all around. "We are sitting around this table for the first time as a family with the one objective of winning the war," said FDR. "Meetings of this type are to be conducted as between friends, with complete frankness on all sides but also knowing that nothing that is said will be made public. I am confident that this meeting will be successful and that our three great nations will not only work in close cooperation for the prosecution of the war but will also remain in close touch for generations to come."[36]

Churchill spoke next. He pointed out that this was the greatest concentration of power in one place the world had ever seen. "In our hands here" he said, "is the possible certainty of shortening the war, the much greater certainty of victories, but the absolute certainty that we hold the happy future of mankind." He added that he prayed that they all would be worthy of this God-given opportunity.[37]

Stalin then spoke. "History had given us a great opportunity and it is up to the representatives here to use wisely the power which our respective peoples have given to us and to take full advantage of this fraternal meeting."[38] Then, as his last words were translated, and satisfied that the proper tone had been set, Stalin added, "Now, let us get down to business," and there was not a hint of dissent.[39]

FDR spoke first. He began by reviewing the war fronts and gave particular emphasis to the Pacific, which, as he put it, was largely a U.S. war. After the attack on Pearl Harbor and then the defeat in the Philippines, he said, the United States had been fighting back towards Japan up through two fronts: one advancing from the south through China-Burma-India, and the other across the islands of the Central Pacific. China was helping by engaging the Japanese on the western front, with American support and supplies of course, but in addition, over one million American soldiers were committed to the Pacific theater. But the logistics were daunting, he said. "The whole operation covers a huge territory, and a large number of ships and men and planes are necessary to carry it out," said Roosevelt. "A large number of ships."

Ships were no less important to the war in Europe, said FDR, which, he added, had the highest manufacturing priority in the eyes of the United States. Germany so completely occupies and controls Europe that the only way to get onto the continent is to come ashore over the beaches. Bare beach operations—landing soldiers on sand—were entirely new to both the United States and to Great Britain but they were learning. Several types of specialized ships had to be designed and built, which they had done. Some of these were very small landing craft, which were in plentiful supply, but others were large, ocean-going, three hundred-foot-long ships that were in short supply. These larger ships, Landing Ship, Tanks or LSTs, could transport tanks and motor vehicles and as many as two hundred soldiers in each. LSTs were absolutely necessary in beach assaults because they carried armored vehicles and had a special bow that opened to discharge their cargo over sand. "Not only do we want to get across the English Channel," said Roosevelt, "but once we are across we intend to proceed inland into Germany," meaning these LSTs were essential for the tanks, trucks, jeeps, artillery, and everything else they needed to support the movement of the front inland to Berlin. Everything had to be landed over beaches until French ports were secured and rebuilt. Unfortunately, said Roosevelt, LSTs were ships like any other ship, and they vied for space in the overly crowded shipyards. "There is a definite bottleneck in the matter of war called landing craft," Roosevelt said, and Stalin understood this perfectly—ships were in short supply in the Soviet Union, too.

Roosevelt then talked about Europe. He said that at the last two or three military conferences with Prime Minister Churchill, all of the discussions had revolved around the question of relieving the pressure on the Soviet Union, but until the recent meetings in Quebec, it had not been possible to set a date for the cross-Channel operations largely because of the ship shortages. "The English Channel is a very a disagreeable body of water, and it is unsafe for military operations prior to the month of May, and the plan adopted at Quebec involves an immense expedition and had been set at that time for May 1, 1944," said Roosevelt. Churchill smiled in agreement and interjected that the English people had many reasons to be thankful that the English Channel was so hard to cross. There was a ripple of polite laughter.

Roosevelt continued. One of the major questions on the table was how to use the considerable Allied military forces in the Mediterranean in such a way so as to bring the maximum aid to the Soviet armies on the Western Front. The Allies were willing to take immediate action should it be required, said the president, and he explained how. "There were several things we could do: A) we could increase the drive into Italy, B) undertake an operation from the Northeast Adriatic, C) undertake operations in the Aegean, or D) operations from Turkey. That is what this military conference is concerned with."[40] Most of these options involved a delay of one, two, or even three months in the cross-Channel invasion, said Roosevelt, so before making any decision, he and the prime minister wanted Stalin's point of view. However, in his opinion, said the president, "the large, cross-channel invasion of France should not be delayed by any secondary operations such as those listed."[41]

The president finished and held his cigarette as the translators finished. Leahy and King were no doubt immensely pleased with Roosevelt's direct presentation and, in particular, his final remark about the invasion. The president had fairly outlined the divide between the British and the Americans and stated his own preferences quite clearly.

Now it was Stalin's turn. "Every American and British eye and ear was fixed on the Soviet leader," said Leahy. "Most of us were hearing and seeing him for the first time."[42]

Stalin lit another cigarette. He said that in regard to the Pacific war, the Soviet government welcomed the successes of the Anglo-American forces against the Japanese and that, while they wished to lend a hand, up to the present, they had been unable to do much because the Soviet armies were too deeply engaged in the West. In Siberia, said Stalin, Soviet forces were sufficient for defensive purposes but would have to be increased threefold before they would be adequate for offensive operations. But once Germany was defeated, said Stalin, Russia would send the necessary reinforcements to Siberia and then join up with the Allies to beat Japan.

Roosevelt nodded in appreciation. This was a new and most welcomed piece of information. The American people would be most pleased to hear of this.

Stalin continued. Since the German offensive in July of this year, the Soviet High Command had been preparing for an offensive of its own, but the Germans had stolen the initiative and attacked first. Following the failure of this German offensive, the Soviets had gone on the attack, said Stalin. The successes that they achieved this summer and this autumn had far exceeded their expectations. For one, they found the German army to be a weaker fighting force than they had expected, but, second, they had also found it was hard to exploit their gains because the Germans were destroying everything behind them as they retreated, including roads and bridges. This was one of the great obstacles encountered by the Soviet armies as they advanced.

Stalin then turned to the Allied operations in Italy and began to address the points Roosevelt raised. He said that from the Soviet point of view, the great value of the Italian campaign was opening the Mediterranean to Allied shipping, but he did not view it as a base of operations from which to attack Germany. At the very least, the Alps made that impossible. Moreover, said Stalin, his military people felt that Hitler was really trying to bottle up as many Allied Divisions in Italy as possible because no real decision could be reached there vis-à-vis the war itself. The best method of ending the war, said Stalin, was to drive a stake into the heart of Germany through France. "Germany's weakest spot is France," he said. "We Russians believe that the best result would be yielded by a blow at the enemy in northern or northwestern France."[43] The Germans would fight like devils, he said, but that was the best way to defeat them.

As to the Balkans, Stalin said he thought it would be helpful if Turkey entered the war and opened the way to the Balkans, but even so, the Balkans were far from the heart of Germany, and Northern France was still the best option. But, he also felt certain the Turks would not join the war in any event.[44]

That said, he gestured towards Churchill, and then he picked up a red pencil and began to scribble on a slip of paper. The conversation passed over to Churchill.

Churchill began his own remarks. "In 1943, operations against Africa and across the Mediterranean were the best that could be accomplished in view of the limitations imposed by the lack of shipping and landing craft," he said. "Great Britain and the United States had set before themselves the objective of carrying an army into France in the late spring or early summer of 1944." This invasion, he said, which was called Overlord, would put sixteen British and nineteen American divisions ashore, and a total of one million men behind them over the first ninety days of the invasion. But Overlord would exhaust England of its last drops of manpower, and thus, it had to succeed, he said. The Americans, by contrast, could provide a steady stream of reinforcements—some fifty divisions were being prepared to come over from the United States, each numbering fifteen thousand soldiers including support elements.[45]

But the summer of 1944 was a long way off, said Churchill, and he had five hundred thousand soldiers in the Mediterranean theater that would have nothing to do until May of 1944. He did not want that; he didn't want his soldiers idled. Churchill then dove into his plans and talked at great length about his desire to wage war in Italy, how the front would advance, and how he wanted to engage and destroy Germans there. He talked in detail about combat in Yugoslavia and Greece and how each of these actions would benefit the Allies. Churchill talked at length about bringing Turkey into the war to join forces with them and opening the Bosporus by taking the islands in the Aegean. But, said Churchill, he and the president could not make any decision until they knew the Soviet views on the subject and therefore had drawn up no definite plans.[46]

Churchill's remarks were not playing well with the Soviets. The flow of his remarks was frequently interrupted so translators could catch up and it came off without Churchill's usual oratorical zeal. Worse, it ran contrary to what everyone had just heard from both Roosevelt and Stalin, a fact no doubt reflected in the wooden stares he was receiving from Stalin's right-hand men Molotov and Voroshilov. Churchill stumbled to a halt and finally asked, "Were any of the possible operations in the Mediterranean of sufficient interest to the Soviet Union if these operations involved a two or three months delay in Overlord?" Attack now, or wait until the spring of 1944?[47]

All heads turned to Stalin. He seemed "grumpy," said Bohlen of Stalin, as he prepared to answer Churchill's question.[48] Stalin spoke and repeated some of his earlier comments about the war on his own fronts. Germany had invaded the Soviet Union with two and a half million men. German soldiers had thrust deep into Russia sending the Red Army dangerously back on her heels. The attack had been so swift and so devastating that for a time Russia's survival was at stake, he said. Buying time—time to reinforce the Red Army, time to manufacture guns and arm his soldiers, time to move tanks to the front, time to reinforce the lines—this was all the Red Army had been able to accomplish at first. But now, said Stalin, they had "accumulated sufficient munitions, supplies, reserves, etc. to pass from the defensive mode to the offense." Still, they faced 210 German Wehrmacht divisions—2.4 million soldiers with another 23 divisions pushing in towards Kiev. "Some difficulties," said Stalin, "may, therefore, be foreseen in the future."[49]

Allied operations to date had helped, Stalin said. The invasions of North Africa and Italy had cleared the shipping lanes in the Mediterranean and were of great value to the overall picture, but, he said, continued American and British military operations there, in Italy, or elsewhere in the Mediterranean were of "no further great importance as regards the defeat of Germany." Italy was a trap, Stalin repeated. "Hitler is trying hard now to contain as many Allied divisions in Italy as possible because he knows things cannot be settled there."[50]

Stalin asked Churchill what would happen to the soldiers in Italy if, as Churchill indicated, they went north and captured Rome? What would happen to those soldiers after the capture of Rome? Churchill said that there were twenty to twenty-three Allied divisions in Italy and that they would go on fighting either up the boot's east into the South of France or the west into the Adriatic. That could be decided, but either way, said Churchill, whatever they did there in Italy would not affect Overlord.

Stalin frowned. Stalin said he questioned the wisdom of dispersing Allied forces across so many fronts—Italy, Turkey, the Adriatic, Greece, and so on—because there would be no direct connection between them. This was bad military doctrine, said Stalin. It would be far better to make Overlord the basis for all 1944 operations, he said. Instead of sending the soldiers up the boot of Italy, it would be far better to allocate those available divisions to Overlord and to launch a second invasion of Europe, in coordination with Overlord, perhaps in southern France. If you did this, said Stalin, you would have a classic pincer operation, which would truly contribute to Overlord's main assault.[51]

There was a ripple of surprise. Stalin's comment about an invasion in southern France caught the American Joint Chiefs off guard, but not unpleasantly so. Such an operation around Marseilles or Cannes had been considered by the American planning staffs some months earlier. It had merit, but for other reasons it had been rejected and largely forgotten. However, in the context of Stalin remarks, it made surprising sense. There were murmurs of discussion around the table. "Stalin thought Overlord represented a very large operation and that it would be facilitated and, in fact, would be certain of success, if the invasion of Southern France was undertaken some two months before Overlord." wrote Bohlen, the translator. "This would divert German troops from the northern part of France and assure the success of the invasion.

He said that as an extreme measure he would be inclined to leave 10 Divisions in Italy as a holding force and postpone the capture of Rome in order to launch the attack in Southern France two months in advance of Overlord."[52]

Roosevelt liked it, and he said so. He quibbled some with Stalin's suggestion, particularly that an operation in southern France should *precede* Overlord, but he took no issue with the general concept of a pincer operation. Roosevelt said he thought the question of timing was important because he personally felt that nothing should be done that might delay Overlord, even this proposed second invasion in southern France, but he liked the idea of a pincer operation and suggested the military staff work out a plan of operations for striking through southern France.

Stalin nodded and continued. Pincer operations had worked so well in the past that the Soviet Army now used them as their basic offensive thrust when mounting attacks against the Germans. "Stalin pointed out that the Russian experience had shown that an attack from one direction was not effective and that the Soviet armies now launched an offensive from two sides at once which forced the enemy to move his reserve back and forth," recorded Bohlen. "He added that he thought such a two way operation in France would be very successful."[53]

Churchill saw his own plans fading away, and he was impatient and wanted to talk but he had to wait until the translators finished. He finally got the floor, and he emphatically returned to the subject of Rhodes, the Mediterranean, and Italy and his ideas for combat around the Bosporus. He repeated again that he did not like so many British soldiers sitting idle until May 1, 1944, and he thought that instead they should fight the Germans wherever they were. The forces in Italy were entirely separate from those for Overlord, he said, they should fight their way up the boot of Italy, take Rome and press on. Anything less would seem like a defeat to the general public. Plus, he said, Turkey would be foolish not to join the war against Germany.

Stalin waved off Churchill with his cigarette. Yes, perhaps the Turks were foolish, he said, but that would not change their unwillingness to fight. Foolish people often think the men who are fighting wars are *more* foolish, said Stalin. Stalin repeated his desires—he wanted Overlord, he wanted southern France and he wanted them soon, and no more. Stalin said that it was not worthwhile to scatter the British and American forces all over the Mediterranean. The plans presented by Churchill seemed to indicate that part of the Allied military forces would be sent to Greece and part to northern France and part to Italy and part for operations across the Adriatic in Yugoslavia. That was too far flung to be effective, too diluted. He said that Overlord must be accepted as a basis for operations in 1944 and all other operations should be considered as diversionary, a distraction. "It would be much better to focus, than to scatter forces in several areas distant from each other," said Stalin. France was the weakest area of occupied Europe, and there you should attack. Plus, he repeated, there was no hope of Turkey entering the war, no hope at all.[54]

Churchill persisted. "The Prime Minister said he dreaded the six months' idleness between the capture of Rome and the mounting of Overlord," wrote Bohlen. "Hence, he believed that secondary operations should be considered in order to deploy forces available."

Stalin again disagreed, but Churchill asked to have the opportunity to "develop his arguments why it was necessary," but Stalin waved him off, saying that he did not expect to have technical discussions about military operations.[55]

Stalin's blunt reproach stopped Churchill, and one could quickly feel tension in the air. All eyes turned to the president. Roosevelt offered a conciliatory comment by suggesting that perhaps some further study was warranted. "Roosevelt said that Marshal Stalin's proposals concerning southern France were of considerable interest to him," said Bohlen. "He would like to have the planners make a study of the possibilities of this operation."[56]

That was not helpful and Churchill knew it. He grew increasingly agitated and interrupted: the second front in southern France was merely cementing Overlord and fixing its date. Why should British forces be standing idle merely to keep a firm date for Overlord? Why should a firm date be the deciding factor? He asked why their flexibility was not particularly important in the face of opportunity.

Stalin was impatient. He and Roosevelt were in agreement, he thought the issue was decided, and they could move on. But he conceded another day to Churchill, and said so. "I had not expected that the conference would deal with purely military questions and therefore I had not brought a large military staff," said Stalin. "However, Marshal Voroshilov is present and will be available for military discussions."[57]

Roosevelt said that he would have his staff work with the Russians to prepare a plan for a second invasion in southern France, but Churchill quickly and firmly dissented. He said he wished to go on record as saying that it would be difficult, if not impossible, to sacrifice all activity in the Mediterranean in order to keep an exact date for Overlord. He expressed the hope that careful and earnest consideration would be given to making certain that operations in the Mediterranean were not injured solely for the purpose of keeping the May date for Overlord. "Agreement between the three powers is necessary and will be reached," said Churchill, hinting that he could force the issue if he wanted to, "but I hope that all factors will be given careful and patient consideration before decisions are reached. I suggest meditating on the discussions of this meeting and reviewing them at the meeting of the next day."

Both Stalin and Roosevelt looked at Churchill. "He was the strongest personality in the capitalistic world," said Stalin some weeks later showing his grudging admiration of Churchill. He disagreed with the British Prime Minster, but Stalin always knew where Churchill stood. [58] Largely because of this, it was agreed to give this issue back to the military chiefs and reconvene tomorrow. On that note, they adjourned.

Despite the flair up, it had gone well, at least in the sense of personalities meshing, of three highly independent world leaders getting along. And although Churchill and Stalin had clashed it was not a stumbling block, this was simply part of diplomacy. "The initial session had been pleasant, polite, and agreeable," wrote Leahy. "The three principals stated their respective views and sounded out each other."[59] King agreed with that assessment. "The first day was spent getting to the meat of the matter, which was what to do about helping the Russians at once."[60] Stalin's position boiled down to a plan centered on D-Day, essentially the American plan, with a slight twist. He rejected the Baltics and the Mediterranean but deftly inserted his own agenda—the South of France. The South of France would complement Overlord with peripheral combat yet would keep the core of Overlord intact. Said Leahy, "The Soviets and the Americans seemed to be nearly in agreement."[61] Stalin wanted Overlord.

More than anything, they had met Stalin, the larger-than-life Stalin, the dictator whose caricature had been prominent in editorial cartoons over the decade past, the outsized Stalin, the dark Stalin, the evil Stalin, and they were all fascinated, intrigued, startled, enamored of the man. Although quiet and brooding, Stalin had filled the room with a certain presence and focus that was felt by all. He dressed modestly, a single red stripe down dark blue trousers, was plain looking but also plain speaking. "They say he is a peasant from one of the least progressive parts of Russia, but he had an elegance of manner that none of the rest of us had," Roosevelt would later say.[62] Leahy was just as impressed and thought Stalin had fundamentally altered all of their opinions of him. "Most of us, before we met him, thought he was a bandit leader who had pushed himself to the top of his government," wrote Leahy. "That impression was wrong. We knew at once that we were dealing with a highly intelligent man who spoke well and was determined to get what he wanted for Russia. No professional soldier or sailor could find fault with that."[63]

Bohlen, the translator, noted Stalin's speech patterns and his methods of persuasion, which he felt were convincing in a subtle way. "He spoke quietly, never raised his voice, and frequently used expressions designed to indicate a certain humbleness—phrases like 'I could be wrong, but I think,' and 'I believe,' with no hint of the arbitrary dictator."[64] Roosevelt's friend Hopkins agreed. He was a model of unwasted motion, a blunt man who went a long way on a few words, said Hopkins. "He does not repeat himself. There is no waste of word, gesture, or mannerism...His voice is harsh, but ever under control. What he says is all the accent and infliction his words need."[65] King, who had not spoken and would be largely quiet in the coming days, noticed another thing. Stalin doodled. "[He] used words in Russian which he would write and rewrite ...after the meeting he would fold and refold [the paper] until he would have made it into a compact wad then put this wad into one of his pockets." The hard-as-nails admiral was so interested in Stalin that he could not help himself; he tried to claim one of the "wads" the Soviet leader left behind but a British officer got it first.[66]

Churchill, of course, had been Churchill, the relentless bulldog Prime Minister employing "all the debater's arts, the brilliant locutions and circumlocutions," as Sherwood put it, while Stalin "wielded his bludgeon with relentless indifference to all the dodges and feints of [the Prime Minister]." On the other hand, Roosevelt had been surprisingly quiet and somewhat subdued.[67] He was "wise, conciliatory, and paternal," said one of the British generals, neither as blunt as Stalin nor as impassioned as Churchill.[68]

At 7:20 P.M. they adjourned after the lengthy three-hour session, their first summit, three world leaders trying to decipher a course of action that would affect hundreds of millions of people. Now they would eat. Roosevelt was hosting the dinner that night, Churchill, Stalin, the diplomats Harriman and Molotov, and the translators were invited. FDR went to his quarters and opened a newly arrived mail pouch that contained several congressional bills for his review. He signed four and he approved one proclamation. As he did that, Roosevelt's Filipino cooks were putting together the night's meal. Because he carried with him all of the necessary china and silver, it would be a very grand and very Rooseveltian affair.[69]

It would also be very American.

The menu was steak and potatoes.

CHAPTER 20: DINNER

Diplomacy is sometimes best conducted informally and, often, after hours of meetings. The three world leaders were eager to continue their talks, and they would now do so over a fine evening meal. Roosevelt's dinner that night was both intimate and revealing. Hopkins, Averill Harriman, and Bohlen, his translator, were seated around the table with the president while Churchill brought Secretary Eden, Sir Archibald Clark Kerr, the British Ambassador to Russia, and his translator. Stalin, cautious yet efficient as always, came with just Molotov and a translator—and a dozen bodyguards. Between the clinking of glasses and the courses of food, they talked about post-war Europe. It began, surprisingly, with France. Stalin came back to his earlier theme and said that the French were corrupt and deserved to be punished for helping the Nazis. "Stalin described in considerable length the reasons why, in his opinion, France deserved no considerate treatment from the Allies and, above all, had no right to retain her former empire," wrote Bohlen. "He said that the entire French ruling class was rotten to the core and had delivered over France to the Germans and that, in fact, France was now actively helping our enemies. He therefore felt that it would be not only unjust but dangerous to leave in French hands any important strategic points after the war. Roosevelt replied that he in part agreed with Marshal Stalin. That was why this afternoon he had said that it was necessary to eliminate in the future government of France anybody who was older than 40 years old and particularly anyone who had formed part of the French Government."[1]

Hitler was the next topic, and both FDR and Stalin shared their views on the German leader. Roosevelt ventured the opinion that Hitler was mentally unbalanced, if not a mad man. Stalin disagreed and said he had a different view of Hitler. The others turned to hear the Soviet Marshal's thoughts. While it was well known that Stalin and Hitler were bitter enemies, somewhat surprisingly, Stalin was even-handed in his analysis. He said that Hitler was a sort of genius, albeit one whose ends were abhorrent to him. "He said that Hitler was a very able man but not basically intelligent, lacking in culture and with a primitive approach to political and other problems," wrote Bohlen, who recorded this historic moment. "He did not share the view of the President that Hitler was mentally unbalanced and emphasized that only a very able man could accomplish what Hitler had done in solidifying the German people, whatever we thought of the methods." Stalin did feel, Bohlen recorded, that Hitler had been stupid in attacking Russia, and because of that he had thrown away all the fruits of his previous victories.[2]

FDR allowed the translators to finish then said he thought the word "Reich" should be stricken from the language forever. Churchill said Germany should be permitted "no aviation of any character—neither military nor civilian—and in addition, that the German general staff system should be completely abolished," recalled Bohlen. He proposed a number of other measures such as constant supervision over her industries and "territorial dismemberment of the Reich." Stalin strongly disagreed with the point about her industry, reminding Churchill that any German manufacturing was "subject to deceit, that a furniture factory could be transformed into an airplane factory, and that a watch factory could make fuses for shells."[3]

Stalin continued on to a broader point. The Germans, said Stalin, were robotic people who were easily controlled. They were a nation of habitual followers that were "dangerous if programmed by the wrong people." The German working class, said Stalin, too easily took orders, too easily abused power, and lacked the sort of self-awareness that kept other people morally in check. This made them the hands and feet of Hitler, unthinking and easily programmed to do wrong. Stalin went so far as to say that he thought the German working classes were animals who, if instructed to do so, pillaged, raped, incinerated, and destroyed. He said that he had German prisoners of war shot if they said that they were "only following orders" after they had raped and pillaged the Russian people. Stalin wanted Germany dismembered after the war and forcefully so.[4] The very Reich itself must be rendered impotent to never again to plunge the world into war, said Stalin.[5]

Roosevelt agreed with the idea of dismemberment and outlined his own thoughts on the mater. He said he would divide Germany into three states, including a three-part division of Berlin. Stalin liked that idea but felt it did not go far enough, because nothing was too severe when it came to post-war measures to police Germany. Said Bohlen, "In the detailed discussion between the President, Marshal Stalin, and Churchill, Marshal Stalin took the lead, constantly emphasizing that the measures for the control of Germany and her disarmament were insufficient to prevent the rebirth of German militarism and appeared to favor even stronger measures. He, however, did not specify what he actually had in mind except that he appeared to favor the dismemberment of Germany."[6]

Stalin turned the conversation back to the French and expressed how he felt they should be treated. He said that France had made a choice, that they had preferred to enter into an agreement with Germany rather than with their former allies, Great Britain and the United States, and because of that, they deserved no consideration at all. Churchill objected to Stalin's rather draconian measures and said so. Wrote Bohlen, "When the Prime Minister stated that he could not conceive of a civilized world without a flourishing and lively France, Marshal Stalin somewhat contemptuously replied that France could be a charming and pleasant country but could not be allowed to play any important role in the immediate post war world."[7]

Other borders were discussed as if they were pieces of a grand post-war puzzle. Stalin brought up Indochina and repeated that the colonies should not be returned to the French. Roosevelt agreed. On the other hand, Poland deserved to have her borders returned to her, and Churchill agreed—this was the main reason England had gotten into the war in the first place. Using three match sticks on a table Churchill indicated where Poland's borders should be relative to Germany and Russia, which enlarged Poland at the expense of Germany. Stalin murmured his approval.[8]

Roosevelt brought up Africa. Dakar, Africa was vital to international air travel, said FDR. He suggested that it become a "strategic point" controlled by the United Nations. Stalin agreed with this. "Churchill at this point intervened to say that Great Britain did not desire, and did not expect to acquire, any additional territory out of this war," wrote Bohlen, "but since the four great victorious nations—the United States, the Soviet Union, Great Britain, and China—will be responsible for the future peace of the world, it was obviously necessary that certain strategic points throughout the world should be under their control. Stalin agreed with the idea of these strategic points but again repeated and emphasized his view that France could not be trusted with any strategic possessions outside her own border in the post-war period."[9]

Owing to the hour, the dinner came to a conclusion, and the leaders repaired to their quarters for some well-deserved sleep. There was much to be done the next day including a vitally important discussion between the three military staffs on the issue at hand—a pincer operation, or Italy and Rhodes?

CHAPTER 21: STALIN'S HOUR

Roosevelt started the morning with his large cup of coffee. He had been gone for nineteen days, and his whereabouts remained a secret to most of the world. Yet the mundane tasks of the presidency followed him even on his clandestine journey. With Prettyman by his side, he worked through another new pouch of mail. There were no congressional bills that required his attention.

Naturally, many impressions had been formed. Leahy thought Roosevelt had come across as diplomatic and had conducted the meeting with skill.[1] Arnold had the same feelings—Roosevelt had been "reserved, listening and enjoying the meeting, talking when he thinks necessary, master of the situation."[2] Likewise, Stalin had been exactly as billed, blunt but also smart and intuitive, "hewn out of granite," as Roosevelt later observed.[3]

The British now appeared to be on the defensive and that boded well for a rapid conclusion favorable to the original D-Day plan, but one never knew with them. Handy noted, "When we left Cairo for Tehran... the U.S. planners felt rather glum and the British were correspondingly elated, because they felt Stalin would want a supporting operation nearer to his own front, which of course pointed to the eastern Med. The British were rather taken aback, to say the least, when Stalin came out so definitely supporting our views and in fact using many of the arguments we had repeated over and over again."[4]

But there was an ominous hitch. Several weeks earlier a troubling story had circulated that Stalin might reconsider his plans if the Allies did not draw off the Germans. Stalin was frustrated by the delays, and while he wanted the invasion to go ahead, if it was not going to happen, he had options. Leahy had already warned then that Stalin was at the end of his rope: "Russia would remain at war with Germany at least until the following Spring, at which time, if there had not been started by the

British and Americans an effective second front in Europe, the whole problem would be reconsidered by Stalin."[5]

Evidently, Stalin had repeated this same thing to U.S. diplomats in Moscow some days earlier—certainly not by accident, either—and it was resurfacing again in Tehran. "Will this take place or not?" Stalin was quoted as saying. "If it takes place, that is good, but if not, I wish to know in advance in order to be able to prevent these feelings which the absence of this operation would provoke. This is the important question."[6]

Did this mean that, if the Allies delayed Overlord again as the British were proposing, then Stalin might negotiate his own peace with Hitler? At some point would Stalin say enough was enough? And if so, where would that leave the Americans? Could the United States defeat Hitler's massive Wehrmacht without the Russians? Not likely. In any event, of all things to come out of Tehran, the last thing any of them wanted was to be left alone against Hitler.[7]

This day, perhaps, would tell.

The Monday schedule started with a meeting of the Allied military staffs in the main boardroom of the Russian Embassy to reconsider the British plan, as requested by the Prime Minister. This would be followed by a late lunch and then a 4 P.M. plenary session with Roosevelt, Churchill, Stalin, and the Combined Chiefs and then dinner at 8:30 P.M.

The American, British, and Russian military chiefs arrived at the Russian Embassy at 10:30 A.M. and took their seats. The room crackled with electricity. Technically, this was called a Military Conference but only Leahy and Marshall were present from the American sides, although the records are unclear why Arnold and King were not. Equally, only Portal and Brooke represented the British side, while the Russians were represented solely by Voroshilov. United States Army Colonel Andrew J. McFarland kept minutes for the Americans.

British General Sir Alan Brooke, erect and tall in his uniform as the Chief of the British Imperial Staff, stood up and opened the conference with a brief welcome and an overview of the status of the war from the

British perspective. He invited George Marshall to interject at any time.[8]

Brooke opened with a recitation of the British position. The crux of it all, said Brooke, was the relationship between Overlord and the rest of the war. One of the most important things for the Allies to do, he said, was to keep German divisions actively engaged in combat. Overlord would do just that but it could not be mounted until May 1st at the very earliest. Therefore, said Brooke, there would be a period of some five or six months during which no combat offensives were planned but during which something ought to be done. In his mind, that something was combat in the Mediterranean.

Brooke tapped a wall map with his pointer and indicated where the current Italian front was and indicated how he proposed to advance up the boot of Italy to Rome. Landing craft would be used to flank the Germans, tapping the map, he pointed out where soldiers would be put ashore. Eisenhower had clearly stated the day before that Italy was the one place where they could do the most damage to the Germans, said Brooke, and he agreed. Eisenhower had also said that he could complete this advance by early January, said Brooke, boding well for the current D-Day plans.

Brooke then pointed to Yugoslavia. It was rough, mountainous terrain, he conceded, but it was poorly defended and therefore represented an opportunity. The Axis powers had reduced their garrison forces in the Balkans and were vulnerable to attack from several points. This was too good to pass up, said Brooke; now was the time to strike.

He turned to Turkey and tapped the map at several points while discussing the advantages of bringing Turkey into the war. With Turkey on their side, they could open new bomber bases and mount more aggressive raids against the German oil refineries and airplane factories in Rumania, Hungry, and Czechoslovakia, he said. The Bosporus Strait could be reopened, and supplies destined for Russian could again move through them into the Black Sea, thus saving precious time in transit. This would require they capture the island of Rhodes and some of the other smaller islands in the Aegean Sea, said Brooke, tapping the maps as he talked, and would require some of the landing craft earmarked for D-Day. This would necessitate a slight delay in the invasion, he said, but it would be a short one and certainly an acceptable one considering the expected German losses.

Brooke paused to allow Admiral Leahy to speak. Leahy's patience had run thin—after all this was more of the same from the British—but he saw a contradiction in Brooke's argument. "Damn," said Leahy. "Your Prime Minister wants to keep all Allied Forces actively engaged but the two-and-a-half months delay you propose would immobilize thirty-five divisions waiting in United Kingdom for Overlord."[9] Brooke's plan, said Leahy, meant that nearly 400,000 soldiers in England would be idled in exchange for meaningless gains in places like Yugoslavia.

A discussion ensued and it went around the table, but as it quieted down, Brooke moved on to Stalin's proposal, which he also dismantled. If the Allies adopted a defensive posture in Italy and moved soldiers to Southern France, as Stalin had suggested yesterday, said Brooke, they would still have to maintain combat divisions in Italy strong enough to contain the Germans. What would be left over for the South of France, contrary to what had been said, would be insignificant. In addition, the landing craft available for such an operation would be limited too, thus assuring that it would be a small assault force. An attack against Southern France launched two months prior to Overlord would, by necessity, be a small force and was certain to be defeated. Far better would be a nearly simultaneous execution of those operations, but, even so, there were so few landing craft available that this, too, was a problem.

Brooke said that he agreed with Marshal Stalin's pincer strategy but that a pincer strategy was better used in a land assault than a sea assault, which was what the invasion of France was. In a somewhat condescending tone, Brooke then laboriously explained that in sea assaults the two forces are not self-sustaining and thus cannot reinforce each other and will not work.[10]

There were other problems with Stalin's strategy, the most worrisome of which was the potential build-up of enemy forces. If the Germans were not engaged in combat elsewhere, they would have ample time to recuperate, reequip, strengthen, and concentrate more and more divisions in Western France until an invasion there would be too bloody to even consider.

Brooke waited for the translators to finish then asked Marshall if he cared to add his thoughts. Marshall said he did. He flatly disagreed with Brooke. D-Day was an enormous operation on a scale that was truly reflective of global war. Unlike any of the British plans, said Marshall, Overlord would be a massive, overwhelmingly fatal attack on the Germans; there was simply no other way to see it. The momentum behind D-Day was unstoppable no matter how many divisions the Germans had or would be able to bring forward. The Allies were going to be landing tanks, artillery, trucks, guns, shells, bullets, gasoline, and soldiers by the hundreds of thousands, said Marshall, and they would keep coming and coming and coming without let up. "In contrast to the usual difficulties of war, there is no lack of troops and no lack of supplies. There are now more than fifty divisions in the United States which we wish to deploy as soon as possible, in addition to those already overseas," he said. "The military problem, therefore, resolves itself almost entirely into a question of shipping and landing craft." So long as they had the means to transport soldiers and tanks and land them on the beaches, in a sense it wouldn't matter what the Germans did, their forces coming ashore would just keep coming. This was why any diversion of ships to another theater was a terrible mistake, said Marshall. D-Day would require every available landing ship with no dilution of effort, no diversion of focus.[11]

As evidence of the profitability of this strategy, Marshall highlighted the United States Army Air Forces in England. Fighters and bombers, and the pilots and gunners to man them, were pouring into England and the only bottleneck has been getting them across the ocean, not finding the men, not building the planes or opening the bases. "Our air forces have been sent overseas just as soon as they were trained and, hence, the air battle is far more advanced than the situation on land," said Marshall. "One reason for favoring Overlord from the start was that it is the shortest oversea transport route. After the initial landings, transports will be sent directly from the United States to the French ports because there are about fifty divisions in the United States to be put into Overlord."

As to air superiority, he said, because of the intense bombing conducted to date, and the great number of fighters arriving in England, the guarantee of air superiority over Normandy was a certainty. That could not be said for combat in any other region. The current bases were too far away to provide effective air cover over Greece or the Aegean Sea. However, in France, this was assured. The sole issue was more landing ships, and they would need all they had.[12]

The question then, as Marshall saw it, was what to do over the next three months, and how that would affect the next six months. He agreed with Brooke that an immediate landing in southern France would be dangerous because it would happen before there was sufficient control of the skies over France. Without fighter cover, a landing would be too risky. Plus, the entire German command was expecting an invasion at any time anyway, so a small force would walk into the maw of an excited German defense. He agreed with Brooke that an invasion of southern France two months ahead of Overlord would fail, but something coordinated to within a few weeks of Overlord had a good chance of succeeding.

Marshall pointed out that any military invasion required overcoming many significant obstacles, but the ones Brooke mentioned were the sort of problems they had anticipated and were planning for. The problem Brooke alluded to—the Germans building up their strength—was already factored in. Take the Italian campaign, said Marshall. What they did in Italy was an indication of what they could do in France. All of the ports in Italy had been sabotaged by the Germans or bombed by the Allies in the course of the preparations for the American assault, which meant that everything had to be delivered over bare sand. Nonetheless, he said, with air cover, the U.S. had landed more than 189,000 soldiers and 30,000 motor vehicles during the invasion of Salerno. This had taken eighteen days in Italy—but all of this would be done in *one* day on D-Day.

Marshall let that fact sink in then repeated that if the Allies agreed to undertake Mediterranean operations, Overlord would inevitably be delayed or diminished and continued combat up the Italian peninsula was unnecessary and would be costly.[13] He spelled out what he meant. "For every mile of advance there were seven or more miles added to the perimeter," said Marshall. "We [do] not have enough men in the expedition to advance."[14] Marshall wanted what could be taken cheaply, to be sure, but Italy was not the objective, Germany was the objective.

Nor were the Balkans, said Marshall. The logistics of a shift there were impossible. "Supplying of great armies in the Balkans would have been an insoluble problem," said Marshall. "There was also difficulty of terrain, which in the Balkans was worse than in Italy."[15] Plus, the Balkans were like quicksand, he said. "Once you start a war of attrition you are lost, you are ruined," he said.[16] The only way to keep Overlord on track was, in fact, to reduce combat operations in the Mediterranean, now. Marshall immediately summed it up. "To the U.S., Overlord is the number one priority and nothing I have heard from Brooke, and nothing I know in terms of Germany's defenses, is a reason to delay it."[17]

Marshall let his words echo through the room. He then looked over to Voroshilov. Kliment Efremovich Voroshilov was Stalin's defense commissar and had been consumed by the war, and, because of that, he was less well known to the Americans. Of medium build, fleshy with a full head of hair and a thick mustache, Voroshilov had been with Stalin as far back as the Battle of Baku in 1907 and they had worked together ever since. Like Molotov, Voroshilov had served as Stalin's right hand man and had been involved with the purges. He himself had been a military commander in the field, although a relatively undistinguished one. Voroshilov later served for a time as the minister of cultural affairs.

He had a good mind and was a deliberate thinker who carefully reasoned the subtleties of critical military situations. Stalin brought him back to help him run the war as the Soviet equivalent to a secretary of defense. "Voroshilov performed well at critical moments," said Molotov. "He always supported the party political line."[18]

Voroshilov thanked Marshall, said he would like to ask some questions first, and then he would speak. He addressed Marshall, asking what type of air cover the U.S. was proposing for D-Day and what was being done to build more ships. Marshall answered that the air cover on D-Day would be provided by several thousand U.S. P-51s, P-47s, and P-38s plus British Spitfires. But that was just part of it, he said much had to be done now to weaken the Luftwaffe in advance of D-Day. The B-17s were already bombing German airplane factories to halt the flow of new planes forward, as well as their training bases, repair facilities, and in particular their forward air bases to the tune of some fifteen thousand tons of bombs dropped each month. Losses in the air on both sides were heavy, said Marshall, in some cases forty percent of the Allied bombers had been shot down or badly mauled, but they were not letting up. More had to be accomplished before a landing could be attempted, but more was coming, and soon.

As to the landing ships, Marshall answered that every shipyard in the United States was building ships for the war and that LSTs were large ships that took several months to build. The problem was under control, though, and the Allies would be ready to land soldiers and tanks on the beaches of France in May. Moreover, said Marshall, with so many tens of thousands of soldiers already prepositioned in England, and hundreds of thousands more arriving in the next few months, should we take landing craft away from Overlord to conduct other operations and delay it, would lose any element of surprise. No, the invasion was paramount and it trumped everything. "The troops are in motion," said Marshall. "The air forces are already there and are proceeding with their expansion."[19]

Voroshilov thanked Marshall for his clear answer, then turned to

Brooke. "I wish to apologize for my failure to understand clearly," said Voroshilov facing Brooke. "I attach great importance to the remarks made by General Marshall from which I understood that the U.S. considers Operation Overlord of the first importance. I wish to know if General Brooke also considers the operation of the first importance."[20]

The room quieted as all eyes shifted to the British general. "We have always considered the operation an essential part of this war," said Brooke. "However, we have always stipulated that the operation must be mounted at a time when it would have the best chances of success. The fortifications in Northern France are of a very serious character, the communications are excellent, and therefore the Germans have an excellent opportunity of holding up the landings until they can bring their reserves into play. This is the reason for our stipulations as to the conditions prerequisite for launching the operation. We consider that in 1944 these conditions will exist, but, as General Marshall said—and I wish to say again— landing craft constitute our tactical necessity. In order to maintain the 1 May 1944 date for Overlord it will be necessary to withdraw landing craft from the Mediterranean *now*. If this is done, it would bring the Italian operations almost to a standstill. The British wish, during the preparations for Overlord, to keep fighting the Germans in the Mediterranean to the maximum degree possible. In our view, such operations are necessary not only to hold the Germans in Italy but to create the situation in Northern France which will make Overlord possible."[21]

Voroshilov considered that for a moment then looked at Brooke and repeated his question. "I wish to apologize for my failure to understand clearly, but I am interested in knowing know whether General Brooke, as Chief of the Imperial General Staff, considers Overlord to be as important an operation as General Marshall has indicated that he does. I would like General Brooke's *personal* opinion."[22]

Again, all eyes again turned to Brooke. As Chief of the Imperial General Staff, said Brooke, he considered Operation Overlord to be vital but there was one stipulation. The defenses of northern France were formidable, and he did not wish to see the operation fail. In his opinion, under certain circumstances, Overlord was bound to fail.

Voroshilov considered that for a moment then began his own remarks. He looked around the table. "Marshal Stalin and the Soviet General Staff attach great importance to Overlord and feel that the other operations in the Mediterranean can be regarded only as auxiliary operations. I recall that Marshal Stalin said yesterday that he and the Soviet General Staff consider that Overlord was a very serious operation and would prove a difficult one. But, the accomplishments of the U.S. and U.K. in the war to date, especially the brilliant operations of their air forces over Germany, and your superiority in the Mediterranean, serve to indicate the might of your two nations. If there is added to this the firm will and desire of the U.S. and British staffs, I feel sure that Overlord will be successful, and it will go down in history as one of our greatest victories. I repeat, the excellent fighting in North Africa and the impressive operations of the Allied air forces over Germany are proof of this, and, I have no doubt that you will find a way to produce the necessary landing craft."[23]

Voroshilov continued, pausing only be let the translators catch up. One of the points he wanted to make, he said, was that the Russians favored combat against the Germans in the Mediterranean, there was just a difference of opinion as to where. In their minds, Italy and Rhodes were the wrong places. "I entirely agree with General Brooke that some small operations in the Mediterranean are necessary as diversions in order to draw German troops away from the Eastern Front and from northwestern France, but, as a military man, and as probably all other military men would think also, Overlord is the most important operation and that all the other auxiliary operations, such as Rome, Rhodes, and what not, must be planned to *assist* Overlord and certainly not to hinder it. It is possible now to plan additional operations that may hurt Overlord. This must not be so. These operations must be planned so as to *secure* Overlord, which is the most important operation, and not to hurt it. The suggestion made yesterday by Marshal Stalin that simultaneous operations should be under taken from Northern France and Southern France is based on the idea that the Mediterranean operations are *secondary* to Overlord. The troops saved by defensive operations in Italy would be available for launching an amphibious operation against Southern France. Marshal Stalin does not insist on this, but he does insist on the execution of Overlord on the date already planned."[24]

That was as clear as he could state it, but he had more to say.

Voroshilov talked about the Russian military experiences with cross-channel operations in general. His advice was that it could be done. The Russians had successfully crossed many wide rivers and, while it was a difficult maneuver, they had learned how to do it. He was certain this would be the same for the Allies. Voroshilov shared his advice. "With respect to the difficulties of the cross-channel operation, it is understood, of course, that crossing the Channel will be more difficult than crossing a large river, however, during the recent Soviet advances to the west we crossed several large rivers, the most recent of which was the Dnieper," he said. "In the latter case the ordinary difficulties of a river crossing were greatly increased by the high, steep western bank and the low eastern bank, but with the help of machine gun, mortar, and artillery fire—and the employment of mine throwers—it had been found possible to lay down a fire so intense that the Germans could not endure it. With similar aids it will be possible for you to land in Northern France."[25]

George Marshall smiled politely but took exception to one point. The difference between a river crossing and a landing from the ocean was that the failure of a river crossing was a reverse that could be corrected and tried again while the failure of a landing operation from the sea was a catastrophe. Failure in the latter case, said Marshall, meant the almost complete destruction of the landing craft and personnel involved.

Voroshilov nodded slightly and said that he appreciated the frankness of that statement.

Marshall said that his military education had been based on roads, rivers, and railroads, and that his war experience in France had been concerned with the same. During the last two years, however, he had been acquiring an education based on oceans, and he had had to learn new things all over again. Prior to the present war, he had never heard of any landing craft except a rubber boat. Now he thought about little else.

Voroshilov looked at Marshall. "If you think about it, you will do it."

George Marshall replied evenly: "That is a very good reply. I understand thoroughly."[26]

Voroshilov continued. He said that he wished to emphasize that if Overlord forces were launched against the hostile coast without previously destroying the enemy positions, there could, of course, be no success. He thought that the procedure must be similar to that followed for an assault across land. "First the enemy positions have to be destroyed by artillery fire and bombing from the air; then light forces, including reconnaissance groups, can land and take the first ground; when that has been done, the larger forces would come in later," said Voroshilov. "In that matter, if the advance forces are unable to land and are destroyed in the attempt, the larger forces would not also be destroyed." Voroshilov felt that if operations were conducted in this way, they would prove to be a brilliant success and not result in catastrophe.[27]

"No catastrophe is expected," Marshal said, firmly.[28] Voroshilov smiled in agreement.

Brooke waited for the translators to finish and then suggested that, it now being three hours into this meeting, they adjourn and reconvene in the morning. Voroshilov suggested they reach a consensus and come to a conclusion but Brooke suggested that that could come tomorrow. It had been a long day, said Brooke. They had been at the table for several hours, and there were meetings yet that afternoon and evening. Voroshilov relented and gave his consent. They agreed to meet again at 10:30 in the morning the next day, November 30th. On this point there was unanimous agreement.[29]

THE AFTERNOON

The meeting had gone so long that Leahy and Marshall had to hurry down the cavernous hall to the president's quarters to brief him. It took fifteen minutes. Marshall and Leahy laid out the essence of the Soviet position and their firm support for Overlord, including their insistence that it proceed without interference from any other operations and that it begin on the scheduled date of May 1944. But the British disagreed and had not yielded to Voroshilov, and thus no consensus had been reached, so they were meeting again in the morning to hash it out. That said, they expected Churchill would repeat the British position this afternoon and that he would be difficult. Roosevelt thanked them, and they left to have their own lunch.

At 2:30 P.M., Roosevelt welcomed Agent Reilly and Major Bryan to go over his travel schedule. Bryan had the latest weather forecast, which called for clear skies for the next several days. So long as there was good weather, the president wanted to stay in Tehran through the 1st of December. Bryan said that appeared to be possible.

There was a photo session scheduled for that afternoon on the front portico of the Soviet embassy, and he had a lengthy list of state visitors tomorrow. He told Reilly he wanted to spend his last night at Camp Amirabad and review the troops. Reilly said he would schedule his Secret Service agents accordingly.

At 2:45 P.M., Stalin walked over to Roosevelt's quarters with their translators, and sat down with FDR. Bohlen kept minutes. The America' air staff wanted to start shuttle bombing, Roosevelt said, and he as' Stalin if his crews could be given permission to land American B Soviet air bases, refuel them, stay overnight, and then fly back home bases the next day. Stalin thought that would be okay.

Roosevelt said how happy he was that the Soviet Union would join the U.S. in the defeat of Japan, a reference to Stalin's earlier remark, and, to help the Russians understand the situation there, he wished to share some data from his planning staff. To that end he gave Stalin three papers prepared by the American Joint Chiefs, one on the shuttle bombing issue, one on air operations against Japan, and one on naval operations in the Pacific. Stalin thanked the president for the papers and said he would study them carefully then he put them aside.

Roosevelt paused then brought up another subject. "I have a great many other matters relating to the future of the world that I would like to talk over informally and obtain your view on them," said Roosevelt. "I hope to discuss some of them before we both leave Tehran. I am of course willing to discuss any subject, military or political, which you desire, too"

"There is nothing to prevent us from discussing anything we wish," said Stalin.[30] They both smiled, eyeing each other closely.

"The question of a post-war organization to preserve peace has not been fully explained and dealt with, and I would like to discuss with you the prospect of some organization based on the United Nations," said Roosevelt.[31] He went on to explain that this "United Nations" would be an international body of some thirty-five countries that would debate world issues and make determinations for the rest of the nations of the world. A separate policing body, composed of China, Russia, Great Britain, and the United States, would enforce their resolutions and conduct military operations as needed to preserve the peace. As Roosevelt termed it, these nations would be the Four Policemen.

Stalin was well aware of this proposal and said he had already been briefed on some of the details. He asked, somewhat skeptically, if the "small nations," as he put it, would like the idea of the Four Policemen conducting military operations on their soil, for instance, the Chinese "policemen" fighting in, say, France. Rather, he suggested that there be some sort of regional policing board beneath the main body of the

United Nations, a European Commission, for example, that would carry out enforcement regionally, a Far East Commission for the Far East, and so on. Roosevelt said he had his doubts about that. He thought the United States Congress would object to the involvement of the U.S. in regional governing bodies but that they could be persuaded to intervene when decisions were made by a world governing body. World War II was an example of that. "It would take a terrible crisis, such as at present, before Congress would ever agree to combat again," he said. "If the Japanese had not attacked the United States, I doubt very much if it would have been possible to send any American forces to Europe."[32]

Roosevelt paused for the translators, then said he saw two methods of dealing with threats to world peace. "In the one case, if the threat arose from a revolution or developments in a small country, it might be possible to apply the quarantine method, closing the frontiers of the countries in question and imposing embargoes. In the second case, if the threat is more serious, the four powers, acting as policemen, would send an ultimatum to the nation in question and if refused, it would result in the immediate bombardment and possible invasion of that country."

Stalin frowned. He told the president about a conversation he had the night before with Churchill. He said he found Churchill to be naïve on the subject of Germany. "I discussed the question of safeguarding against Germany with Mr. Churchill and found him optimistic on the subject in that Mr. Churchill believed that Germany would not rise again," said Stalin. "It is my belief that that unless prevented, Germany would completely recover within 15 to 20 years, and therefore we must have something more serious than the type of organization per this current proposal," said Stalin. "The first German aggression had occurred in 1870 and then 42 years later in the 1st World War, whereas only 21 years elapsed between the end of the last war and the beginning of the present. I do not believe the period between the revival of German strength would be any longer in the future, and therefore I do not consider the proposed organization to be enough. What is needed is the control of certain strong physical points either within Germany, along German borders, or even farther away, to insure that Germany would not embark on another course of aggression. Dakar could be one of these points. The same method should be applied in the case of Japan. The islands in the vicinity of Japan should remain under strong control to prevent Japan's embarking on a course of aggression. Any commission or body which was set up to preserve peace should have the right to not only make decisions but to occupy such strong points against Germany and Japan."

Roosevelt waited for the translator to catch up, and smiled. He had used a nearly identical term on the *Iowa* to describe a similar concept, "I agree 100% with you," said Roosevelt. "Regarding your statements as to the ease of converting factories, a strong and effective world organization of the Four Powers could move swiftly when the first signs arose of the beginning of the conversion of such factories for warlike purposes."

Stalin smiled. "The Germans had shown great ability to conceal such beginnings."

"Yes," said Roosevelt. "I accept that..."[33]

*

As the afternoon sessions approached, the admirals and generals milled about in the main hall and passed the NKVD agents and bodyguards. Stalin was there and walked down to see Hap Arnold to ask about the U.S. bombers. "Stalin surprised me with his knowledge of our planes," said Arnold. "He knew details of their performance, their characteristics, their armament, and their armor much better than many of the senior officers in our own Air force. He asked me for improved airplanes, and he asked me for heavy bombers. I told him if he wanted heavy bombers he would have to send his engineers and maintenance and combat crews to the United States to go through our schools, or we could send the necessary personal to instruct his men in Russia. He thought those two suggestions over for a while and finally agreed that something like that could be done." Arnold came away feeling that Stalin knew some English, but he was not letting on. He also came away impressed.[34]

During their afternoon breaks it was tea time, a tradition for both the British and the Russians. "Every afternoon, at about four o'clock … were treated to 'tea and cakes,'" Wrote King, "Stalin poured the first day with some Russian tea, the next day the British managed the 'tea' with cream which apparently Stalin didn't like, nor did he like the American tea on the last day, especially the lemon."[35] This afternoon, though, tea was accompanied by ceremonies, the first of which was to honor Stalin and the Red Army's successful but bloody defeat of the Germans at Stalingrad.

King George V of England had commissioned a ceremonial steel sword in commemoration of the resilience of the "steel-hearted citizens of Stalingrad" who had so bravely repelled the German advance. The King asked Churchill to do the honors, and an elaborate presentation unfolded in the ballroom of the Russian Embassy. At 3:30 P.M. the band broke out in the national anthems of England and Russia, and Soviet and British soldiers marched into the hall and lined opposite walls. The Soviet soldiers were resplendent in their blue uniforms with red epaulettes, the British in full regalia with rifles and ceremonial bayonets. In the middle of the room was a great oval table and on it was a presentation case, several times the size of a gun case, in which lay the sword, nested on a bed of red velvet. With great fanfare, Churchill, dressed in his own military uniform with a chest full of medals and a single braid on his sleeve, read the King's message to Stalin as a British soldier lifted it up. The soldier formally passed the sword to Churchill who turned, and with both hands, presented it to Stalin. The scabbard was removed to reveal a blade of near perfect proportions. Stalin was noticeably moved. He admired the sword then handed it over to one of his soldiers who goose stepped it over to Roosevelt for his inspection.

Roosevelt held the heavy sword in both hands and brought it close to his face read the inscription. "It is a fine gift," he said, then praised the citizens of Stalingrad himself.[36]

The sword given, the group moved to the front portico of the Russian embassy where the Big Three took their seats and were photographed. In the background out of the main photograph were King, Marshall, Leahy, and Arnold. King casually lit a cigarette; Leahy was introspective. "If we succeed in destroying Nazi Germany this [conference] will be recorded in history as comparable to The Field of the Cloth of Gold."[37] For security reasons the photo was not released for nineteen days, although it remains an iconic image of the war and of the first of only two meetings of the Big Three.[38]

A second meeting of Roosevelt, Stalin, and Churchill followed immediately after the photo session, and no one knew for certain what was going to happen. The Americans had momentum, but the British seemed unwilling to yield. Said Bohlen, "As we went into the second plenary meeting, the conference was approaching a crisis; there was a real question whether it was to be a success."[39] Roosevelt had with him Hopkins, Harriman, Leahy, Marshall, King, and Arnold, plus four others including his translator, Bohlen. Churchill had his foreign officers, Eden and Kerr, and his military chiefs, Brooke, Porter, Cunningham, plus Dill, Ismay, a translator, and a secretary. Stalin brought Molotov, Voroshilov, and his translator. Every seat at the table was taken; foremost on everyone's mind was the outcome of the morning's military conference.

The president opened the meeting by asking Brooke to summarize. Brooke was happy to oblige. Bohlen took minutes.

The military committee had not finished its work, said Brooke, it merely made a survey of the various operations available to them. He said that the committee considered the fact that if active operations were not undertaken in the Mediterranean during the period of time that must elapse before Overlord, it would provide the Germans with an opportunity to remove their forces from Italy and Yugoslavia and transfer them to the Soviet front or to France to defend against the planned invasion. In that light, the committee had examined the advantages of continuing military operations up the leg of Italy and had reviewed the question of providing the Partisans in Yugoslavia with aid and supplies in order to assist them in containing German forces.

The advantages of Turkey's participation in the war were also considered, said Brooke, as well as the possibility of an operation in southern France in connection with Overlord. But, nothing had been decided; it was all preliminary and there was another meeting scheduled for the next morning.

General Marshall said he had little to add, and he did not intend to go into any detail. Nonetheless, Overlord should be kept on track, he said. He said the chief problems with Overlord were landing craft suitable to carry forty tanks, and airfields to afford fighter protection for the operations, but these were being corrected. He emphasized that the question of adequate landing craft came first in importance, and that production of these ships had been stepped up. He said that he had endeavored to make it clear to all, the manner in which preparations for Overlord were proceeding. The flow of troops from the United States was on schedule, he said. More than one million tons of material had already been shipped to England, and veteran divisions from Italy had already been moved to England to get them ready for the invasion.[40]

Voroshilov spoke next. He turned to Stalin and said that Brooke and Marshall had fairly represented the morning's discussions.

Voroshilov looked at Stalin. Stalin was doodling wolf heads on his tablet using a red pencil.[41] Stalin put down his cigarette as he looked around the table. "Every American and British eye and ear was fixed on the Soviet leader," said Leahy.[42]

"Who will command Overlord?" he asked.

There was silence.

Roosevelt answered that it had not yet been decided.

"Then nothing would come out of the operation unless one man is made responsible, not only for the preparation, but for the execution of the operation."[43]

Churchill objected and said that British General Frederick Morgan had been in charge of planning the invasion for some time, although it was true that the actual commander had not yet been appointed. He said the British government was willing to have a United States general in command of D-Day in view of the fact that the United States would land the bulk of the troops, and that possibly the commander in chief in the Mediterranean would be a British general.

Stalin was unimpressed. He said that a commander could easily change even the most advanced plan unless he made those plans himself. A commander needed to be named, he said.

Again there was silence, an awkward silence.

"Stalin kept asking who was to be commander of Overlord. He kept asking this," said Marshall. "Strictly speaking this was none of his business. Stalin of course knew of the discussion about the commander. Stalin knew I had been proposed. There was nothing very secret about this." Marshall felt this was Stalin's way of nailing the allies down to doing something and forcing them to stick to it. "Stalin knew that Churchill was opposed to the operation and Stalin didn't understand why Roosevelt was holding back on the operation," said Marshall.[44]

The attention shifted to the president.

Roosevelt said that this was a very important decision and the conclusions reached at this conference would most certainly affect his choice of a commander.

Stalin understood that, but said he would like a name as soon as possible.[45]

Churchill spoke again to argue the Mediterranean, and it was a terrible miscalculation. Churchill began what was no doubt the longest, most unwelcome soliloquy of the conference. He repeated nearly everything he and others had said so far and tried to curry favor with Stalin by underscoring how the British plans would directly benefit the Russians. Roosevelt, Marshall, Hopkins, and the other members of the Joint Chiefs were uncomfortably silent. Churchill talked on and on, spelling out in minute detail why he felt the American plan to pin all hopes on D-Day was short sighted and, in that dismissive vein, continued for more than thirty minutes. Blessedly, Churchill finally came to an end, no doubt aware that everyone had wearied of his oratory.[46]

Stalin took the floor. He told Churchill that he was well aware of the options as described and well aware of what the British were advocating, but that it had come down to Overlord and it must be concluded. "He said that Overlord was the most important [plan] and nothing should be done to distract attention from that operation," said Bohlen of Stalin's answer to Churchill's final appeal. "[Stalin] felt that a directive should be given to the military staffs, and proposed the following one: (1) In order that Russian help might be given from the east to the execution of Overlord, a date should be set and the operation should not be postponed. (2) If possible the attack in southern France should preced Overlord by two months, but if that was impossible, then simultaneously or even a little after Overlord. An operation in southern France would be a supporting operation as contrasted to diversionary operations in Rome or in the Balkans, and would assure the success of Overlord. (3) The appointment of a commander in chief for Overlord as soon as possible. Until this was done, the Overlord operation could not be considered a reality, he said. Stalin added that the appointment of the commander in chief was the business of the President and Mr. Churchill, not his, but that it would be advantageous to have the appointment made here."[47]

Churchill simply would not give up. He stood again and repeated his arguments and then began another long-winded explanation of the advantages of his plans, this one almost forty-five minutes long, but his words fell on deaf ears.

Through it all, Roosevelt had been quiet, but now he spoke and sided with Stalin. Wrote Bohlen, "Roosevelt said he had been most interested

in hearing the various angles discussed and that he attached great importance to the question of logistics and timing. He said it is clear that we
are all agreed as to the importance of Overlord and the only question was
one of when. He said the question was whether to carry out Overlord at
the appointed time, or possibly postpone it for the sake of other operations in the Mediterranean. He felt that the danger of an expedition in
the eastern Mediterranean might be that, if not immediately successful,
it might draw away [resources] which would delay Overlord. He added
that, in regard to the Balkans, the Partisans and other questions are pin-
ning down some forty Axis Divisions, and it was therefore his thought
that supplies and commando raids be increased to that area to ensure
these Divisions remaining there."[48]

The president paused as the translators caught up, then, being particularly careful in his choice of words, he declared his position. "I am
in favor of adhering to the original date for Overlord set at Quebec," said
Roosevelt, "namely, the first part of May."[49]

Stalin quickly said an enthusiastic "*Yes!*," and said that he would like
to see Overlord during the month of May but that he did not care whether it was May 1st, 15th or 20th, but that a definite date was important.

Churchill was clearly not in agreement. He said that his point of
view was not as far apart from the others as it seemed. The British
Government was anxious to begin Overlord as soon as possible but did
not desire to neglect the great possibilities in the Mediterranean merely
for the sake of avoiding a delay of a month or two.

Stalin shook his head. The operations in the Mediterranean were
only a diversion.

Churchill disagreed again. The British forces in the Mediterranean
should not stand idle but should be pressing the enemy with vigor, said
Churchill. To break off the campaign in Italy, where valiant Allied forces were holding a German army from returning to the Russian front
through their hard combat, would be impossible, unthinkable.

Stalin snapped back. "It looks as though Mr. Churchill thinks that the Russians were suggesting that the British army do nothing."[50]

Churchill shot back that if the landing craft were taken from Italy then they would be doing nothing.[51]

Roosevelt intervened and suggested a compromise. He said that the military staffs should reconsider this matter with a simplified directive to put Overlord as the main operation and to consider another operation in the area that would not delay Overlord.

Stalin disagreed: "What can such a committee do," he asked. "We Chiefs of State have more power and more authority than a committee. General Brooke cannot force our opinions, and there are many questions which can he decided only by us."[52]

Stalin said he wished to ask Mr. Churchill a question, and, as the translation was completed, the room came to a hushed quiet. He leaned forward. "Do the British really believe in Overlord, or are they only saying this to reassure the Russians?" asked Stalin.[53]

Churchill listened to the translation and turned red. "Churchill was irked, to put it mildly," remembered Bohlen. "He glowered and 'chomped on his cigar' as he formulated his answer." Churchill mustered up his best oratory and answered. "So long as plans were carried out as presently agreed to, it would be the duty of the British government to hurl every scrap of strength across the Channel."[54]

Stalin turned away. If there is to be a committee to discuss these matters, he said, that committee should know their wishes as the heads of state. "First of all," said Stalin, "this directive must be specific with regard to the fact that Overlord should not be postponed and must be carried out by the limiting date. Secondly, the directive to the committee should state that Operation Overlord must be reinforced by a landing in the South of France a month or two before undertaking the Overlord assault. If not possible two or three months earlier, then the landing in the South of France should be at the same time. If a landing cannot be effected in the South of France at the same time as Overlord, possibly this operation could be mounted a little later than Overlord. This operation in the South of France would be an auxiliary or supporting operation and would help and be considerably effective in contributing toward Overlord. On the other hand, operations against Rhodes and other operations in the Mediterranean would be diversions. Operations in the South of France would influence and contribute directly to Overlord. The directive to the ad hoc committee must also state that the appointment of the Supreme Commander for Overlord should be made forthwith. The decision regarding the Overlord commander should be made here in Tehran. If it cannot be done here, it should be done within a week at the latest."[55]

Roosevelt said he was certain that a commander could be named shortly, and he agreed with the directive and said that it should be given to the committee and deliberated forthwith. He then changed the subject to Yugoslavia. The president said that all possible aid short of impinging on Overlord should be given to Yugoslavia to help them bottle up the German divisions there. Commando-style raids were a possibility, but anything to keep the Germans contained had to be done *without* diverting resources from Overlord.

"You are right! You are right!" said Stalin slapping the table. No diversions, no distractions.

Roosevelt went on to say that timing was the issue and we should agree that Overlord would take place in May.[56]

Churchill disagreed. The possibilities for effective combat in the Mediterranean should not be cast aside for a fixed date, he said.

"All the Mediterranean operations are diversions, aside from that into Southern France," answered a frustrated Stalin. He emphasized that he had no interest in any other operations other than those into southern France. Nothing will come out of the other proposed diversions, he said. In his opinion, Overlord should be done in May. He added that there would be plenty of suitable weather in May.[57]

Roosevelt sensed the meeting had grown too tense to continue, so he suggested they adjourn. FDR said that in an hour a very fine dinner would be awaiting all, and everyone should be very hungry. He suggested that the military staffs meet tomorrow morning and discuss the matter and that a few political problems might be discussed during the next day's luncheon with the Foreign Secretaries and Hopkins.

Stalin objected. "It is unnecessary," he said. "The staffs will not in any way speed our work; they will only delay matters. It is proper to decide matters more quickly."[58]

Stalin turned to Roosevelt and asked how many more days he thought these meetings would go?

Roosevelt thought two days at the most.

Stalin said he must leave on the first, in any event, but that he might stay over until the second of December, but then he absolutely must go. Stalin reminded the president that he had said he could come to the conference for only three or four days, the war back home being pressing.

Roosevelt nodded and asked if the three heads of state could agree, for the sake of expediency, that the proceedings from this afternoon's conference would act as the directive to the military staffs. They have been confronted with every suggestion made at this afternoon's meeting, he said, and in this way they would have only one directive.

Stalin said that he believed that all that needed to be solved was the selection of the commander for Overlord, the date for Overlord, and the matter of supporting operations in southern France. He considered that all matters had been solved here and that committees were unnecessary.

Roosevelt held firm on his idea and said he preferred that the committees iron this out so he read a proposed directive:

"The Committee of the Chiefs of Staff will assume that Overlord is the dominating operation.

The Committee recommends that subsidiary operation(s) be included in the Mediterranean, taking into consideration that any delay should not affect Overlord."[59]

Stalin asked why there was no date in the directive to which Roosevelt answered that it had been fixed in Quebec by agreement.

Stalin waved his hand: "Then at four o'clock tomorrow, after noon, we will have our conference again."

Roosevelt looked over to Leahy, and Leahy confirmed the timing. The Combined Chiefs would meet at 9:30 in the morning, the Secretaries of State in their own meetings at 1:30 P.M., and the heads of state would adjourn until 4 P.M. the next day.[60]

Adjourn formally, but the day was far from over for Roosevelt, Churchill, and Stalin. Evenings were an integral part of the Tehran Conference, and tonight would be no exception. By nature, both Roosevelt and Churchill were social creatures and looked forward to a cordial at the end of the day. Stalin too was well known to enjoy the evening activities and, more than the others, was a late-nighter, often sleeping well past the breakfast hour as the price for his long evenings. Tonight, however, was special. A grand dinner was on the schedule to be hosted by Stalin in the Russian embassy. There would be no military meetings and no officers from the combined Chiefs—just the three heads of state with their various diplomats and, in a few instances, even some family members. Per usual, the night would be filled with pleasantries and the standard number of toasts, but tonight would take an unexpected turn, one that would be remembered and recorded in memoirs for generations to come.

THE DINNER

It had been a long day, one marred by "controversial discussion(s)," as Leahy graciously put it in his diary. Now they needed to tie up the loose ends.[61] Marshall, Arnold, Leahy, and King returned to their quarters at Camp Amirabad, called in General Handy, and told him they wanted to put the debate to bed once and for all. Marshall told Handy to draft a plan to invade southern France as a flanking operation to Overlord. There was an earlier draft of such an operation, Marshall said. Handy said there was and that it had even been updated some on the *Iowa* and then again in Cairo. With a little more work he thought his team could have something fleshed out by morning. Marshall was pleased; he would need it in the morning.

Marshall then asked Handy to do an analysis of the landing craft problem. Marshall said he wanted to know how long it would take to replace landing craft under various scenarios, and he wanted data that were unassailably accurate. Whatever he presented had to survive the fine-toothed comb of the British.

"When General Marshall returned from a meeting with the British Chiefs of Staff, he told me that now the Southern France operation had been accepted," said Handy. "The British said it couldn't be done, resources would not be available, etc. Gen. Marshall said they were to meet again the next morning (it was then evening) and asked me to get him some notes for the meeting. [General Brehon D.] Somervell, [head of Army supplies], [Admiral Charles M.] Cooke, [chief planner on King's staff], [Col. Emmett] O'Donnell [chief planner on Arnold's air staff], and I got together that night after dinner and drew up an outline plan for the operation—Somervell handling the shipping support and supply factor, Cooke the landing craft and naval support, O'Donnell the air, and I the divisions and other combat troops. We did have a very sketchy study made some time before, but all of us had given a lot of thought to this operation. The outline plan we drew up was reproduced by some early hour in the morning, possibly about 3 A.M. Our Chiefs of Staff took it to the meeting the next morning with copies for the British."[62]

*

Back at the Soviet embassy, a grand affair was underway. Hopkins and Roosevelt had retired to the president's residence and changed into their formal attire for a formal dinner that evening hosted by Stalin. It would be an elegant affair with endless toasting, such being the way of Russian dinners. The table was filled with the very best of their ornate silver, china, and stemware. "I have never seen such an elaborate table service," said Deane of the Soviet dinners. "The center pieces were huge silver bowls...beautiful cut glass ... the inevitable vodka glass...silver platters of Russian *zakouska*, including fresh large-grained dark caviar ... raw salmon and sturgeon...knives, forks, and spoons were gold, and service plates of the finest china heavily encrusted with gold."[63]

The lights were bright in the ballroom and the mood was good. Churchill and Roosevelt brought with them their diplomats while Stalin came only with Molotov, his translator, and, of course, his bodyguards. The dinner began nicely enough—meats, potatoes, and plenty of vodka—but it inexplicably turned ugly. Chip Bohlen made notes after it was over. Said Bohlen: "The most notable feature of the dinner was the attitude of Marshal Stalin toward the Prime Minister. Marshal Stalin lost no opportunity to get in a dig at Mr. Churchill. Almost every remark that he addressed to the Prime Minister contained some sharp edge, although the Marshal's manner was entirely friendly. He apparently desired to put and keep the Prime Minister on the defensive."[64] Oddly, Roosevelt not only stood out of the way, but seemed to enjoy it, particularly when Stalin started boasting about the dismemberment of Germany after the war. "I did not like the attitude of the President, who not only backed Stalin but seemed to enjoy the Churchill-Stalin exchanges," wrote Bohlen.

"Roosevelt should have come to the defense of his close friend and ally, who was really being put upon by Stalin."[65]

It began with yet another discussion on the need to dismember Germany after the war, but Stalin took it a step further. "Stalin developed the thesis that he had previously expressed, namely, that really effective measures to control Germany must be evolved, otherwise Germany would rise again within 15 or 20 years to plunge the world into another war," said Bohlen. "He said that two conditions must be met: (1) At least 50,000 and perhaps 100,000 of the German Commanding Staff must be physically liquidated. (2) The victorious Allies must retain possession of the important strategic points in the world so that if Germany moved a muscle she could be rapidly stopped."[66]

In hindsight most of the attendees agree that Stalin was talking in jest, but Churchill somehow missed the humor. Churchill responded by saying that Great Britain would have nothing to do with such a thing. "War criminals should pay for their acts," he said, "but I could never approve the cold-bloodied execution of simple soldiers."[67]

Stalin was quick to respond and said the British were soft on the Germans. "Fifty thousand must be shot," said Stalin.[68]

Stalin laughed, but then Roosevelt said he agreed with that but perhaps only 49,000 German officers should be "liquidated."

"Churchill had enough and pushed back his chair and stood up to leave," remembered Admiral King, but Eden stopped him "Stalin got 'W.C.' really mad," wrote King. "So much so that 'W.C' stood up and told Stalin that he couldn't talk to him and anyone in Britain like that, and kept 'sounding off,' walking to and fro until Mr. Eden stood up and spoke with 'W.C' in a low tone after which 'W.C.' resumed his seat and seemed to get calmed down."[69]

But it started again. Harry Hopkins recalled that the barbs directed by Stalin and Roosevelt towards Churchill were "unremitting."[70] Awkwardly, Elliot Roosevelt, who was also at the table, chimed in. He rose to toast the Russians and in doing so he joined in the digging.

"The U.S. Army would support this plan," he joked, meaning the executions of German officers. That was the final straw. Churchill stood up, turned, and left the room and went into the next hall, which was cloaked in semi-darkness. Unbeknownst to the prime minister, Stalin followed. "I had not been there a minute before hands were clapped upon my shoulders form behind, and there was Stalin, with Molotov at his side, both grinning broadly and eagerly declaring that they were only playing," wrote the prime minister. "Stalin has a very captivating manner when he chooses to use it, and I never saw him do so to such an extent as at this moment."[71]

Churchill returned, the conversation seemed to relax, and the topic of territories again surfaced. Roosevelt again talked about holding the strategic points in a sort of world trusteeship while Churchill said Great Britain had no territorial ambitions resulting from the war. Stalin was asked the same question and, perhaps ominously foreshadowing the future, he dismissed the question with an abrupt wave of his hand. "There is no need to speak at the present time about any Soviet desires, but when the time comes, we will speak."[72]

CHAPTER 22: THE BRITISH CAPITULATION

Churchill knew Stalin better than most and with a degree of such intimacy comes a degree of contempt. Months before, he and Stalin had gotten into a row over the war in Europe. Churchill had complained to Stalin that he had not been allowed to visit the Russian front. Stalin replied, "Maybe it can be arranged sometime, Mr. Prime Minister, perhaps when you have a front that I can visit, too. Goodnight."[1]

Such treatment was hardly deserved. From the earliest days of the war, Churchill had been the first to do something to help relieve the Soviet front even as London itself was reeling under the weight of the attacks by the German Luftwaffe. Despite his own crisis and his own need for resources, Churchill ordered his Royal Air Force to bomb German cities at great loss of British bomber crews but with the result that the British air strikes were forcing hundreds of thousands of German soldiers to be diverted from the Russian front to the defense of Germany, and every little bit helped the Red Army.

Moreover, the British-manned convoy ships coming across the Atlantic were supplying Russia with badly needed material but at great loss of British life. As but one example, a recent convoy of thirty-four ships lost twenty-three to the U-boats, leaving just eleven vessels that made it to Russia. Of the six hundred tanks the ships had carried, only one hundred got across the ocean. Harry Hopkins said of this sort of self-sacrifice: "I believe the British have saved our skins twice—once in 1914 and again in 1940. They, with the French, took the brunt of the attack in the First World War, and the Germans came within a hair's breadth of licking them before we got into it. This time it was the British alone that held the fort and they held the fort for us just as much as for themselves because we would not have had a chance to have licked Hitler had Britain fallen."[2]

Still, Stalin bullied. "You British are afraid of fighting," he said to Churchill in August of 1942 after Churchill flew to Moscow to meet Stalin to discuss the widening war. Churchill was there to tell Stalin that the second front would not be opened in 1942; a brave enough thing to do, personally delivering bad news, but Stalin attacked the messenger. "You should not think the Germans are supermen. You have to fight sooner or later. You cannot win a war without fighting," he said.[3] But Churchill had another message. The invasion of North Africa was about to be launched. To that news Stalin had proposed a toast.

And now as D-Day approached, Stalin belittled his friend again. One toast stood out as particularly demeaning. "Stalin referred to both the President and Churchill as his 'fighting friends' or 'comrades-in-arms'," said Bohlen, "but in the case of Churchill he added the observation, 'if it is possible for me to consider Mr. Churchill my friend.'"[4]

Such rudeness raised in Churchill an ugly tendency to heap similar criticism on the Americans by belittling the American soldier the way Stalin belittled the British. At his dinner with George Marshall in Cairo, the Prime Minister had questioned the fighting qualities of the American soldier. This of course struck a nerve. Yes, said Marshall, the American soldier had gotten off to a slow start, but they had come about and faced the Germans rather well. "They didn't realize the brutality of the war," said Marshall of his men. "They didn't realize the determination and ruthlessness of the Germans.... But they quickly got over this ... they became magnificent fighting men."[5]

To build some respect for his army, Marshall took his British counterparts to visit his American army bases and observe their maneuvers. "General Marshall said he missed no opportunity, when occasion presented itself, to take Mr. Churchill, Mr. Anthony Eden, Lord Louis Mountbatten, and other distinguished British visitors to training areas in the United States to convince them of the army that was being built," wrote two historians after an interview with the general. "[Marshall had] absolute confidence that troops could be so superbly trained that in their first battle engagement they could cope with, and succeed against, any enemy."[6]

But Marshall was honest with himself, and he knew the British had been in the war a lot longer than his soldiers had, so he accepted their initial skepticism and some criticism, but only so far.[7] "[British Army] General Alexander spoke rather patronizingly of American troops," remembered Marshall. "He continued to have this attitude long after the situation had radically changed, and when American troops in Italy had to bear the brunt of the fighting because of exhaustion of the British divisions. Alexander remarked to me: 'Of course your American troops are basically trained.' I said, 'Yes, American troops start out and make every possible mistake, but after the first time they do not repeat these mistakes. The British troops start out in the same way and continue making the same mistakes over and over, for a year.' The Prime Minister was with us and quickly changed the subject."[8]

Despite Churchill's extraordinary faith in the ultimate outcome of the war, Overlord remained his Achilles heel. Despite diplomatic and military agreements to proceed, despite his own public proclamations and the communiqués to the contrary, he was afraid of it. "You are fighting the battle of Somme," Churchill's personal physician once confided to George Marshall of this aspect of Churchill, referring to the gore of WWI and the bodies that were stacked in mud-filled trenches. "This was the root of his reserve about Overlord."[9] But there was another reason: England had run out of men. If the cross-Channel invasion failed, it would be their last attack against Germany. "They were completely exhausted and under strength," said Marshall sympathetically.[10] Thus depleted of reserves, the invasion of France was the all-in bet that would leave Churchill with no chips on the table. Such was not the case with combat in Greece, Italy, or Yugoslavia. The British could survive the winds of war however they blew in the Mediterranean, but not D-Day. D-Day had to work.

*

Handy's group worked through night on their analysis of the landing craft bottlenecks and on war plans to invade southern France, the results of which Marshall now had in his folder. The Tuesday morning meeting was gaveled to order at 9:30 A.M. in the conference room at the British Legation with Brooke presiding. Brooke opened by saying that the problem they faced today was to arrive at an agreed upon strategy to present to the Soviets at this afternoon's plenary meeting. Brooke then went into a repetitive, slow review of the various military options, but he placed an emphasis on Churchill's position. He said that it was agreed that the Allies should advance to Rome, and probably as far as the Pisa-Rimini line. For that thrust, he said, General Eisenhower had requested that he keep his landing craft until January15, but this would have repercussions on the Overlord date, said Brooke.

In Yugoslavia, he said, it was important to give all the help they could to the Partisans, and there was general agreement on this.

As regards Turkey and operations in the Aegean, an agreement was much more up in the air, said Brooke.

Finally, he said, if combat in the South of France proved to be feasible, it had been proposed to provide landing craft for that, too.

The sequence of events to be agreed to or not, said Brooke, would begin with the advance up to Rome in the Italian campaign, then Yugoslavian support, followed by Rhodes, and then the South of France, with the date for the South of France determined by Rhodes, if this was undertaken.[11]

Clearly, this did not comport with the directions given them yesterday, and Leahy rose from the table to speak. This was not what the heads of state had asked of us, he said firmly. We were given a specific directive to see that Overlord was carried out and not to reopen the Rhodes debate, said Leahy. "The problem seems to be a straightforward one of the date of Overlord. The Russians want Overlord on a fixed date in May.

They also want an expedition against the South of France at the same time, or perhaps a little earlier or a little later. As far as I can see it, the date of Overlord is the only point confusing the issue. If this matter is settled, everything will be settled."[12] Leahy continued. The retention of landing craft by Eisenhower in Italy until January 15 would not cause a delay in Overlord, he said, nor would an invasion in the South of France, said Leahy. If the landing craft were to be kept in Italy until 15 January, the U.S. calculations were that they could still be back in time for Overlord.

Brooke interrupted and said that those figures disagreed with the ones the British had. Leahy expected that—this was precisely the opening he wanted. With that he motioned to Marshall who pulled out Handy's reports. "Four questions had been put to the U.S. Planners," said Marshall. "Firstly, assuming that the operations against the South of France were undertaken, could Overlord take place on 15 May 1944? In this connection, the answer had been ['yes.']" However, said Marshall, it should not be carried out more than two to three weeks before Overlord.

The second question was related. How long could the landing ships remain in the Mediterranean and still arrive in time for an Overlord date of 15 May? Given time for repairs and training the crews, said Marshall, the U.S. calculation had been that the landing craft must be released two-and-a-half months before Overlord. This gave a date of 1 March as the last possible date to move them, which was plenty of time for Eisenhower to take Rome and advance as far north as the Pisa-Rimini line. The U.S. calculations show that, after allowing for losses, the landing craft that would be allowed to remain in the Mediterranean after the departure of the ones needed for Overlord would be sufficient to lift 27,000 troops and 1,500 vehicles—plenty for Eisenhower's needs.

Marshall went to the third scenario. If the Rhodes operation had to be undertaken, as well as the operation against the South of France, how would Overlord be affected? It was difficult to get an answer to that, he said, but assuming that Rome was taken by the end of January, and Rhodes by the end of April, then allowing a month for the repairs and extra time for transit and training, the South of France invasion could take place by July 15.[13]

Marshall continued. The Planners were also asked how long Overlord would be delayed if the LSTs used for Italy and Rhodes were lost to enemy fire and never returned for Overlord. The answer to that was three months. It would take three months to build new ships, and thus there would be a three-month delay to Overlord if landing craft were lost, which was a certainty.

In summary, because Overlord is now the determining event, Rome could and will be taken, but nothing more, said Marshall. The rest had to be tabled in favor of the May invasion of France. Those were the facts, said Marshall and he welcomed any review of them. Marshall had copies passed around the table.[14]

Brooke cleared his throat and suggested that they look at two alternate timelines for an invasion: one based on combat in the Mediterranean with Turkeys support and the other with no support from Turkey.

Nonsense, said Leahy. Brooke hesitated. Certain that he had done all he could to advance Churchill's position but convinced that it was no longer possible to advocate Rhodes, he conceded the British position. "Unless we can give the Russians a firm date for Overlord," he said, "there is no point in proceeding with the Conference." There were smiles of agreement, and the tension drained from the air. "As far as I can see," said Brooke, "we could do Overlord in May if we did not undertake other operations."[15] A robust discussion followed to fine tune the details—how many divisions were needed here, how many there?—but a consensus had formed, and it was in favor of the Russian plan: Overlord in May, with a near simultaneous invasion in the South of France.

And there it was. Brooke was magnanimous in defeat, there were no smug smiles, and the meeting simply moved on to the next topic.

The Combined Chiefs rustled their papers and moved to the language of a written resolution that they agreed would be given to their respective leaders immediately after their meeting. It read as follows:

Agreed:

a. That we should continue to advance in Italy to the Pisa-Rimini line.

b. That an operation shall be mounted against the South of France on as big a scale as landing craft permit. For planning purposes, D-Day to be the same as Overlord D-Day.

c. To recommend to the President and Prime Minister respectively that we should inform Marshal Stalin that we will launch Overlord during May, in conjunction with a supporting operation against the South of France on the largest scale that is permitted by the landing craft available at that time.[16]

They had done it. Ten days sailing a sub-infested Atlantic Ocean, the glide bombs, the risky flight through the Alborz, the threat of German assassins, the unknown of Stalin. Seven thousand miles, and now there was a D-Day. Churchill and Stalin had a private meeting with Roosevelt in his quarters in the Russian embassy. They were alone accompanied only by their translators. Bohlen took minutes. Roosevelt handed out freshly typed copies of the resolution. Stalin had it translated, then broke out in a generous smile. He said that he was completely satisfied. He immediately offered to initiate a Soviet military offensive at the same time to draw off German soldiers that might otherwise rush forward to the Normandy coast as reinforcements.[17]

Roosevelt said he would name a supreme commander in a matter of a few days and that this commander would operate from England. There would be an entirely separate commander in chief for the Mediterranean area, he said, which Stalin thought was sound military doctrine. Churchill said that commander would be British. Churchill, too, was magnanimous in defeat.

They shared a short lunch together in what was perhaps the warmest meeting of their war careers. They were relaxed, a great task accomplished—perhaps several great tasks—and now they could share it. "The President and Stalin are highly pleased with the results of our efforts," wrote Leahy. "This practically accomplishes the purpose of our meeting of the three staffs. And if the decisions are adhered to, it justifies our journey half around the word to get here."[18]

Churchill was quick to let the past be the past and move on. He turned to Stalin and asked if he had read the communiqué from Cairo regarding Japanese territories. The communiqué stipulated that Japan would be stripped of all of the islands occupied by her since 1914. It also said that she would return Formosa, Manchuria, and a cluster of islands off Formosa to China, and that she would be forced out of any land she had taken during the war, including, specifically, Korea.[19] Stalin said he had, and that he agreed with the contents, although he said that the Chinese must be made to fight. Roosevelt and Churchill murmured their agreement.

Churchill continued. A large land mass such as Russia deserved to have better access to warm-water ports, he said. As it was, the Soviet Union had only one such port. Churchill said that the question of a new port would of course form part of the peace settlement, but that it could be settled agreeably and as between friends.

Stalin replied that at the proper time that question could be discussed, but since Mr. Churchill had raised the question he would like to inquire as to the regime of the Dardanelles. He said that since England no longer objected, it would be well to relax that regime. Churchill assured Stalin that England had no objection to Russia having access to a new warm water port there; however, he questioned the advisability of doing anything about the straits at the moment, as we were all trying to get Turkey to enter the war. Stalin said there was no need to hurry, that he was merely interested in discussing it here in general.[20]

Roosevelt brought up the Baltic Sea and access to the German ports in the north. He said he liked the idea of establishing the cities of Bremen, Hamburg, and Lubeck into some form of a free zone, with the Kiel Canal put under international control and guaranty, with freedom of passage for the world's commerce. Stalin thought that was a good idea, and then asked what could be done for Russia in the Far East. Roosevelt said he thought that the idea of a free port might be applied to the Far East, and mentioned Dalian as a possibility. Stalin said he did not think that the Chinese would like such a scheme, to which Roosevelt replied that he thought they would like the idea of some sort of free port under international guaranty. Stalin said that that would not be bad, and added that Petropavlovsk on the Kamchatka Peninsula was an excellent port.[21]

So it went among the Big Three, parceling out bits and pieces of the world, one piece here for world trade, one piece there for national interests, one for peace. But Churchill had a far nobler reason for it all. "It is important that the nations who would govern the world after the war, and who would be entrusted with the direction of the world after the war, should be satisfied and have no territorial or other ambitions," said Churchill. "Hungry nations and ambitious nations are dangerous, and I would like to see the leading nations of the world in the position of rich, happy men." If the Big Three could walk away from this terrible war satisfied with their spoils, a lasting peace might be possible.[22]

Roosevelt and Stalin understood his sentiment completely and nodded their agreement.

The final plenary session started at 4 P.M., and while it would go for almost three hours, it was now largely a formality. As always, Stalin's secret police were seemingly everywhere, their jackets noticeably bulging as the admirals and general walked past them in the halls. "It wasn't the United States Secret Service who held the balance of power," noted Hap Arnold. "It was the Russian guards. The Russian guards controlled everything. Even when Stalin visited the President of the United States or the Prime Minister there were Russian guards within the building when and where Stalin was present." Today was no different. They were walking in front and behind Stalin.[23]

As before, today's meeting was held in the conference room of the Russian embassy. Roosevelt brought with him Hopkins and Harriman, Marshall, Leahy, King, and Arnold, and his translator. Churchill had his foreign officers as well as his military chiefs, and Stalin had Molotov, Voroshilov, and Pavlov. Again, every seat was taken.

Roosevelt opened the proceedings by saying that, while most of those present were aware of what had occurred this morning at the meeting of the British and American staffs, he wished personally to express his happiness at the decision, which he hoped would be satisfactory to Marshal Stalin. Stalin smiled to no one in particular and gave a slight wave of his hand. Roosevelt then proposed that Sir Alan Brooke report for the Combined Chiefs.

Brooke said that the United States and British staffs had reached agreement that Overlord would be launched during the month of May, 1944, and that a supporting operation would be undertaken in southern France on as large a scale as possible, based of course on the number of landing craft available to them. There was more, but that was the sum and substance of it, he said, and now it was on to D-Day. Brooke acknowledged the grateful, and relieved, smiles around the table.

Churchill took his cue and said that they now must closely coordinate D-Day with Marshal Stalin and the Soviet general staff since "it was important that in closing on the wild beast all parts of the narrowing circle should be aflame with battle."[24] He said that Overlord should be delivered with "smashing force" and he hoped to "place that man [Hitler] in a position where there was no way out for him; if he put force in the west he would be smashed on the Soviet front, and if he attempted to hold firm in the east he would be smashed on the west."[25] The room broke into a round of enthusiastic applause.

Stalin was next and said he fully understood the importance of the decision reached and the difficulties that would be encountered by the soldiers in the execution of Overlord. To that end he said the Red Army would help. The critical danger would be in the beginning of the operation when the Germans might attempt to transfer troops from the Eastern front to oppose the invasion. In order to deny the Germans that possibility, the Red Army would launch a large-scale offensive in a number of places simultaneous to the invasion. That, he said, would pin down German forces and prevent them from being transferred to the west. He said that he had already made the foregoing statement to the president and Mr. Churchill, but he thought it necessary to repeat it to the conference.

Again, appreciative smiles.

Roosevelt took his turn. He said that his next step would be the appointment of a commander in chief for Overlord, and he was confident that it would be made within three or four days or immediately after he and the prime minister had returned to Cairo.

Because of the significance of this conference and of the gravity of the decision reached, Roosevelt brought up the subject of a communiqué. He suggested the military staffs draft something for their approval as soon as practical. Stalin agreed, and Churchill noted that it should include mention that all future military operations were to be orchestrated between the three great powers.

An invasion such as D-Day depended to a large degree on surprise, so the conversation turned to general question of deception plans, and it was here that the three leaders again acted like old friends. Churchill said that the preparations for Overlord were bound to be known to the enemy. Numerous supply depots were being constructed in southern England, and in fact the entire appearance of the coastline was changing. He said it was difficult, if not impossible, to hide such a large operation from the enemy. Stalin acknowledged the point. The prime minister asked Stalin how he had gone about it. Stalin said that the Soviets had achieved some success fooling the enemy as to their real intentions by building fake tanks, airplanes, and airfields. They built these airfields in sectors in which no operations were planned, and such movements were immediately picked up by the German intelligence. He noted that at times up to five thousand false tanks and two thousand false airplanes had been used, as well as the construction of a number of airfields that were not actually intended to be used. Another method of deception was by the use of radio, he said. Red Army unit commanders freely communicated by radio giving the Germans false information, which evoked immediate attacks from the German air forces in areas where such attacks would do no harm.

Churchill beamed a generous smile.

"The truth deserves a bodyguard of lies."[26]

A great deal of discussion ensued that continued until the dinner hour approached. Roosevelt suggested that if Marshal Stalin and the prime minister had no objection, it would be advisable for the British and American military staffs to return to Cairo tomorrow, as they had a great deal to of work to do on the details of the decisions reached today. Stalin nodded his approval. Churchill reminded them that they were invited to a black tie dinner that evening at the British Legation. It was his 69th birthday.[27]

*

The Soviet secret police had been busy all week. Stalin's NKVD had bugged all of the guest quarters inside the Soviet embassy including Roosevelt's suite and Sergo Beria, Lavrenti's son, had listened in. "I have never done anything with such enthusiasm," the young nineteen-year-old later confessed. "I was able to establish from my eavesdropping that Roosevelt felt great respect and sympathy for Stalin." On his part, Roosevelt assumed he was being bugged and thought that was grand.[28]

Stalin, who had to adjust his sleeping schedule for this conference—
he was a notorious night owl and usually woke up quite late in the
morning—met with Beria each day at 8 A.M. Beria briefed him on the private conversations he listened in to and on what Roosevelt had said in his
various meetings. Stalin could not believe the president talked so freely.
Beria was convinced he had no idea his suite was bugged.[29] Stalin asked
about the president's emotions or if Roosevelt had placed any particular
emphasis on an idea or a thought. "Did he say that with conviction or
without enthusiasm," Stalin asked Beria. "How did Roosevelt react?"[30]
In general, the eavesdropping did not help much. More or less the only
insight that Stalin came away with was that FDR seemed to like him, and
that the President was somewhat of an idealist.[31]

In anticipation of the evening's black tie dinner, the NKVD swept
into the British Legation and for two hours turned every room upside
down and even walked the corners and crevices of the roof. They were
looking for booby traps, assassins hiding in the shadows, or hidden
microphones. The elder Beria, who himself had stayed in the shadows,
led the search.[32]

That night a celebration of unity was wrapped in the exuberance
of a festive party on the occasion of Churchill's sixty-ninth birthday,
and it was a grand affair. The dinner bells chimed at 8:30 P.M. sharp,
and a magnificent meal for thirty-four was served. The dinner table was
thirty feet long and festooned with the luminescent china, sparkling
silver and crystal, and ornate centerpieces. The evening was gay, the
mood was upbeat—a fitting end to such a high occasion as the Tehran
Conference—and the toasts were nearly endless. "The party developed
into an international exchange of compliments," said Leahy. "Our common hopes for a new world order in the world were stressed by the
principal speakers."[33]

Leahy, Marshall, Arnold, and King attended. So did Hopkins and
Harriman, as well as the British and Soviet diplomatic and military staffs.
Also seated were assorted sons and daughters—Hopkins' son, Robert;

Roosevelt's son, Elliott; his son-in-law, John Boettiger; Churchill's son, Randolph; and his daughter, Sarah Churchill Oliver. Roosevelt sat on Churchill's right, Stalin to his left. As the dinner plates were removed, a birthday cake was presented to Churchill and placed in front of him. He beamed.

Hap Arnold observed the world leaders and felt giddy from the sense of occasion. "Three truly great men: the President, Prime Minister, and Stalin, at a birthday party, the Prime Minister's 69th. Toasts and more toasts; everyone toasting his opposite, but the Prime Minister trying to outshine, carrying on true to form. The Prime Minister in one speech after another, glorifying the President, Stalin, the USA, our Army, Air Force, Navy, the Red Army, General Marshall and just making a toast... Stalin: the man of steel, fearless, brilliant mind, quick of thought and repartee, ruthless, a great leader, courage of his convictions as indicated by his half-humorous, half-scathing remarks about the British, the PM, and Brooke. I doubt if either was ever talked to like that before. Harry Hopkins made the best speech; his memory of things that passed is wonderful. Practically everyone at the table was toasted; Stalin went all the way around the table to click glasses with all military men, not with diplomats or civilians. History was made and how."[34]

Roosevelt's son-in-law took notes and later wrote of the occasion. "It was clear that those present had a sense of realization that historic understanding had been reached, and this conception was brought out in the statements and speeches. Back of all was the feeling that basic friendships had been established which there was every reason to believe would endure."[35]

And history made was not ignored. Of particular note was a toast offered by Stalin, which went straight to the heart of the herculean contribution America had made to the war effort. "I want to tell you, from the Russian point of view, what the President and the United States have done to win the war. The most important things in this war are machines," said Stalin. "The United States has proven that it can turn out from 8,000 to 10,000 airplanes per month. Russia can only turn out at most 3,000 airplanes a month. England turns out 3,000 to 3,500 airplanes a month, which are principally heavy bombers. The United States therefore is a country of machines. Without the use of Lend-Lease, we would lose this war."[36]

The room broke out in boisterous applause and a chorus of '*Hear! Hear!*' rang out. FDR no doubt beamed broadly as did Marshall, Leahy, King, and Arnold who, above all, knew what it had taken to build those machines. Churchill's eyes sparkled too, but he was lost in a private thought. How had Stalin so correctly known the output of his own factories? Clearly, deduced Churchill, Stalin had Soviet spies working in his own backyard.[37]

Churchill's thoughts were interrupted by the sound of one more fork tapping a goblet. It was Roosevelt. Perhaps fittingly, his toast would be the last of the evening and possibly the most poignant.

"There has been discussion here tonight of our varying colors of political complexion," said Roosevelt. "I like to think of this in terms of the rainbow. In our country the rainbow is a symbol of good fortune and of hope. It has many varying colors, each individualistic, but blending into one glorious whole. Thus with our nations. We have differing customs and philosophies and ways of life. Each of us works out our scheme of things according to the desires and ideas of our own peoples. But we have proved here at Tehran that the varying ideals of our nations can come together in a harmonious whole, moving united for the common good of ourselves and of the world. So as we leave this historic gathering, we can see in the sky, for the first time, that traditional symbol of hope, the rainbow."[38]

CHAPTER 23: DIVIDING THE SPOILS

The morning came all too soon. It was departure day for the admirals and generals, their next set of meetings would be in Cairo, but first, they had a day off, something Leahy was grateful for. "The pressures of war business at this conference which prevents an examination of these colossal antiquities will always be a matter of sharp regret," said Leahy, but now he was about to rectify that.[1] The British had coordinated a tour of Jerusalem, and so at 8:30 A.M., Leahy, Marshall, Arnold, King, and their British counterparts boarded their airplanes in Tehran and winged their way down to the Holy City. They landed in Palestine just after lunch.

The American and British chiefs checked into the magnificent King David Hotel, and they spent the day like any other tourist might. They saw the Jaffa Gate, the Wailing Wall, and the Dome of the Rock; they walked the Stations of the Cross, saw Gethsemane, and visited the Pool of Siloam.[2] After the thread-bare quarters of an Army camp in Tehran, Arnold could not help but add an entry in his diary about his new accommodations and the five-star view from his window. "Delightful rooms at [King] David Hotel," he wrote. "Portico that looks out on Mount of Olives across to mountain other side of Jordan River, bougainvillea, green pines and shrubs, beautiful roses, star pines, the walls of Old Jerusalem opposite me on the hill."[3]

Roosevelt remained in Tehran for a day of political discussions with Stalin and Churchill, post-war issues mainly, plus he wanted to visit the U.S. soldiers at Camp Amirabad. He was up at his usual hour and went through a new pouch of mail, which once again contained no Congressional bills.

At noon, he met with Churchill and Stalin in the Russian embassy. They opened with a lengthy discussion about Turkey and the possibility of her entering the war against Germany, but all three leaders agreed that nothing should be done to induce her into it, particularly in light of the new agreement on Overlord. Stalin, of course, believed that Turkey would do nothing no matter what they said or did.

The next topic was Finland, which was a touchy one. Finland was an old enemy of Russia and had in fact supported the German invasion in 1941 and declared war on the Soviet Union. They were now on the losing side of their war so they were sending overtures to Stalin through the Swedish ambassador for a meeting in Moscow. Stalin was unmoved. The details were vague as to the terms of peace they were proposing, and they failed to mention a dissociation from Germany, leaving Stalin with the impression that they were simply hedging their bets.

Both Roosevelt and Churchill said they hoped to see an independent Finland after the war and asked Stalin for his views. Stalin said he too wanted an independent Finland but expected some land concessions as well as reparations for the damage they had done to Russia. Payments, said Stalin, could be in kind—timber, paper, and other natural resources—but payments nonetheless. Molotov put it in perspective. Some twenty-one Finnish divisions had manned artillery batteries that for twenty-seven months pounded Leningrad. Roosevelt saw his point and agreed that for any visit to Moscow, Finland first had to replace its current pro-Hitler leaders. Stalin said he was willing to accept any assistance in these matters from the United States.[4]

The second meeting of the day was a lesson in the awkward humility politicians must occasionally endure to survive in democracies. Roosevelt met privately with Stalin in his residence at 3:30 P.M. Said Roosevelt to Stalin, America had elections in 1944 and that, while personally he did not wish to run again, if the war was still in progress, he might have to. This was touchy in the sense of their meetings here in Tehran, said Roosevelt, because there were six to seven million Americans of Polish extraction, and as a practical man, he did not want to lose their vote. He said he personally agreed with the views of Marshal Stalin as to the necessity of the restoration of a Polish state but he would like to see the

Eastern border moved further to the west and the Western border moved as far as the River Oder. This would of course appease this voting bloc, said FDR. Roosevelt said he hoped that Stalin would fully appreciate that, for the political reasons, he could not participate in any decision here in Tehran, or even next winter, on this subject and that he could not publicly take part in any such arrangement at the present time. Stalin said he completely understood.

In a similar vein, Roosevelt inquired about the nations of Lithuania, Latvia, and Estonia. Nationals from these countries were also naturalized Americans and could vote, aiding Roosevelt, and he hoped some measure of self-determination could factor in the reoccupation of these states by the Soviet Union. Stalin was non-committal but said that there would be many opportunities for the peoples of these states to express their will. It was not much, but FDR seemed satisfied with it.[5]

Having concluded his somewhat awkward request, Roosevelt thanked Stalin, and they both returned to the conference. Stalin no doubt marveled at the difficulties of ruling in a democracy—or perhaps the foolishness of it altogether.

The final meeting in Tehran was a tripartite political conference that convened at 6 P.M. in the main conference room of the Soviet embassy and was largely devoted to the dismemberment of Germany.

Roosevelt and Churchill both asked how soon Russia might start to negotiate with Poland. This was tricky, said Stalin. The Polish government-in-exile was closely connected to the Germans, and their agents in Poland were killing true partisans. The USSR had broken off diplomatic relations with Poland, not because of a whim, but because the Poles in exile had joined in the "slanderous propaganda with the Nazis" against Russia. Stalin liked Poland, he said, but he did not like the government-in-exile.[6] Stalin said it was impossible to imagine what was truly going on in Poland, but Russia was interested in having friendly relations with them since the security of Soviet frontiers was involved. The Russians were in favor of the reconstitution and expansion of

Poland's borders, but only at the expense of German territory. Just as FDR had done on the USS *Iowa*, Stalin asked for a map to show what he had in mind. They found one from a newspaper, but it wasn't very detailed, so Bohlen came up with a solution. "I took a book over to Stalin, who looked at one map and asked me on what data these lines had been drawn. The map showed the ethnic divisions of eastern Poland. I informed the Marshal that, as far as I knew, the only data available came from Polish sources. Stalin grunted and took his ever present red pencil and somewhat contemptuously marked the map to show what would be returned to the Poles and what would be kept for the Soviet Union."[7]

The division of Germany was next. All agreed that the best way to prevent Germany from rising again as a belligerent power of consequence was to break it apart. Churchill was primarily interested in seeing Prussia, the "evil core of German militarism," as he put it, separated from the rest of Germany. Roosevelt was more aggressive about it and said he had a plan to divide Germany into five parts. None of this was enough, said Stalin. If Germany were to be dismembered, he said, it should really be dismembered, and it was neither a question of five or six states, or two, but rather in preventing them from ever coming together again. Stalin said that he did not believe there was any real difference between the Germans living in one region or the other. They were all bad, he said. He said that the Prussian officers and staffs should be eliminated, but as to the inhabitants, he saw little difference between one part of Germany and another. Stalin said he was against any confederation of German states because they would just give Germany a chance to revive itself. Such an idea that created five or ten or even a hundred artificial states would not last. Austria, for example, had existed as an independent state and should be again, as should Hungary, Rumania, and Bulgaria. But Germany had to be permanently dismembered. He said that no matter what measures were adopted, there would always be a strong urge on the part of the Germans to unite, so the measures had to be severe. Stalin said he felt the whole purpose of any international organization meant to preserve peace should be to neutralize the tendency on the part of the Germans to reunite, apply against them economic and other measures, and, if necessary, use force to prevent reunification. He said the victorious nations must have the strength to beat the Germans if they ever start on the path of a new war.

Churchill asked if Stalin contemplated a Europe composed of little states, disjointed, separate, and weak.

Not Europe, Stalin said, but Germany, yes. Poland would be a strong country, as would France and Italy, but Rumania and Bulgaria would remain as they always had been—small States.[8]

The translations slowed things down and created a delay that resulted in a degree of confusion, so much so that before the obvious question could be asked—*what was Stalin's plan*—the meeting was adjourned. Unspoken was the idea of occupation. Apropos of the Rankin discussions held on the *Iowa*, whose soldiers were where at the end of the war could have long lasting consequences.[9] As FDR biographer Black succinctly put it, "The struggle for Germany would determine who really won the war."[10]

*

The President hosted the final dinner of the Tehran Conference. Fine china, cut crystal glasses, platters of perfectly prepared foods, and numerous toasts. After it was over, Churchill, Stalin, and Roosevelt huddled together to work on a communiqué to be issued to the press after FDR's departure from Cairo. The president bade Stalin and Churchill goodbye and was whisked away to the nearby U.S. Army Camp Amirabad where he and his party spent the night. Weather reports indicated that a cold front was approaching and might close off the mountain passes by Friday, so it was decided to make every effort to leave the next morning, Thursday, for the journey back to the United States. En route to Washington, Roosevelt had stops in Cairo and Italy.

Stalin left the next morning. He boarded his plane at Gale Morghe airfield and flew to Baku where he took off his uniform and changed into his greatcoat, cap, and boots. He took the train to Stalingrad for what would be his only wartime visit to the city that bore his name. Afterward that, he returned to Moscow.[11]

CHAPTER 24: STATESMAN

The president spent the night at Camp Amirabad and was up early to review the troops. He was lifted into a jeep and rode the grounds with his trademark cape over his shoulders. He stopped at the base hospital and talked to some of the patients there, then returned to the main compound where some three thousand soldiers had gathered. His driver slowly inched the jeep up an elevated wooden platform specially built so he could see and be seen. FDR thanked the soldiers for their service.

The president left Amirabad for Gale Morghe airport and departed Tehran for Cairo. In the president's plane were his usual passengers: Hopkins, Leahy, McIntire, Watson, Rigdon, Prettyman, his Secret Service detail, and some others. After a flight of 1,600 miles, Roosevelt landed in Cairo at 2:30 P.M. and moved back into the Mena Hotel, where he went through a new mail pouch. That night he had dinner with Churchill and their respective aides.

For the next several days, the American chiefs and the British chiefs met to clean up the plans, and the atmosphere was collegial yet again. The movements of more than three million Allied soldiers, 15,000 aircraft, 40,000 small Higgins boats, 6,000 ships, and several million tons of guns, bullets, and bombs required daily conferences between the Joint Chiefs of the United States and Britain. Most of the meetings were long ones and lasted between three to four hours with the president and the prime minister hovering about, interjecting their own ideas as to the plans and the invasion. "We had to see 'F.D.R' and 'W.C' almost every day in the morning at 11 A.M. because W.C. had 'fixed ideas' about what the Allies should do about going into France," remembered Admiral King. Churchill had not changed entirely—he was nudging Rhodes back onto the table and the chiefs were nudging it back off. "He didn't like the idea of Nazis there," said King with a smile, Churchill simply could not help himself, but it was of no particular importance now.[1]

The issue of the D-Day command remained unresolved. George Marshall had figured prominently in the discussions in Tehran and it seemed that whenever military strategy reached an impasse, Marshall was there to shape the information and give the leaders perspective. Wrote Hap Arnold: "He had more mature judgment and could see further in the future. What he said was said in a way that carried conviction."[2] His discerning voice was a distinct center of gravity even in the midst of domineering personalities, and Roosevelt was an observant president. Marshall had grown in his eyes, too.

But had his stature changed? Had "statesman" replaced "military commander?"

"History traditionally pivots on giants whose persistence, solidity, and courage fashion the events that shape the lives of lesser men," wrote the great Army commander General Omar N. Bradley. "Among the Western Allies, three of these giants towered above all others during the last World War—Roosevelt, Churchill, and Marshall."[3]

And history's time to pivot was at hand.

CHAPTER 25: THE SUPREME ALLIED COMMANDER

The Supreme Allied Commander of the D-Day invasion would be entrusted both with a grave responsibility and with the most powerful military force in world history. Ironically, the American Joint Chiefs had made no recommendations as to who that man should be. Eisenhower was now a proven commander on the field of battle, but Marshall out ranked him. Marshall, though, had recused himself. "I was determined," said Marshall, "that I should not embarrass the President one way or the other—that he must be able to deal in this matter with a perfectly free hand in whatever he felt was in the best interests... I was utterly sincere in the desire to avoid what had happened so much in other wars—the consideration of the feelings of the individual rather than the good of the country."[1]

Secretary of War Stimson believed that Marshall deserved the command and, more importantly, even wanted it. Stimson spoke to FDR about this and argued his case. "I said that I knew that in the bottom of his heart it was Marshall's secret desire above all things to command this invasion force into Europe," he said to Roosevelt, but FDR saw it differently and replied that he thought Marshall wanted to stay on as chief of staff. Stimson knew better than that, but Marshall made it hard to argue otherwise. "[His] matchless power of self-sacrifice and self-control gave that appearance, the appearance that he was happy to stay in Washington, but an Army officer wants to command in the field, and Marshall was a field commander, a brilliant one, a proven commander in WWI, one of the most capable battlefield planners around. But Marshall refused to state his preference, feeling that a President should make his own choices." Stimson urged Marshall to speak up, but Marshall said he would not. "I had begged him not to sacrifice what I considered the interest of the country to the undue sensitiveness of his own conscience in seeming to seek a post," said Stimson. But Marshall had been cast in an unbreakable mold of self-sacrifice. "This institution," Marshall later said of his years at VMI, "gave me not only a standard for my daily conduct among men, but it endowed me with a military heritage of honor and self-sacrifice." In Marshall's mind the decision was rightly—and exclusively—the president's.[2]

Omar N. Bradley was able to watch from afar and saw the contrasts between the possible candidates "Ike was admirably equipped for the job," said Bradley. "For after having defeated the Axis in Tunisia and Sicily, Eisenhower was now fording his way up the Italian peninsula in that agonizing winter campaign."[3] And yet FDR was not wrong: there was something special about Marshall. He transcended mere soldiering.

Marshall, of course, had too much self-awareness not to know that he was overqualified for the job; that it would be a step down from the most senior position the Army had. If he took on Overlord, his authority would be on par with the generals who now reported to him—Spaatz, Doolittle, Eisenhower, and so on—and yet he wanted the command very badly. In that small logic-proof compartment that occupies every man's mind the seductive siren song of Overlord played loudly, and Marshall could no more dismiss it than renounce his very name.

The selection was made and the unpleasant duty fell to Harry Hopkins, the plain spoken Iowan and FDR's close friend. "Hopkins came to me at Cairo and told me that the President was very much concerned because he felt he had to make a decision," said Marshall. "So I went to see the President, I think after luncheon, at his villa in Cairo... I just repeated again in as convincing language as I could that I wanted him to feel free to act in whatever way he felt was to the best interest of the country and to his satisfaction and not in any way to consider my feelings. I would cheerfully go whatever way he wanted me to go, and I didn't express any desire one way or the other. Then he accepted that as the evident—then he evidently assumed that concluded the affair and that I would not command in Europe. Because he said, 'Well, I didn't feel I could sleep at ease if you were out of Washington.'"[4]

And that was the way he was told.

In his own handwriting, Marshall drafted the order for the president's signature. "The immediate appointment of General Eisenhower to command the Overlord operation has been decided upon," it said, and Roosevelt scribbled his name below it, thus completing the last major combat decision of World War II that Roosevelt would have to make.[5] FDR asked that his order be sent to Churchill and Stalin.

Marshall left the meeting and wired his aides in Washington to have a set of summer clothes sent to the Pacific. This they did, but it was puzzling because he was supposed to be flying home via Italy. "Tell Mrs. Marshall I am well and the weather is fine," he said in closing "I cannot say more for reasons of secrecy."[6]

It was December 6, 1943.

*

For the next several days, Roosevelt's schedule was packed. As the Second Cairo Conference came to a close, he received various dignitaries in his villa and attended the final meetings of the Joint Chiefs and the Combined Chiefs. Most nights he dined with Churchill, knowing the final, substantive portions of his lengthy trip were over, save for one final message.

On December 7, 1943, Roosevelt began his return trip home. He boarded the *Sacred Cow* and departed the Cairo airfield for Tunisia where he would finally meet with Eisenhower to talk things over. He flew over the battlefields of Alamein, Tobruk, Benghazi, and Tripoli, securely nested in a cocoon of fighter planes.[7] Eisenhower elected to pick the president up at the airport and drive him to his villa, but he had just been handed orders to go to England in a matter of days. He was confused. His present command was in the Mediterranean, not England, and as far as he knew, he had no business in England. Nonetheless, he met the president at the airport and found out what this was all about.

"The President arrived in mid-afternoon and was scarcely seated in the automobile when he cleared up the matter with one short sentence," wrote Eisenhower in his memoirs. "He said, 'Well, Ike, you are going to command Overlord' ... I did manage to say, 'Mr. President, I realize that such an appointment involved difficult decisions. I hope you will not be disappointed."[8]

Marshall kept FDR's order and had it sent to Ike with his own note scribbled on the bottom. It was dated December 7th. "Dear Eisenhower. I thought you might like to have this as a memento. It was written (for) Roosevelt by me as the final meeting broke up yesterday, the President signing it immediately. G.C.W."[9]

Eisenhower was moved by Marshall's generosity of spirit. "Marshall's thoughtfulness in sending me a memento he knew I would value was certainly not the action of a disgruntled and defeated opponent for a job," he wrote. "While I have never discussed the matter directly with him, I have always been confident that it was his decision, more than anyone else's, that sent me to the Overlord post."[10] While that was a nice thing to say, Eisenhower was of course wrong, and he very likely knew it; it was Roosevelt's absolute dependence on Marshall that gave Eisenhower his command.

As the word spread, so did the initial reactions. "His selection was somewhat of a surprise," said Leahy. "The Joint Chiefs never recommended Eisenhower or anyone else. We had thought it was going to be George Marshall."[11]

Not so General Bradley, who was seasoned to such unexpected things in the Army: "In the Army we often scoff at the myth of the indispensable man," said Bradley, "for we have always maintained that Arlington Cemetery is filled with indispensable men. General Marshall, however, was an exception for if ever a man was indispensable in a time of national crisis, he was that man."[12] But not in Europe. In Washington.

On December 8, Roosevelt flew to Malta to review the troops, then on to Sicily for another official visit. He wore his business suit and hat with the brim of his hat slightly turned up and was in good spirits at each stop. Eisenhower was with him, as was General George Patton, and his son-in-law John Boettiger, as well as Bohlen. As they prepared to depart Castelvetrano on yet another leg of the trip home, Roosevelt asked where George Marshall was. No one knew. Hap Arnold happened to be among the soldiers milling about the plane, so Roosevelt beckoned him over. "He asked me where General Marshall was," wrote Arnold in his memoirs. "I told him he was returning [to the United States] by way of Australia. The President seemed surprised and wanted to know when that had been decided. I said I was sure I could not answer that question, but I thought General Marshall must have received approval from either him (the President) or from Admiral Leahy before he went on the trip."[13]

In fact, Marshall had asked no one. Marshall needed some time alone so he decided to go to the Pacific to meet with General MacArthur and then return to Washington, D.C. He asked his aide and good friend General Frank McCarthy of the war staff to come with him. McCarthy would later write that he sensed Marshall's "anguish" but that no words were spoken on the plane trip out to the Pacific, and there was no outward display of emotion. Marshall simply desired to be alone.[14] "If he would have shown emotion to anyone except his wife he would have shown it to me," said McCarthy. But he did not. "He was a really solid man. He was really a duty-bound man."[15]

Roosevelt nodded to Hap Arnold and let it go. He understood. "The President never commented on Marshall's sudden decision," wrote Marshall's biographer, "nor did Marshall."[16]

The first draft of the joint communiqué from the Tehran Conference was just one page long, yet it contained two paragraphs that spelled out the intent of the Allies.

"We say to the German people. We do not seek to enslave you. We do mean to destroy not only your military forces, but also the false leaders who have led a generation of Germans into bitter excesses against common decencies, culminating with your being plunged, by this same leadership, into a useless war which has caused millions of your sons to die and may sacrifice millions more. No power on earth can prevent our destroying the German armies by land, their submarines by sea, and their war plants from the air. Our attacks will be relentless."[17]

It was signed Roosevelt, Stalin, and Churchill.

EPILOGUE

Roosevelt's suite of rooms in the Soviet embassy in Tehran went untouched for months; the round table became something of a curiosity for the dignitaries who later visited there. The meeting halls remained silent, and in time all eyes would eventually turn towards a second conference in Yalta.[1]

As the great trip to Tehran neared its end, FDR was again in his C-54 bound now for Dakar, French West Africa. It was a long flight across the western half of North Africa, some 2,400 miles in length, with little by the way of scenery to entertain him. As always, Roosevelt was mildly cranky and less than pleased to be in the air again. "I am now on a 12-hour plane trip which I hate," wrote FDR in a letter home, but it would soon be over.[2]

On arrival in Dakar the president was off to a nearby naval base where he boarded a French destroyer. They put out to sea, rendezvoused with the USS *Iowa* off the coast, and steamed alongside as cables were fired between the ships. As if his travels had not been dangerous enough, Roosevelt was strapped into a bosun's chair, attached to one of the cables, and winched from one ship to the other. Below him, the ocean rushed just a dozen feet away.

On December 16, the *Iowa* entered the Hampton Roads channel and steamed up the Chesapeake Bay to the mouth of the Potomac River. It was a bitterly cold December day as FDR sat before the ship's company and thanked them for his safe travels. "As heads of governments we represented between two-thirds and three-quarters of the entire population of the world we had the same fundamental aims—stopping what had been going on in these past four years," said Roosevelt. "We have got to eliminate from the human race nations like Germany and Japan; eliminate them from the possibility of ruining the lives of a whole lot of other nations."[3]

Roosevelt thanked the crew and remarked that the *Iowa* was a "happy ship," words that to a sailor meant it was a good ship. Of course, that was how they felt about their grand old battleship anyway, and they didn't need a president to tell them, but it felt good anyway.

Two days later, on December 18, the president was back in the White House and met with Secretary of War Stimson to close out officially the final chapter. "I have thus brought Overlord back to you safe," said a proud president, "and sound on the ways for accomplishment." Indeed he had.[4]

The plans developed by Hap Arnold and presented to the president on the *Iowa* were approved by the Combined Chiefs during the second meetings in Cairo. As expected, the British refused to allow the RAF to be put into a unified bombing command, and they likewise balked at one overall Supreme Commander for Europe and the Mediterranean.

Hap Arnold's United States Strategic Army Air Forces was a brilliant success and his two new generals, Spaatz and Doolittle, animated their forces with the fighting spirit of their own personalities. By war's end, Hap's bombers and fighters had flown 1,693,000 combat sorties against Germany, dropping 8,200,000 bombs. German aircraft factories, chemical plants, auto factories, metal fabrication plants, engine plants, truck plants, ball bearing plants, coal mines, electrical power distribution stations, radio towers, railroad stations, and radar stations were gone. In the final four weeks before D-Day, his planes swarmed over western France and bombed every major roadway, bridge, airfield, and railroad between Germany and the Atlantic Ocean at least once and some a dozen times. On D-Day, there was not a single bridge left standing south of Paris, nor a single rail yard untouched, nor a single airfield in France, Belgium, Holland, or Western Germany that had escaped. These totals included the great commercial airports of Orly and Le Beurgot in Paris and Schiphol in Amsterdam, which had long ago been converted to German air bases but whose runways were now rubble. Because of Hap's bombing and his D-Day air cover not a single combat-effective attack mission was flown against the landings on D-Day and the forward movement of German reinforcements was so badly interfered with that their pace was slower than a company of soldiers on the move during the Civil War. Hap's United States Strategic Air Forces was a stroke of genius and an overwhelming success. Hap himself soldiered on despite numerous heart attacks and died just years after the war was won.

"D-Day in Washington was more a day of prayer than elation," wrote Katherine Marshall, General Marshall's wife. "The churches were crowded. There was no celebration such as there had been on the night of the African landings. Our hospitals by now were filled with the wounded, Nazi prison camps held innumerable Allied prisoners, many wives had been widowed, parents had lost their sons."[5]

Overlord was of course a beginning, not an end. "Do you realize," said the British Prime Minister to his wife, Clementine, in the early hours of June 6, 1944, "that by the time you wake up in the morning, twenty thousand men may have been killed?" The words hung in the air, the image of such death simply too much to bear.[6] Churchill's fear of another stalemate on the continent never materialized. The Allies stormed ashore and fought inland as thousands of tons of war materials flowed in behind them over the sands of the Normandy beaches. On June 6, 1944, 150,000 soldiers landed on the beaches of Normandy, France, and breached the vaunted Atlantic Wall. On August 15, 1944, another 100,000 soldiers landed on the beaches between St. Tropez and Cannes in the South of France invasion, thus bringing to fruition Stalin's pincer strategy.

Stalin delivered on his promised diversionary thrusts on the Eastern Front. The Germans were so tied up there that they were unable to shift soldiers to oppose the landing.

The combat was hard and went one hard mile at a time. Paris was liberated on August 25, 1944. Germany surrendered on May 8, 1945.

Operation Rankin had been unnecessary. American soldiers entered Berlin alongside the Red Army.

FDR never saw the surrender of Germany or Japan. After Tehran, he was reelected, but his health steadily declined. "The terrific burden of being in effect the Commander-in-Chief of the greatest global war yet recorded in history began to tell on the President in 1944," observed Admiral Leahy. "He required more rest and it took him longer to shake off the effects of a simple cold or the bronchitis to which he was vulnerable."[7]

On April 12, 1945, George and Katherine Marshall were sitting on the porch of their home enjoying a splendid afternoon of fair weather tinged with the first hints of spring. Theirs was a handsome two-story, red brick home with a wrap-around porch built on a ridge on the grounds of Fort Meyer, an Army base at the confluence of the Anacostia and Potomac Rivers. Their home commanded a magnificent view that on any other day they would have enjoyed until sunset, but as they sat there Marshall saw a car hurrying towards his house and he immediately feared the worst. A new German weapon? Something gone wrong in the Pacific? The driver was not his regular driver but his good friend Frank McCarthy, and that was unusual, too. McCarthy pulled to the curb in front of Quarters One and leaped out. "The President is dead," said McCarthy. Marshall let the words register then silently rose, took Katherine by the hand, and without saying so much as a word, got in the backseat and was driven to the White House.

Marshall was ushered into the Cabinet Room where members of the Supreme Court had assembled along with FDR's cabinet. It was a moment too difficult to comprehend. "Everyone in the room appeared completely stunned," Marshall said to Katherine, who had waited outside. The newly sworn-in President, Harry S. Truman and Marshall spoke briefly, but what they said has been lost to history.[8]

Truman was overwhelmed, too. He had no in-depth knowledge of the war, nothing about the intentions of the former president, and an absence of information so complete that he felt compelled to explain it to his daughter. "Roosevelt," Truman said, "never did talk to me confidentially about the war, or about foreign affairs, or what he had in mind for peace after the war."[9] But in death, things left undone rarely fit together. The day after FDR's death, Truman called in his Joint Chiefs and asked them for a briefing. Secretary of War Stimson, Admiral Leahy, General Marshall, and Admiral King arrived promptly at 11 A.M. Stimson turned and asked King to brief Truman on the Pacific. King, who utterly disdained the new president, a "pipsqueak" as he once put it, could scarcely look Truman in the eye as he spit out his words, disgusted that such a man could be allowed to take such a high office. A bad speaker anyway, King sent a clear message. He retired shortly thereafter.

An embarrassed Stimson turned to Marshall, and Marshall was brilliant. Marshall collected his thoughts and, in his characteristically soft but clear voice, spelled out the war situation on both fronts including the expected consequences of the various combat initiatives then underway. It was a magnificent, compassionate, sensitive briefing entirely fitting to the grave burden Truman had inherited. His biographer Mosley wrote of that morning, "Stimson got the impression that Truman had found the steadying hand he needed to grasp, and it was at the end of Marshall's arm."[10]

After the end of the war, Marshall made sure his victorious field generals received the appreciation of a grateful nation. He arranged for parades to be held in the hometowns of each of his commanders. One by one, they were brought back from Europe and sent home to receive the applause they so richly deserved. Marshall never accepted a parade for himself.

Eisenhower was the face of victory over Nazi Germany, and his parade was the grandest of any yet seen in the nation's capital. "Washington gave General Eisenhower a tumultuous welcome when the Supreme Commander, who had led our forces to victory over Germany, returned to the capital on June 18," recorded Leahy in his diary. "The crowds were said to have been the largest even seen in Washington."[11]

Marshall purposefully stayed away lest his own presence take away from the attention focused on his generals. But what he had accomplished had not gone unnoticed. *Time Magazine*, in their cover story when he was designated the 1943 Man of the Year, wrote, "George C. Marshall, was at year's end the closest thing to 'the indispensable man.'"[12]

Fitting to be sure, Marshall's real parade would be a very private affair. On VE Day, Secretary of War Stimson assembled his generals and admirals in his private conference room in the Pentagon building and called in George Marshall. An unsuspecting Marshall walked down the halls and into a room filled with his close friends and one empty chair. He sat down. "I want to acknowledge my great personal debt to you, sir, in common with the whole country," said Stimson to Marshall. "Seldom can a man put aside such a thing as the Commanding General of the greatest army in the whole of history. The decision was made by you for wholly unselfish reasons. But you have made your position as Chief of Staff a greater one." Stimson continued and concluded with words that no doubt meant more to Marshall than any medal or accolade. "I have seen a great many soldiers in my lifetime, but you, Sir, are the finest soldier I have ever known."[13]

Tears welled up in the eyes of many of those present, and it was a day they would scarcely forget. Here before them were two men of great character, Stimson, who was George Marshall's "Rock of Gibraltar," and "the General" who to Secretary Stimson had no peers.

In October of 1945, Marshall's third and final report on the state of the war was presented to Congress and published. So popular was he that the commercial edition sold more than 100,000 copies and it climbed to number two on the *New York Times* best seller list where it remained for twelve weeks. Such was the nation's love for "the General."

The lines sketched on the *Iowa* set into motion an imperative to go to almost any lengths to prevent Germany from rising to power again. The Western allies wanted to weaken Germany by chopping it up. For Roosevelt the solution was to break Germany into three smaller states, for Churchill the number was six, but nothing satisfied Stalin, who told Roosevelt and Churchill in Tehran that the Allied plans were not strong enough to render Germany impotent for the coming decades. He did not, however, reveal his own plan. Here history leaves us with a conundrum. On the one hand, the Soviets unilateral actions to take over most of Eastern Europe clearly led to the Cold War. On the other hand, it accomplished the aims of the Tehran Conference. As we now know, Stalin's solution was to occupy East Germany and, through puppet dictatorships, establish a Soviet-friendly buffer zone around Russia that would become known as the Soviet bloc. History harshly judges this and no doubt it should, but in truth Stalin, at least from a Russian perspective, did what he, Roosevelt, and Churchill all vowed to do—to take measures sufficient to divide, weaken or otherwise prevent Germany from rising again. Would a "cow-like federation" have been more palatable? Perhaps. Would FDR or Churchill have gone along with Stalin had he outlined the landscape of Eastern Europe as it came to be? Certainly not. But both Western leaders clearly signaled their desire to take draconian action and in a sense they gave Stalin a dim green light. Stalin, whose country lost between twenty-five and forty million dead during the war, did what he thought best to protect Russia. In the end, Germany would remain all but impotent for the next forty-five years, just as Stalin, Roosevelt, and Churchill would have had it in Tehran.

*

Europe desperately needed food; the homeless needed shelters. Arnold's B-17s sprang into action and began dropping supplies and airlifting help. So many cities had been destroyed that the traditional models of human self-sufficiency were gone. It was no longer possible for one German city to come to the aid of another, for nearly every city in Germany was to some degree suffering heavy damage and extensive loss of life. "It is a rubble heap, a charnel house, a breeding ground of pestilence and hate," said Winston Churchill as he surveyed the land-scape of Europe. Across the continent some five million homes and apartments were completely gone.[14]

Truman saw a solution. "I'm here to make decisions," he said to one of his callers just days after Roosevelt's death "and whether they prove right or wrong I am going to make them."[15] On January 21, 1947, George Catlett Marshall was confirmed as Truman's new Secretary of State by a unanimous vote of the United States Senate. "He was a man you could count on to be truthful in every way," said Truman, "and when you find someone like that, you hang on to them."[16]

Marshall immediately toured the European capitals and came back convinced that help could not wait. He had his own ideas of what form that aid should take. He envisioned a pool of money, approved by Congress and administered independently, from which any of the war-ravaged nations could draw funds to stimulate their own econo-mies. Marshall ran it past Truman, then did most of the leg work to implement it. He went before Congress and persuaded them to release the unheard of sum of seventeen billion dollars, and crafted the pacts with the European governments. Monies flowed; Europe began to stand upright again.

Truman refused to call this plan his own plan; it was Marshall's idea and it would be named after him, said the president. Nations that before had been at war with America would now be revived by the same general who had built the armies that defeated them. The Marshall Plan was a triumph of human compassion, but Marshall persistently ducked any praise for it. It was only an offhanded remark of his, years later in 1956, that summed up his perspective of this grand accomplishment. Modestly, Marshall called the Marshall Plan "an entirely selfish move," to ensure the future prosperity of the United States by rebuilding Europe so they could become healthy trading partners and "keep turning" America's economy. Yes, perhaps that was true, but there was more to it than that as scores of families would later attest.[17] Historian David McCullough addressed the enduring impact of Marshall as Secretary of State: "The appointment of Marshall was one of the best, most important decisions of Truman's presidency. One wonders, as Truman must have in later years, how differently history might have unfolded had Marshall declined to serve as Secretary of State at that particular moment in world affairs."[18]

One wonders, too, how history might have unfolded if Marshall had been given the D-Day command he so coveted. If he had been named Supreme Commander, he would have been on the battlefields of France and not in Washington, D.C. to make such a lasting impression on Truman in the aftermath of Roosevelt's sudden death. Would they have ever met?

How to put it all in perspective?

Said British foreign service diplomat Robin Edmonds, "The Tehran Conference was certainly the most significant Allied meeting of 1943 and—arguably—of the entire war. It was the first occasion on which the two most powerful political leaders in the world, Roosevelt and Stalin, met face to face; it was the last on which Churchill was able to confer with them on equal terms and, even so, had to fight hard to maintain his position. Military historians—with justice—record this meeting as the moment when the decision to invade France in 1944, finally became irreversible."[19]

Charles Bohlen, who later rose to prominence in the U.S. State Department, believed it all turned on Tehran. "There is no doubt however that Tehran was the most successful of the wartime Big Three conferences...the military decisions made at Tehran led to the defeat and surrender of Germany."[20]

Yes, but there was more to it than that. It was perhaps Stalin's finest hour, too, a moment in history when he held sway over and stood hand-in-hand with the Western World, united to cross the bridge before them. As the divide deepened it was Stalin's steady, sure, blunt voice that arced over the meetings and forced the unity that had to be found.

It was unexpected, this Stalin they encountered, but it was what he was for these decisive days in Tehran.

Harry Hopkins asked his good friend the playwright and historian Robert Sherwood to help him write his biography. For months they worked on it, Hopkins in failing health, the one-time confident to Franklin D. Roosevelt, forty-seven years of a life to record, the college years, the Great Depression, the war years; Sherwood meticulous, detailed, together going over papers, talking, remembering.

Some months into the project Hopkins looked up from his sickbed to ask Sherwood a question. Hopkins understood how against all odds the American factories had scaled up production and had produced tens of thousands of bombers and tanks. He understood how the seemingly impossible legislative bottlenecks had been broken. He even understood how scarce resources like aluminum and rubber and even uranium had been acquired and sourced from around the world. But that wasn't all of it. Wrote Sherwood: "There was one miracle he could not explain. How did it happen that the United States, an unwarlike nation and unprepared country if ever there was one, was suddenly able to produce so large and so brilliant a group of military leaders , competent to deal with situations that had never before existed in the world?"[21]

How, indeed. An army general from Uniontown, Pennsylvania, an admiral from Ohio, an undistinguished graduate from West Point, a president with no military service—how did they all do it?

Hopkins searched Sherwood's face for an answer, but it was not there to be found. Rather that answer, and an inspiring story, began on that cold, rain-swept morning in November of 1943 on those wide, teak decks of the battleship USS *Iowa* when World War II was in its darkest hours. These five men would depart the sovereign waters of the United States with an uncertain future and would return with the strategy that, at the 11th hour, would reshape the world.

This was their story.

NOTES

FOREWORD

1. Paraphrased from the translation quoted in Edmonds, Robin, The Big Three: Churchill, Roosevelt and Stalin in Peace and War, New York: Norton & Co., 1991, p.356
2. Bohlen, Witness to History, p. 133
3. Maurice Matloff, Strategic Planning for Coalition Warfare, 1943-1944, a volume in the United States Army in World War II [Washington: GPO, 1959], p. 335

CHAPTER 1: WINTER 1943

1. FRUS, p.77
2. FRUS, p. 80
3. Rigdon, White House Sailor, p. 57
4. http://uboat.net/allies/warships/ship/8881.html, last accessed 10.11.12
5. THE PRESIDENT'S LOG, FRUS Tehran Conference, Preconference Papers, p. 274

CHAPTER 2: THE *IOWA*

1. Larrabee, p.185.
2. Whitehill, Fleet Admiral King, A Naval Record, p. 438
3. Reminiscences of Vice Admiral John L. McCrea, USN (Ret.), p. 221
4. McCrea, History of the USS *Iowa*, no page numbers
5. Helvig, Tom, Editor, *The Iowan*, Vol. 1., Number 1, p. 6, http://www. ussiowa.org/general/html/specifications.htm, last accessed 8.15.12

6. Helvig, Tom, Editor, *The Iowan*, Vol. 1., Number 1, p. 7, http://www. ussiowa.org/general/html/specifications.htm, last accessed 8.15.12
7. Hall, USS *Iowa*: BB-61, p. 62
8. Hall, USS *Iowa*: BB-61, p. 65
9. McCrea, History of the USS *Iowa*, no page numbers
10. McCrea, History of the USS *Iowa*, no page numbers
11. Rogers, J. David, Development of the World's Fastest Battleships, p. 4
12. THE PRESIDENT'S LOG, p. 274

CHAPTER 3: LEAVING PLYMOUTH

1. Churchill, Closing the Ring, p. 287
2. I Was There, p. 105
3. I Was There, p. 106
4. Gilbert, Churchill, p. 767
5. Gilbert, Churchill, p. 767
6. Interviews, p. 9
7. Quoted in Pogue, Organizer of Victory, p. 300
8. Black, Franklin Delano Roosevelt: Champion of Freedom, p. 852

CHAPTER 4: IT CAN BE DONE

1. Friedel, Franklin Roosevelt, the Apprenticeship, p. 345
2. Friedel, Franklin Roosevelt: The Apprenticeship. p.5
3. Cross, Sailor in the White House, p. 196
4. Reilly, Reilly of the White House, p. 109
5. Cross, Sailor in the White House, p. 200
6. McCrea, History of the USS *Iowa*, no page numbers
7. McCrea, The History of the USS *Iowa*, Chapter titled Ghost of the Chesapeake, no page numbers.
8. Hall, USS Iowa: BB-61, p. 62
9. *The Iowan*, Vol. 1, No. 4, p. 12
10. Rigdon, White House Sailor, p. 57
11. McCrea, History of the USS *Iowa*, no page numbers
12. Cross, Sailor in the White House, p. 198
13. Cross, Sailor in the White House, p. 198
14. FRUS, p. 81
15. McCrea Reminiscences , p. 228
16. McCrea's War, p.656 Tobey, ed.

CHAPTER 5: BAKU

1. FRUS, p.22
2. Commander-in-Chief, Larrabee, p. 4
3. Winston Churchill's address before The House of Commons, February 11, 1943.
4. Rigdon, p. 85

5. Paraphrased from the translation quoted in Edmonds, Robin, The Big Three: Churchill, Roosevelt and Stalin in Peace and War, New York: Norton & Co., 1991 P.356
6. At Stalin's Side, p. 333
7. Montefiore, p. 497
8. Montefiore, Stalin, p. 463

CHAPTER 6:
THE JOINT CHIEFS OF STAFF

1. THE PRESIDENT'S LOG, p. 279
2. Roosevelt and Hopkins, p. 834
3. Roosevelt and Hopkins, p. 932
4. Interviews, Guyer and Donnelly, p. 9
5. Interviews, Mathews, Smythe, Lemson, Hamilton, p. 7
6. Quoted in Matloff, STRATEGIC PLANNING FOR COALITION WARFARE 1943-1944, p. 306
7. Truman, p. 533
8. Larrabee, Commander-in-Chief, p. 99
9. Truman, p. 535
10. Mosley, Leonard, Marshall: hero for our Times, p. 22
11. Pogue, Education of a General, p. 152
12. Pogue, Education of a General, p. 189
13. Interviews, October 5, 1956, p. 593
14. Quoted in Marshall: Hero for our Times, p. 200
15. Master of Sea Power, p. 332
16. Larrabee, p. 255
17. Larrabee, Commander-in-Chief, p. 207
18. Sugrub, Starling of the White House, P.321
19. Larrabee, p. 252
20. Larrabee, p. 252
21. Larrabee, p. 224

22. Arnold Diary
23. Arnold Diary
24. Interviews, p. 451
25. Black, Franklin Delano Roosevelt: Champion of Freedom, p. 858

CHAPTER 7: TORPEDO

1. Sherwood, Roosevelt and Hopkins, p. 768
2. Sherwood, Roosevelt and Hopkins, p. 768
3. Sherwood, Roosevelt and Hopkins, p. 768
4. Sherwood, Roosevelt and Hopkins, p. 768
5. Rigdon, White House Sailor, p. 64
6. Hall, USS *Iowa*: BB-61, p. 104
7. McCrea Reminiscences , p. 234
8. Gregory A. Freeman World War II Magazine, Dec, 2005
9. Sherwood, Roosevelt and Hopkins, p. 768
10. McCrea Reminiscences , p. 234
11. McCrea Reminiscences , p. 234
12. Helvig, To, Editor, *The Iowan*, Vol. 1., Number 1, p. 12, http://www.ussiowa.org/general/html/specifications.htm, last accessed 8.15.12
13. Hall, USS *Iowa*: BB-61, p. 104
14. Quoted in Master of Sea Power, p. 332
15. Larrabee, p. 230
16. Larrabee, p. 230
17. Interviews, p. 15.
18. Leahy, I Was There, p. 195
19. McCrea, The History of the USS *Iowa*, Chapter titled n Historic Voyage, no page numbers.

1. H Handy AFHRA, p. 45
2. Werner, Iron Coffins, p. 304
3. Whitehall, Fleet Admiral King, p. 485
4. I Was There, p. 198
5. Three members of the Joint Strategic Survey Committee, six members of Joint Staff Planners, 12 members of the Joint War Plans Group, and four members of the Joint Logistics Committee
6. Cline, Roy S., Washington Command Post: The Operations Division, p. 213, p.228, p. 312
7. Whitehill, Fleet Admiral King, p.482
8. Interviews, p. 30
9. Interviews, p. 30
10. Maurice Matloff, STRATEGIC PLANNING FOR COALITION WARFARE 1943-1944, p. 337
11. Larrabee, p. 173
12. Interviews, p. 31
13. Matloff, p. 336; JCS Minutes, RG 165, Box 6, Testimonials, Conferences, Minutes, etc.
14. Matloff, p. 303
15. Matloff, STRATEGIC PLANNING FOR COALITION WARFARE 1943-1944, p. 304
16. Matloff, p. 334
17. Cross, Sailor in the White House, p. 198
18. FRUS, p. 86
19. Mosley, Marshall: A Hero For Our Times, P. 282
20. FRUS, p. 86
21. FRUS, p. 86
22. FRUS, p. 88; see also Matloff, p. 337
23. Matloff, p. 339

24. The concept of strong points endured and are the precursors to the Cold War network of quick-reaction air and naval forces that the United States and Great Britain operated for essentially these same reasons.

25. Arnold Diary

26. Buell, p. 410

27. King Diary, LOC

28. Leahy, I Was there, p. 192

29. Quoted in Matloff, p. 275

30. Leahy, I Was There, p. 191

31. This ultimately became moot as the structure of the SHAEF crystallized. Presumably FDR thought the D-Day landing forces and the British forces coming in through Holland have separate commands.

32. FRUS, November 15 Meeting Notes, p. 198; see also Matloff, p. 338

33. McCrea, The History of the USS *Iowa*, Chapter titled n Historic Voyage, no page numbers.

34. Helvig, Tom, Editor, *The Iowan*, Vol. 1., Number 3, p. 10, contributed by Judy Tobey, http://www.ussiowa.org/general/html/specifications.htm, last accessed 8.15.12

35. Quoted in http://www.usnavyoilers.com/Time/index.html, last accessed 8/7/12

36. The President's Log, p. 273

37. McCrea, The History of the USS Iowa, Chapter titled Ghost of the Chesapeake, no page numbers

1. Interviews, p. 598

2. I Was There, p. 103

3. Interviews, p. 6

4. Mosley, Marshall: Hero For Our Times, P. 256

5. Interviews, p. 8

6. Interviews, p. 62

7. Cray, p. 412

8. History of COSSAC, Chief of Staff to Supreme Allied Commander, Supreme Headquarters Allied Expeditionary Force, May 1944, P. 21, http://www.history.army.mil/documents/cossac/Cossac.htm, last accessed Oct 22, 2012

9. McCrea, The History of the USS Iowa, Chapter titled n Historic Voyage, no page numbers.

10. Helvig, Tom, Editor, The Iowan, Vol. 1., Number 2, p. 3, contributed by Arthur F. Lockwood, http://www.ussiowa.org/general/html/specifica-tions.htm, last accessed 8.15.12

11. Rigdon, White Sailor, p 63

12. Cross, Sailor in the White House, p. 196

13. Cross, Sailor in the White House, p. 169, 170

14. Hall, USS *Iowa*: BB-61, p. 89

15. Fox, FDR and the Guns: memories of the USS *Iowa*, The Philadelphia Inquirer, July 30, 1986

CHAPTER 10:
THE JOINT CHIEFS OF STAFF

1. Blair, Hitler's U-Boat War, The Hunted, 1942-1943,p.419, p. 445
2. Gilbert, Churchill: A Life, p. 747
3. Churchill, Closing the Ring, p. 287
4. Gilbert, Churchill: A Life, p. 756, p. 758
5. Black, Franklin Delano Roosevelt: Champion of Freedom, p. 852
6. Reilly, Reilly of the White House, p. 166
7. Reilly, Reilly of the White House, p. 166
8. Eisenhower, Crusade in Europe, p. 171
9. Eisenhower, Crusade in Europe, p. 171
10. Rigdon, White House sailor, p. 65
11. Arnold Diary, p.
12. Arnold Diary, p.
13. Churchill, Closing the ring, p. 288
14. FRUS, p. 98
15. Eisenhower, Crusade in Europe, p.193
16. Reilly, I was Roosevelt's Shadow, p. 88
17. Reilly, Reilly of the White House, P. 151
18. Slocum, Reilly of the White House, p. 174
19. McCrea, The History of the USS Iowa, Chapter titled n Historic Voyage, no page numbers.

CHAPTER 11: OPTION A

1. Quoted in Last Stand of the Tin Can Sailors, p. 29
2. Tobey, A Naval Life, p. 662
3. Mosley, Marshall: Hero For Our Times, P. 274
4. Goodwin, p. 473
5. Cross, Sailor in the White House, p. 199
6. FRUS, p. 204
7. Handy Interview, AFHRA, p. 41
8. Handy Interview, AFHRA, p. 33.
9. Gilbert, Churchill: A Life, p. 752, p.761
10. Gilbert, Churchill: A Life, p. 743
11. Gilbert, p. 757
12. Gilbert, p. 758
13. I Was There, p. 198
14. Reilly, Reilly of the White House, p. 164; Dates of attacks per Combat Chronology, USAF

CHAPTER 12:
DISMEMBERING GERMANY

1. Rigdon, White House Sailor, p. 62
2. Hall, USS Iowa: BB-61, p. 68
3. Tobey, A Naval Life, p. 664
4. FRUS chart, p. 207
5. FRUS chart, p. 207
6. FRUS, p. 249
7. Interviews, p. 8
8. FRUS, p.252
9. FRUS, p. 788
10. Interviews, p. 10
11. FRUS, p.253
12. Interviews, p. 13
13. FRUS, p. 254
14. Interviews, p. 10
15. Matloff, p. 342
16. FRUS, p. 258
17. Interviews, p. 37
18. FRUS, p. 259
19. This expression is used in part or whole or in substance in several documents but it is clearly stated in Sherwood's biography of Hopkins.

20. Cray, p. 408
21. FRUS, p. 253; see also Sherwood,
    p. 711
22. Matloff, p. 342
23. Map courtesy Marshall Library
24. Interviews, p. 15
25. I Was There, p. 198
26. Cross, Sailor in the White House,
    p. 159
27. Tobey, A Naval Life, p. 664
28. Muir, The *Iowa* Class Battleships, p.42
29. Reilly, Reilly of the White House,
    p. 166
30. McCrea, The History of the USS *Iowa*,
    Chapter titled n Historic Voyage,
    no page numbers.
31. McCrea, The History of the USS *Iowa*,
    Chapter titled n Historic Voyage,
    no page numbers.

CHAPTER 13: TUNIS

1. McCrea, The History of the USS Iowa,
   Chapter titled n Historic Voyage, no
   page numbers.
2. Roosevelt, As He Saw It, p. 133
3. Arnold Diary
4. Roosevelt, As He Saw It, p. 133
5. Arnold Diary
6. McCrea, p. 239
7. Eisenhower, At Ease, p. 251
8. Crusade in Europe, p. 195
9. Box 34, Flight Log Book 1942-1943,
   Ernest King Papers, Manuscript
   Division, Library of Congress; see also
   Fleet Admiral King, p. 504
10. Box 34, Flight Log Book 1942-1943,
    Ernest King Papers, Manuscript
    Division, Library of Congress; see also
    Fleet Admiral King, p. 504
11. Pogue Tape 11M, p. 45
12. Crusade in Europe, p. 196

13. Interviews, Tape 16, unnumbered
    pages
14. Interviews, Tape 16, unnumbered
    pages
15. Fleet Admiral King, p. 502
16. Box 34, Flight Log Book 1942-1943,
    Ernest King Papers, Manuscript
    Division, Library of Congress
17. The President's Log, p. 219
18. Interviews, p. 3
19. Cray, p. 423
20. Sherwood, Roosevelt and Hopkins,
    p. 770
21. Eisenhower, Crusade in Europe, p. 197
22. Dorr, p. 28
23. There is no universally accepted
    explanation for the nickname save
    the idea that a 'sacred cow' was some-
    thing that was protected and the
    Secret Service protected the President.
    It may well have been a Secret Service
    codename for the plane, but it was
    embraced by the President and often
    attributed to FDR who had a good
    sense of humor about such things.
24. Leahy Papers, Leahy Diary, LOC

CHAPTER 14: TUNIS

1. Reilly, Reilly of the White House,
   P. 149
2. Reilly, Reilly of the White House,
   P. 150
3. Rigdon, White House Sailor, p. 17
4. FRUS, p. 301
5. Sherwood, Hopkins and Roosevelt,
   p. 774
6. FRUS, p. 301
7. Slocum, Reilly of the White House,
   p. 174
8. Reilly, I was Roosevelt's Shadow, p. 90

CHAPTER 15: TUNIS

1. Black, Franklin Delano Roosevelt: Champion of Freedom, p. 858
2. Cray, p. 424
3. FRUS, p.296
4. The Strange Alliance, p. 36
5. Stalin, p. 487
6. FRUS, p. 327
7. FRUS, p. 329
8. FRUS, p. 328
9. FRUS, p. 330
10. Pogue, p. 307
11. Pogue, p. 307
12. Pogue, Organizer of Victory, p. 305
13. FRUS, p. 333
14. Leahy Papers, LOC
15. Arnold Diary, p. 85

CHAPTER 16: THANKSGIVING

1. Crusade in Europe, p. 166
2. Crusade in Europe, p. 166
3. Leahy, I Was There, p. 201
4. Leahy, I Was There, p. 201
5. FRUS, p. 409
6. Handy Interview, AFHRA, p. 12
7. Pogue, Organizer of Victory, p. 331
8. FRUS, p. 409
9. FRUS, p. 409
10. Quoted in Pogue, Organizer of Victory, p. 294
11. Cray, p. 426
12. Arnold Diary, p. 86
13. Sherwood, p. 775
14. Quoted in Black, Franklin Delano Roosevelt: Champion of Freedom, p. 859
15. Quoted in Black, Franklin Delano Roosevelt: Champion of Freedom, p. 860

CHAPTER 17: WALKING HOME

1. Gilbert, Churchill: A Life, p. 741
2. 15 Stars, p. 205
3. Master of Sea Power, p. 338
4. FRUS, p. 359
5. FRUS, p. 359
6. FRUS, p. 359
7. Leahy Papers, Leahy Diary, LOC
8. Leahy Papers, Leahy Diary, LOC
9. Montefiore, p. 497
10. Montefiore, p. 464
11. Montefiore, p. 463
12. Arnold Diary

CHAPTER 18:
CAIRO TO TEHRAN

1. Quoted in Black, Franklin Delano Roosevelt: Champion of Freedom, p. 861
2. Roosevelt, As He Saw It, p. 172
3. Quoted in Havas, Hitler's Plot to Kill the Big Three, P.70
4. Reilly, I was Roosevelt's Shadow, p. 91, Reilly, Reilly of the White House, p. 171
5. Pogue, Organizer of Victory, p. 280
6. The Strange Alliance, p. 40
7. Berezhkov, p. 312
8. Churchill, Closing The Ring, p. 302

1. FRUS, p. 477
2. FRUS, p. 478-479
3. FRUS, p. 480
4. FRUS, p. 482
5. Reilly, I was Roosevelt's Shadow, p. 91
6. Mosley, Marshall:
   Hero For Our Times, p. 263
7. Reilly, I was Roosevelt's Shadow, p. 92
8. Reilly, Reilly of the White House,
   p. 178
9. Reilly, I was Roosevelt's Shadow, p. 92
10. Harriman, Special Envoy to
    Churchill and Stalin, p. 264
11. Reilly, Reilly of the White House,
    p. 183
12. FRUS, p.440
13. Reilly, I was Roosevelt's Shadow, p. 93
14. Molotov Remembers, p. 213
15. Stalin, p. 497
16. Stalin, p. 486
17. Rigdon, White House Sailor, p. 83
18. Mosley, Marshall:
    Hero For Our Times, p. 263
19. Rigdon, p. 82
20. Description per Rigdon, p. 83;
    other accounts have Marshall in a
    mustard colored uniform.
21. Montefiore, p. 466
22. Rigdon, p. 80
23. Reilly, I was Roosevelt's Shadow, p. 93
24. Reilly, I was Roosevelt's Shadow, p. 93
25. FRUS, p. 483
26. FRUS, p. 485
27. Rigdon, White House Sailor, p. 81
28. All diarists maintain that Roosevelt
    knew or assumed that his rooms were
    bugged but pretended that he did not.
29. At Stalin's Side, p. 333
30. Reilly, I was Roosevelt's Shadow, p. 93
31. Reilly, I was Roosevelt's Shadow, p. 94

32. King diary, LOC, p. 21
33. King diary, p. 22, LOC
34. Described in Montefiore, p. 466
35. Description from Bohlen, p. 141
36. FRUS, p. 487
37. FRUS, p. 487
38. FRUS, p. 487
39. FRUS, p.513
40. FRUS, p. 499
41. FRUS, p. 489
42. Leahy, p. 204
43. Quoted in Black, Franklin Delano
    Roosevelt: Champion of Freedom,
    p. 866
44. FRUS, p. 490
45. A division is somewhat imprecise.
    Today a division is between 10,000
    and 20,000 combat soldiers but this
    varies in the U.S. and varies among
    the armies of different countries.
46. FRUS, p. 491
47. FRUS, p. 491
48. Bohlen, p. 142
49. FRUS, p. 494
50. FRUS, p. 494
51. FRUS, p. 494
52. FRUS, p. 495
53. FRUS, p. 495
54. FRUS, p. 505
55. FRUS, p. 506
56. FRUS P. 507
57. FRUS, p. 507
58. Montefiore, p. 500
59. Leahy, p. 205
60. King Diary, p. 12, LOC
61. Leahy, p. 205
62. Quoted in Rigdon, p. 83
63. Leahy, p. 205
64. Bohlen, p. 142
65. Quoted in FDR, p. 588

66. King diary, p. 12 LOC
67. Sherwood, p. 789
68. Smith, p. 600
69. Sherwood, Hopkins and Roosevelt, p.781

CHAPTER 20: DINNER

1. FRUS, p. 509
2. FRUS, p. 513
3. FRUS, p. 511
4. Quoted in Black, Franklin Delano Roosevelt: Champion of Freedom, p. 871
5. FRUS, p. 510
6. FRUS, p. 513
7. FRUS, p. 514
8. FRUS, p. 485, p. 510
9. FRUS, p. 509

CHAPTER 21: STALIN'S HOUR

1. Leahy Diary, p. 64
2. Arnold Diary, p. 90
3. Quoted in Rigdon, p. 83
4. Quoted in Strategic Planning for Coalition Warfare, Maj Gen Thomas T. Handy, Comments on Manuscript, Strategic Planning for Coalition Warfare, 1943-1944, 28 Sep 56, OCMH files, Endnotes, Chapter XVn44
5. I Was There, p. 187
6. Paraphrased from the translation quoted in Edmonds, The Big Three: Churchill, Roosevelt and Stalin in Peace and War, New York: Norton & Co., 1991 P.356
7. I Was There, p. 187

8. FRUS, p. 509
9. Buell, p. 432
10. FRUS, p. 514—529
11. 'Communication' is a military term that means the roads or sea lanes by which men and material move from one point to another.
12. FRUS, p. 518
13. Interviews, p. 5
14. Interviews. P. 1
15. Interviews, p. 5
16. Interviews, p. 10
17. FRUS, p. 521
18. Molotov Remembers, p. 225
19. FRUS, p. 522
20. FRUS, p. 523
21. FRUS, p. 523
22. FRUS, p. 523
23. FRUS, p. 525
24. FRUS, p. 525
25. FRUS, p. 526
26. FRUS, p. 526
27. FRUS, p. 528
28. FRUS, p. 528
29. FRUS, p. 528

THE AFTERNOON

30. FRUS, p. 530
31. FRUS, p. 530
32. FRUS, p. 532
33. FRUS, p. 529
34. Global Mission, p. 466
35. King Diary, p. 13, LOC
36. President's Log, p. 467
37. Leahy Diary, Library of Congress, November 30, 1943 entry
38. Klara, FDRs Funeral Train, p. 8
39. Bohlen, p. 145
40. FRUS, p. 534

41. Montefiore, p. 469
42. I Was There, p. 204
43. FRUS, p. 535
44. Interviews, Mathews, Smythe, Lemson, Hamilton, p. 7
45. FRUS, p. 535
46. Cray, p. 434
47. FRUS, p. 537
48. FRUS, p. 538
49. FRUS, p. 538
50. FRUS, p. 538
51. FRUS, p. 538
52. FRUS, p. 551
53. Told in several accounts but quotes are from Bohlen, Witness to History, p. 146
54. Told in several accounts but quotes are from Bohlen, Witness to History, p. 146
55. Records of the Combined Chiefs, November 29, 1600, p. 549
56. Records of the Combined Chiefs, November 29, 1600, p. 551
57. Minutes of the Combined Chief, p. 551
58. FRUS, p. 552
59. FRUS, p. 550
60. FRUS, p. 552

THE DINNER

61. Leahy Diary, Library of Congress, November 29, 1943 entry
62. Quoted in Strategic Planning for Coalition Warfare, Maj Gen Thomas T. Handy, Comments on Manuscript, Strategic Planning for Coalition Warfare, 1943-1944, 28 Sep 56, OCMH files, Endnotes, Chapter XVn44
63. The Strange Alliance, p. 14
64. FRUS, p. 553

65. Bohlen, p. 146
66. FRUS, p. 554
67. Bohlen, p. 147
68. Churchill, p.330
69. King Diary, p. 13, lov
70. Sherwood, p. 790
71. Churchill, p. 330
72. FRUS, p. 555

CHAPTER 22:
SOMEBODY KNEW SOMETHING

1. Reilly, I was Roosevelt's Shadow, p. 94
2. Roosevelt and Hopkins p. 921
3. Gilbert, Churchill: A Life, p. 728
4. FRUS, p. 837
5. Interviews, p. 20
6. Interviews, p. 2, p.9
7. Interviews, p. 8
8. Interviews, p.11
9. Interviews, p. 2
10. Interviews , p. 589
11. FRUS, p. 555
12. FRUS, p. 556
13. FRUS, p. 557
14. FRUS, p. 556-558
15. FRUS, p. 561
16. FRUS, p. 565
17. FRUS, p. 565
18. Leahy Diary, LOC, Nov. 30th
19. FRUS, p. 448
20. FRUS, p. 566
21. FRUS, p. 567
22. FRUS, p. 568
23. Global Mission, p. 467
24. FRUS, p. 576
25. FRUS, p. 577
26. FRUS, p. 581
27. FRUS, p. 576
28. Smith, p. 595
29. Smith, p. 596

30. Quoted in Montefiore, p. 465
31. The Strange Alliance, p. 14; see also Robert Service, Stalin, p. 464
32. Beria, p. 131
33. Leahy Diary, p. 65
34. Arnold Diary, p. 90
35. FRUS, p. 582
36. The President's Log, p. 469
37. The President's Log, p. 469
38. FRUS, p. 585

CHAPTER 23:
DIVIDING THE SPOILS

1. Leahy Diary, LOC
2. Box 34, Flight Log Book 1942-1943, Ernest King Papers, Manuscript Division, Library of Congress
3. Arnold Diaries, p. 92
4. FRUS, p. 591
5. FRUS, p. 594
6. Bohlen, Witness to History, p. 152
7. Bohlen, Witness to History, p. 152
8. FRUS, p. 601-604
9. FRUS, p. 846
10. Black, Franklin Delano Roosevelt: Champion of Freedom, p. 887
11. Montefiore, p. 472

CHAPTER 24: STATESMEN

1. Box 34, Flight Log Book 1942-1943, Ernest King Papers, Manuscript Division, Library of Congress
2. Arnold Diaries, p. 85; Global Command, p.
3. Bradley, A Soldier's Story, p. 204-205

CHAPTER 25:
THE SUPREME ALLIED COMMANDER

1. Pogue, Organizer of Victory, p. 321
2. Quoted in Pogue, Organizer of Victory, p. 321
3. Bradley, , p. 205
4. Interviews, p. 44
5. Eisenhower, P.208
6. Quotes in Pogue, Organizer of Victory, p. 325
7. Leahy diary, p. 70
8. Eisenhower, P.207
9. Eisenhower, P.208
10. Eisenhower, P.209
11. I Was There. P. 215
12. Bradley, p.205
13. Global Mission, p. 475
14. Mosley, Marshall: Hero For Our Times, p. 267
15. Quoted in Cray, General of the Army, p. 438
16. Mosley, Marshall: Hero For Our Times, p. 267
17. FRUS, p. 635. The final communiqué contained only the final paragraph of this draft. The first news of the conference ran in the December 4, 1943 editions of several world papers including those in the U.S. The official communiqué was dateline Tehran, December 6, 1943.

EPILOGUE

1. Conversations with Stalin, p. 21
2. FDR Letters, p. 1471
3. Quoted in Helvig, To, Editor,
   The Iowan, Vol. 1., Number 2, p. 5,
   http://www.ussiowa.org/general/html/
   specifications.htm,
   last accessed 8.15.12
4. Matloff, p. 387
5. Together, p. 197
6. Closing the Ring, p.
7. I Was There, p. 220
8. Mosley, Leonard, Marshall:
   Hero For Our Times, P.319;
   Together, p. 243
9. Truman, p. 355
10. Mosley, Leonard, Marshall:
    Hero For Our Times, New York, P.320
11. I Was There, p. 375
12. Pogue, Organizer of Victory, p. 348
13. Together, p. 250
14. Quoted in Truman, p. 562
15. Truman, p. 384
16. Truman p. 534
17. Interviews, p. 2
18. Truman, p. 532
19. Edmonds, Robin, P.341
20. Bohlen, Witness to History, p. 154
21. Sherwood, Roosevelt and Hopkins,
    p. 807

BIBLIOGRAPHY

Ambrose, Stephen E. *D-Day: June 6, 1944*. New York: Touchstone, 1994.

Arnold, H.H. *Global Mission*. New York: Harper & Row, 1949.

Bailey, Helen McShane, "The Office of the Chief of Staff, United States Army in World War II:A Memoir of Helen McShane Bailey." In World War II-Korean War Memories Project. Lexington, VA: George C. Marshall Foundation, 2001.

Baldwin, J.L. "The Weather in 1943 in the United States." In Monthly Weather Review. Washington, DC: Weather Bureau, 1943. Recovered document found at http://docs.lib.noaa.gov/rescue/mwr/071/mwr-071-12-0198.pdf

Bell, William Gardner. *Quarter's One, The United States Army's Chief of Staff Residence*. Washington, DC: U.S. Army Center of Military History, 1981.

Bekker, Cajus, *The Luftwaffe War Diaries*. Translated and edited by Frank Ziegler. New York: Ballantine Books, 1969.

Berezhkov, Valentin M. *At Stalin's Side, His Interpreter's Memoirs From the October Revolution to the fall of the Dictator's Empire*. Secaucus, NJ: Carol Publishing Group, 1994.

Bishop, Stan D, and John A Hey. *Losses of the US 8th and 9th Air Forces, Vol II*. Suffolk, UK: Bishop Book Productions, 2009.

Black, Conrad. *Franklin Delano Roosevelt, Champion of Freedom*. New York: Public Affairs, 2003.

Bland, Larry I. "George C. Marshall and the Education of Army Leaders." *Military Review* 68, October 1988: 27-37.

Blair, Clay. *Hitler's U-Boat War: The Hunted, 1942-1945*. New York: Modern Library, 2000.

Bohlen, Charles E. *Witness to History, 1929-1969*. New York: W.W. Norton, 1973.

Bonner, Kit & Carolyn, St. Paul. *ALWAYS READY. Today's U.S. Coast Guard. The Power Series*. Minneapolis, MN: MBI Publishing Company, 2007

Bonner, Kit. "The Ill-Fated USS William D. Porter." *The Retired Officers Magazine*, March 1994.

Bradley, Omar N. *A Soldier's Story*. New York: Henry Holt, 1951.

Buell, Thomas B. *Master of Sea Power, A Biography of Fleet Admiral Ernest J. King*. Annapolis, MD: Naval Institute Press, 1980.

Burr, Lawrence. *US Fast Battleships, 1938-91, The Iowa Class*. Oxford, UK: Osprey Publishing, 2010.

Carter, Kit C., and Robert Mueller. *The Army Air Forces in World War II: Combat Chronology, 1941-1945*. Washington DC: Center for Air Force History, 1991.

Churchill, Winston S. *The Second World War, Volume V, Closing the Ring*. New York: Houghton Mifflin, 1951.

Cline, Ray S. *Washington Command Post: The Operations Division*. Washington, DC: U.S. Army Center of Military History, 1990.

Coffey, Thomas M. *Hap: The Story of the U.S. Air Force and the Man Who Built It.* New York: Viking Press, 1982.

Coles, Harry L. "The Army Air Forces in Amphibious Landings in World War II." In USAF Numbered Studies, No. 96. Montgomery, AL: USAF Historical Research Agency, 1953. IRIS No. 467681.

Condit, Kenneth W. *The Joint Chiefs of Staff and National Policy, Volume II, 1947-1949.* Washington, DC: Office of Joint History, 1996.

Craven, Wesley Frank and James Lea Cate, eds. *The Army Air Forces in World War II.* Chicago: University of Chicago Press, 1948.

Cray, Ed. *General of the Army, George C. Marshall Soldier and Statesman.* New York: Cooper Square Press, 2000.

Cross, Robert F. *Sailor in the White House: The Seafaring Life of FDR.* Annapolis, MD: Naval Institute Press, 2003.

Deane, John R. *The Strange Alliance, The Story of Our Efforts at Wartime Co-Operation With Russia.* New York: Viking Press, 1946.

Djilas, Milovan. *Conversations With Stalin.* San Diego: Harvest Books, 1962.

Dorr, Robert F. *Air Force One.* Minneapolis, MN: Zenith Press, 2002.

Doyle, David. *Iowa-Class Battleships, On Deck.* Carrollton, TX: Squadron Signal Publications, 2011.

Edmonds, Robin. *The Big Three, Churchill, Roosevelt & Stalin in Peace and War.* New York: W.W. Norton, 1991.

Eisenhower, Dwight D. *Crusade in Europe.* New York: Doubleday, 1948.

Feis, Herbert. *Churchill- Roosevelt -Stalin: The War They Waged and the Peace They Sought.* Princeton, NJ: Princeton University Press, 1957.

Ferguson, Arthur B. "The Early Operations of the Eighth Air Force and the Origins of the Combined Bomber Offensive, 17 August 1942 to 10 June 1943." Washington, DC: Army Air Forces Historical Offices, 1946.

Fox, Tom. "FDR and the Guns: Memories of the USS Iowa." *The Philadelphia Inquirer,* July 30, 1986.

Friedel, Frank. *Franklin D Roosevelt: The Apprenticeship.* Boston: Little, Brown, 1952.

Fursenko, Aleksandr, and Timothy Nafatali. *Khrushchev's Cold War: The Inside Story of An American Adversary,.* New York: W.W. Norton, 2006.

Gilbert, Martin. *Churchill: A Life.* New York: Henry Holt, 1991.

Goodwin, Doris Kearns. *No Ordinary Time, Franklin & Eleanor Roosevelt: The Home Front in World War II.* New York,: Simon & Schuster, 1994.

Hall, Kenneth. *USS Iowa, BB-61.* Paducah, KY: Turner Publishing, 1997.

Hammel, Eric. *The Road to Big Week: The Struggle for Daylight Air Supremacy Over Western Europe.* Pacifica, CA: Pacifica Press, 2009.

Hansen, Randall. *Fire and Fury: The Allied Bombing of Germany 1942-1945.* New York: NAL Caliber, 2008.

Harriman, W. Averell, and Elie Abel. *Special Envoy to Churchill and Stalin, 1941-1946* New York: Random House, 1975.

Havas, Laslo. *Hitler's Plot to Kill The Big Three.* New York:Cowles Book Company, 1967.

Hingley, Ronald. *Joseph Stalin, Man & Legend.* New York: Konecky, 1974.

Hornfischer, James D. *The Last Stand of the Tin Can Sailors: The Extraordinary World War II Story of the U.S. Navy's Finest Hour.* New York: Bantam, 2002.

Huston, John W., ed. *American Airpower Comes of Age: General Henry H. "Hap" Arnold's World War II Diaries.* 2 vols. Honolulu: University Press of the Pacific, 2004.

Isaacson, Walter, and Evan Thomas, *The Wise Men: Six Friends and the World They Made.* New York: Touchstone, 1986.

Ivie, Tom. *Aerial Reconnaissance: The 10th Photo Recon Group in World War II.* Fallbrook, CA: Aero Publishers, 1981.

Keen, Patricia Fussell. *Eyes of the Eighth: A Story of the 7th Photo Reconnaissance Group 1942-1945.* Sun City, AZ: CAVU Publishers, 1996.

King, Ernest J., and Walter Muir Whitehall. *Fleet Admiral King, A Naval Record.* New York: W.W. Norton, 1952.

Klara, Robert. *FDR's Funeral Train:A Betrayed Widow, A Soviey Spy, And A Presidency in the Balance.* New York: Palgrave Macmillan, 2010.

Knight, Amy. *Beria, Stalin's First Lieutenant.* Princeton, NJ: Princeton University Press, 1993.

Larrabee, Eric. *Commander In Chief, Franklin Delano Roosevelt, His Lieutenants, and Their War.* Annapolis, MD: Naval Institute Press, 1987.

Leahy, William D. *I Was There: The Personal Story of the Chief of Staff to Presidents Roosevelt and Truman Based on His Notes and Diaries Made at the Time* New York: Whittlesey House, 1950.

Marshall, George C. *Interviews and Reminiscences for Forrest Pogue.* Edited by Larry Bland. 3rd Edition. Lexington, VA: George C. Marshall Foundation, 1996.

Marshall, Katherine Tupper. *Together: Annals of an Army Wife.* New York: Tupper and Love, 1947.

Matloff, Maurice. *Strategic Planning For Coalition Warfare, 1943-1944.* Washington, DC: U.S. Army Center of Military History, 1994.

McCrea, John L. "Captain McCrea's War: A Memoir by Franklin D. Roosevelt's Naval Aide and USS Iowa's First Commander." Edited by Julia C. Tobey. Unpublished manuscript.

McCrea, John L. "The History of the USS Iowa." Unpublished manuscript.

McCrea, John L. *Reminiscences of Vice Admiral John L. McCrea, USN (Ret.).* Annapolis, MD: U.S. Naval Institute, 1990.

McCullough, David. *Truman.* New York: Simon & Schuster, 1992.

Mets, David R. *Master of Airpower: General Carl A. Spaatz.* Novato, CA: Presidio Press, 1988.

Molotov, V.M., and Felix Chuev. *Molotov Remembers: Inside Kremlin Politics.* Edited by Albert Resis. Chicago: Ivan R. Dee, 1993.

Montefiore, Simon Sebag. *Stalin: The Court of the Red Tsar*. New York: Vintage Books, 2003.

Mosley, Leonard. *Marshall: Hero For Our Times*. New York: Hearst Books, 1982.

Muir, Malcolm. *The Iowa Class Battleships: Iowa, New Jersey, Missouri & Wisconsin (Weapons and Warfare)*. Dorset, UK: Blandford Press, 1988.

Parrish, Thomas. *Roosevelt and Marshall: Partners in Politics and War*. New York: William Morrow, 1989.

Persico, Joseph E. *Roosevelt's Secret War: FDR and World War II Espionage*. New York: Random House, 2001.

Perry, Mark.*Partners in Command: George Marshall and Dwight Eisenhower in War and Peace*. New York: Penguin Books, 2007.

Pogue, Forrest C. *George C. Marshall: Organizer of Victory*. New York: Viking Press, 1973.

Pogue, Forrest C. *George C. Marshall: Education of a General, 1880-1939*. New York: Viking Press, 1963.

Raafat, Samir. "Mena House, Khedivial Hunting Lodge Turned Hotel." *Cairo Times*, April 3, 1997.

Radzinsky, Edvard. *Stalin: The First In-Depth Biography Based in Explosive New Documents From Russia's Secret Archives*. New York: Anchor Books, 1997.

Ramsey, John F. *Ninth Air Force in the ETO [European Theater of Operations], 16 October 1943 to 16 April 1944*. Washington, DC: Army Air Forces Historical, 1945.

Reilly, Michael F., and William J. Slocum. *I Was Roosevelt's Shadow*. London: W. Foulsham & Co, 1947.

Reilly, Michael F., and William J. Slocum. *Reilly of the White House*. New York: Simon & Schuster, 1947.

Rigdon, William M., and James Derieux. *White House Sailor*. Garden City, New York: Doubleday, 1962

Rogers, J. David. "Development of the World's Fastest Battleships." Unpublished paper found on Missouri University of Science and Technology website http://web.mst.edu/~rogersda/american&military_history/World%27s%20 Fastest%20Batleships.pdf.

Roosevelt, Elliott. *As He Saw It*. New York: Duell, Sloan and Pearce, 1946.

Roosevelt, Franklin Delano. *F.D.R: His Personal Letters, 1928-1945, Vol. II*, Edited by Eliott Roosevelt. New York: Duell, Sloan and Pearce, 1950.

Sainsbury, Keith. *The Turning Point: Roosevelt, Stalin, Churchill, and Chiang-Kai-Shek, 1943: The Moscow, Cairo, and Teheran Conferences*. Oxford, UK: Oxford University Press, 1985.

Service, Robert. *Stalin, a Biography*. Cambridge, MA: Belknap Press, 2004.

Sherwood, Robert E. *Roosevelt and Hopkins, An Intimate History*. New York: Harper & Brothers, 1948.

Smith, Jean Edward. *FDR*. New York: Random House, 2007.

Stanley, Roy M. *World War II Photo Intelligence: The First Complete History of the Aerial Photo Reconnaissance and Photo Interpretation Operations of the Allied and Axis Nations*. New York: Scribner, 1981.

Starling, Edmund D. *Starling of the White House: The Story of the Mman whose Secret Service Detail Guarded Five Presidents from Woodrow Wilson to Franklin D. Roosevelt*. Compiled by Thomas Sugrue. New York: Simon & Schuster, 1946.

Stormont, John W. *The Combined Bomber Offensive, April through December 1943* Washington, DC: Army Air Forces Historical Offices, 1946.

Werner, Herbert A. *Iron Coffins: A Personal Account of the German U-Boat Battles of World War II*. New York: Da Capo Press, 1989.

Weintraub, Stanley. *15 Stars: Eisenhower, MacArthur, Marshall, Three Generals Who Saved the American Century*. New York: NAL Caliber, 2008.

Wills, Matthew B. *Wartime Missions of Harry L. Hopkins.*Bloomington, IN:

AuthorHouse, 2004.

ARCHIVES, MANUSCRIPT COLLECTIONS, ORAL HISTORY AND OTHER SOURCES

Ernest Joseph King Papers, Manuscript Division, Library of Congress, Washington, D.C.

Foreign Relations of the United States Diplomatic Papers, U.S. Department of State, Washington, D.C.

Grace Tully Papers, National Archives and Records Administration, Franklin D. Roosevelt Library and Museum, Hyde Park, New York.

Henry Harley Arnold Papers, Manuscript Division, Library of Congress, Washington, D.C.

Oral History, General Thomas T. Handy, Air Force Historical Research Agency, Maxwell AFB, Montgomery, Alabama.

Oral History, General Thomas T. Handy, George C. Marshall Foundation, Lexington, Virginia.

Papers and Minutes of Meetings from Sextant and Eureka Conferences, National Archives and Records Administration, Office of the Combined Chiefs of Staff, College Park, Maryland.

Papers of Franklin D. Roosevelt, National Archives and Records Administration, Franklin D. Roosevelt Library and Museum, Hyde Park, New York.

Papers of George Catlett Marshall, George C. Marshall Foundation, Lexington, Virginia.

Papers of Harry L. Hopkins, National Archives and Records Administration, Franklin D. Roosevelt Library and Museum, Hyde Park, New York.

Papers of John L. McCrea, Manuscript Division, Library of Congress, Washington, D.C.

Records of the Joint Chiefs of Staff, National Archives and Records Administration, College Park, Maryland.

William D. Leahy Papers, Manuscript Division, Library of Congress, Washington, D.C.

Crew Oral Histories, Pacific Battleship Center, San Pedro, last accessed March 2012 http://www.pacificbattleship.com/alumni/alumnidetail/18

Helvig, Tom, ed. *The Iowan, History Letter*, Vol.1, Mt. Laurel, N.J., 2012

Robert Arnold Interview via telephone, 2012

Informal Minutes of the JCS Meeting 19 Nov-1943, 1943 Aboard Iowa, Joint Chiefs of Staff, FDR Library, Lexington, VA: George C. Marshall Foundation, 2001

Minutes of the Meeting, Between The President and the Chiefs of Staff, Held onboard ship in the Admiral's Cabin, Friday 19 November 1943 at 1500, Lexington, VA: George C. Marshall Foundation, 2001

The Invasion Of Normandy, Operation Neptune, The United States Naval Administration During World War II, United States Naval Forces, Europe, Histories, Volume 5/ Washington, D.C: Naval History & Heritage Center, 1945. Last accessed January 2015. http://www.history.navy.mil/library/online/comnaveu/comnaveu_index.htm

World War II, FDR, Truman, Churchill, Stalin, Conferences Documents. BACM Research, Los Angeles, California. Paperless Archives.com

The Churchill Centre. Selected Speeches of Winston S. Churchill. Last accessed January 3, 2015 http://www.winstonchurchill.org/learn/speeches /speeches-of-winston-churchill.

Helgason, Gudmundur, ed. "USS SC-664." Submarine and Anti-submarine Ship Data Uboat.net. Last accessed October 11, 2012. http://uboat.net/allies/warships/ship/8881.html.

History of Cossac (Chief of Staff to Supreme Allied Commander). U.S. Army Website. History. Last accessed October 22, 2012. http://www.history.army.mil/documents/cossac/Cossac.htm.

Schultz, John E. ed., USS Iowa Veterans Association website. Last accessed August 15, 2012. http://www.ussiowa.org/general/html/specifications.htm.

INDEX

A

Acheson, Dean, 27

Aegean Sea. *See* Greek islands

Air Force. *See* Army Air Forces, U.S.

Alaska, 49

Albania, 91

Aleutians, 49, 50

Alexandria, Egypt, 13, 78, 86

Algeria. *See* Oran, Algeria

American Chiefs of Staff. *See* Joint Chiefs of Staff

American Legation, 173, 192, 195, 199–200, 201

Angilletta, Vincent, 17

Army Air Corps, U.S., 30

Army Air Forces, U.S., 163, 164, 183, 184, 229–231, 239: air cover for D-Day, 93, 112, 154–155, 230–231, 232, 286–287; air cover for FDR's travel, 88, 101, *134. See also* Arnold, Henry A. "Hap,"

Army Corps of Engineers, 149

Army Operations Division, U.S., 48–50

Arnold, Henry A. "Hap," 2, 26, 29–33, 48, 60–61, 63, 65, 67, 70, 90, 92, 96, 103–104, 106–107, 115, 147, 148, 154, 155, 167, 170, 172, 187, 189, 193, 197, 205, 225, 226, 251, 263–264, 267, 268, 269, 271, 283: B-29 Super Fortress bombers, 50–52, 53; on Marshall, 169, 278; military aviation career of, 29–31; personality of, 29, *124;* photographs of, *118, 124, 132, 133, 137, 140,* 242; reorganization of air forces, 32, 39–42, 85–86, 91, 93, *134,* 286–287; on risk of Luftwaffe attack in Cairo, 76–77; Roosevelt and, 31–32, 84; Stalin's interest in U.S. bombers and, 240–241. *See also* Army Air Forces, U.S.

Atlantic Ocean, crossing of. *See Iowa,* USS

Australia, 109

Austria, 86, 274

Azores, 73

B

B-29 Super Fortress bombers, 50–52, 53, 86

Baku, Azerbaijan, 23, 79, 186, 191, 276

Balkans, 54, 57–58, 93, 97–98, 175, 195, 210, 231

Basra, Iraq, 80, 190

Belgium, 96, 109, 286

Berezhkov, Valentin, 22–23, 204

Beria, Lavrenti Pavlovich, 22–24, 79, 156, 186–187, 199, 204, 266–267

Beria, Sergo, 266–267

Berlin, Germany, 68–70, 93–97, 99–100, 223

Bermuda, 35

Block Island, USS, 70

blue water operations, 35

Boettiger, John, 176–177, 268, 283

Bohlen, Charles E. "Chip," 55, *141*, 159, 200, 202, 205, 206, 211, 213, 214, 215, 217, 221, 222, 223, 237, 242, 245–246, 252, 256, 274, 283, 293

Bosporus Strait, 13, 175, 182, 211, 214, 227

Bradley, Omar N., 113, 278, 280, 282

Britain. *See* England

British Chiefs of Staff, 68, *132*, 154

British Legation, *141*, 191, 267–269

Brooke, Alan, *132*, 154, 172–174, 180, 182, 183, 184, 226–229, 230, 231, 233–234, 236, 242–243, 247, 259, 264, 268

Brooklyn, USS, 90

Brooklyn Naval Yard, 6–7

Bryan, Otis F., 104, 115, *131*, 153, 171, 189, 190, 237

Bulgaria, 57, 91, 194, 274, 275

Burma, 49, 150, 184, 196

C

C-54. *See Sacred Cow* (C-54 transport plane)

Cadogan, Alexander, 171

Cairo, Egypt, 13, 60, 86, 91, 155, 169–170, 281: Marshall's dinner with Churchill, 157–158; meetings in, 149–153, 154–155, 157, 159–169, 171–176, 179–186; Mena House Hotel, 76, *132*, *133*, 147–148, 149, 277; Roosevelt's arrival in, 153–154; Roosevelt's sightseeing detour and, 148; security and, 76–78, 80, 111–112, 147–148; Thanksgiving dinner in, 176–177

California, 75

Camp Amirabad, *142–143*, 193, 237, 251, 271, 275, 277

Canada, 109. *See also* Quebec meetings

Capra, Frank, 111

Carlin, Daniel J., 89

Casablanca, Morocco, 80, 105

Casey, Tom, 38

Chiang Kai-shek, *127*, 168–169, 203, 204

China, 53, 238–239, 262

Chinese nationalists, 49, *127*, 150, 154, 157, 168–169, 179, 183–186, 194, 203, 207, 262

Churchill, Clementine, 287

Churchill, Randolph, 268

Iowa, USS, 1, 2, 4, 5–9, 32–33, 87–88: commanding officer of, 6–7, 83, *121*; at high
speed, 70; key military personnel and, 48–49, *121*; meetings on board, 39–44,
48–63, 90–100, 103–104; in Oran, Algeria, 103–105; photographs of, *120, 143*;
Roosevelt's boarding of, 16–19; Roosevelt's request to travel on, 6; Roosevelt's
return home on, *143*, 285–286; route of travel, 5–6, *119*; sailors and, 16–17,
71–72; size and armaments of, 7–8; task force for, 19, 25, 47, 70, 75–76, 83, 89–90,
101–102; threat of German attacks on, 8–9, 25, 47–48, 64–65, 74–78, 81, 101, 105;
time adjustment procedures, 65; torpedo incident, 35–39
Iran. *See* Tehran, Iran
island-hopping strategy in Pacific, 49–50, 52–53, 168
Ismay, Hastings, *132*, 154, 242
Italy, 80, 97, 106, 150, 174, 208: Allied invasion of, 12, 54, 75, 160–161, 164, 212,
230–231; British focus on combat in, 13, 87, 164–168, 175, 179, 183, 211–215,
227–229, 242–243, 246–247, 258; combined command and, 40, 43–44, 85, 91, 93;
Eisenhower on, 171–172, 180–182, 227; Joint Chiefs of Staff on, 58–59, 193–194,
195, 230–231, 259–260; Soviet views on, 210, 212–213, 214, 233–235; Tehran
resolution and, 261

J

Japan, 77: JCS strategy for defeat of, 49–53, 168–169; post-war plans for, 62–63, 240,
262; Stalin's offer to help defeat, 209, 237–238. *See also* Chinese nationalists; Pearl
Harbor, attack on
Jersey, USS, 6
Jerusalem, 271
Joint Chiefs of Staff (JCS), 4, 25–33, 35, 171–172, 277, 281: consolidated command with
British and, 12–13, 41–44, 60–62, 85, 91–92, 286; functions of, 26, 67; meetings
on board USS *Iowa*, 39–44, 48–63, 90–100, 103–104; meetings with Roosevelt,
54–63, 90–100, 103–104, 193–197; members of, 2, 26–32, 39, *118*; Operation
Rankin and, 68–70, 93–97, 99–100; Planning Staff and, 25, 48–50, 84–85,
259–260; reorganization of air war against Germany, 32, 39–42, 85–86, 91, 93,
134, 286–287; Roosevelt's detachment from, 84; selection of D-Day commander
and, 60–62, 107–109, 279; Truman and, 289. *See also* Combined Chiefs of Staff;
specific Joint Chief

K

Kalamaki, Greece, 76, 88
Kennedy, John, 14
Kerr, Archibald Clark, 221, 242
Khartoum, Sudan, 77–78

King, Ernest J., 2, 26, 33, 38, 42, 47, 48, 51, 53, 57, 60–61, 63–65, 67, 84, 90, 95–97, 103, 104, 115, *125*, 147, 148, 154, 155, 172, 180, 184, 189, 193, 196, 197, 205–206, 209, 216, 217, 226, 251, 253, 264, 267, 269, 271, 277: address to officers on USS *Iowa*, 63–64; on naval strategy, 5, 52; personality of, 5, 28–29; photographs of, *118*, *123*, *132*, *140*, *145*, 242; Roosevelt's route of travel and, 5–6; on selection of D-Day commander, 60, 107–109, 111; Truman and, 289

Kirk, Alexander, 153

Korea, 262

Krueger, Walter, 27–28

L

landing craft, 167, 181, 183, 196, 228, 229–230, 232–236, 243, 258–261: Landing Ship Tanks (LSTs), *128*, 207–208

Latvia, 273

Leahy, William D., 2, 18, 26, 33, 42, 44, 45, 48, 49, 53–54, 58, 65, 88, 90, 91, 103, 104, 115, *121*, *141*, 148, 153, 154, 155, 159–160, 161, 168, 169–170, 172, 186, 199, 200, 205, 206, 209, 216, 250, 251, 262, 264, 267, 269, 271, 277, 288, 289: on British, 173; on Combined Chiefs of Staff, 12–13; D-Day vs. Mediterranean strategy and, 182–183, 193–194, 228, 237, 258–259, 260; on de Gaulle, 57, 96; Joint Chiefs of Staff and, 26, 39, 67; Pacific theater and, 183, 185; photographs of, *118*, *132*, *141*, *145*, 242; Roosevelt and, 39; on selection of D-Day commander, 60–61, 282; on Stalin, 217, 225–226

Leathers, Frederick James, 171

Lebanon, 203

Lee, Billy, 36

Lend-Lease program, 16, 80, 190, 269

Lenin, Vladimir, 200

Leros, 13, 74, 92–93, 150, 151, 163, 165, 179, 181, 182

Lithuania, 273

Lockwood, Arthur, 70

Luftwaffe, 8–9, 13, 14, 40, 41–42, 74–78, 81, 88, 101, *134*, 159

M

MacArthur, Douglas, 283

Macomb, USS, 47

Malta, 13, 73, 74, 78, 86, 283

Marianas, 49, 50, 53

Marquart, E.J., 6–7

Marseille, France, 47

Marshall, George C., 2, 33, 42, 47, 48, 54, 55, 57, 59, 65, 90, 92–93, 103, 104, 115, 147, 148, 149, 154, 155, 170, 172, 187, 189, 226, 245, 264, 267–268, 269, 271, 288: on American soldier's fighting qualities, 110–111, 158, 256–257; Churchill, private dinner with, 157–158; commanding presence of, 27, 29, 278; D-Day vs. Mediterranean strategy and, 14, 26, 97–99, 151, 166–167, 173–176, 183, 193–197, 229–232, 233, 237, 259–260; first plenary session, absence from, 205; Joint Chiefs of Staff and, 26, 27–30, 31, 39, *126*; landing craft and, *128*, 229–230, 232, 235–236, 243, 251, 258–260; military career of, 27–28, 29; on Operation Rankin, 94, 95–96, 100; Pacific theater and, 50, 51–52, 157, 168–169, 183–185; photographs of, *118*, *122*, *129*, *132*, *140*, *144*, *145*, 242; recognition of, 290; Roosevelt's detachment from, 84; on Stalin, 67–68, 201; supreme commander for D-Day and, 60–61, 107–108, 114, *144*, 244, 278, 279–283; Truman and, 289, 292–293; on war strategy, 67–68
Marshall, Katherine, 31, 287, 288
Marshall Plan, 292–293
Matloff, Maurice, 54
McCarthy, Frank, 283, 288
McCloy, John J., 171
McCrea, John L., 6–7, 17, 18–19, 37, 38, 45, 64–65, 70, 74, 83, 87, 89, 90, 101, 102, 103, 104–105, *121*, *131*
McFarland, Andrew J., 226
McIntire, Ross T., 2, *131*, 189, 277
media, 3, 61, 76–78, 98
Mediterranean Sea, 8–9, 47, 73, 74–78, 86, 88, 101–102
Mediterranean theater, 43–44, 91–92. *See also* Operation Overlord vs. Mediterranean strategy; *specific country*
Mena House Hotel, 76, *132*, 147–148, 149, 277
Military Conference, 226–236, 242–243
Mitchell, Billy, 30
Molotov, Vyacheslav Mikhailovich, 23, 24, 55, *138*, *140*, 186–187, 200, 206, 211, 218, 221–222, 231, 232, 242, 252, 254, 264, 272
Moran, Lord, 27
Morgan, Frederick, 244
Morocco, 60, 73, 80, 105, 111
Morrell, Sydney, 189
Mountbatten, Louis, 155, 256
Mr. Lucky, 170

N

Navy, U.S., 15, 39, 42, 47, 48, 51, 52
Nelson, Myron E., Sr., 71
New Zealand, 109
Nimitz, Chester, 5

NKVD, 22–24, 79, 156, 186, 197–198, 199, 201, 204–205, 263–264, 266–267

North Africa, 5, 12, 32, 40–41, 43–44, 56, 62, 68, 75, 77, 105–106, 109, 164, 212

Norway, 109

Pershing, John "Black Jack," 28, 61

Phantom of the Opera, The, 33

Philippine-American War, 27–28

Philippines, 30, 60, 207

pincer strategy, 49–50, 212–214, 228–229, 287

Pisa-Rimini line, 175, 181, 183, 258, 259

Pitt, William, the Elder, 33, 158

Plymouth, England, 11

Poland, 109, 223–224, 272–274, 275

"policemen" nations concept, 60, 238–239

Portal, Charles F.A., 154, 172, 184, 226, 242

Postal Service, U.S., 30–31

post-war plans, 86–87, 202–204: aid for Europe, 96, 291–293; for France, 57, 59, 87, 94, 96, 203–204, 221, 223, 224; "free ports" concept, 59, 224, 263; for Germany, 68–70, 86, 93–97, 99–100, 222–224, 239–240, 252–254, 263, 274–275, 290–291; for Japan, 62–63, 240, 262; for Poland, 223–224, 272–274, 275; "policemen" nations concept, 60, 238–239; Stalin and, 203–204, 221, 222–224, 239–240, 252–254, 262–263, 272–275, 291; "strong points" concept, 60, 239–240

Potomac, 1, 3, 4, 16, 17

Po Valley, 172, 180, 181, 194

Prettyman, Arthur S., 1, 2, 4, 16, 17–18, 33, 35, 36, 37, 70, 90, 103, 104, *131,* 154, 200, 225, 277

Princess O'Rourke, 45

"psychological moment," 150

Puerto Rico, 39

Pyle, Ernie, 83

Q

Quantico, Virginia, 1, 4

Quebec meetings, 60, 208, 246

R

RAF (Royal Air Force), 41–42, 73, 76, 78, 85, 91, 110, 153, 255, 286

Rankin plan, 68–70, 93–97, 99–100, 174, 175, 287

Recife, Brazil, 59

reconnaissance flights, 101, 110, *134*

Red Army, 21–22, 190, 201. *See also* Eastern Front

Regensburg, Germany, 41–42

Reilly, Mike, 16, 74–77, 79–80, 102, 103, 147–148, 155–156, 159, 171, 189, 193, 197–199, 201–202, 204–205, 237

Renown, HMS, 11–14, 73–74, 77, 86, 154

Rhodes, 13, 76–77, 93, 161, 163, 165–168, 179, 182, 183, 194, 196, 214, 227–228, 234, 248, 258–261, 277

S

Stalingrad, Russia, 21, *136*, 159, 201, 241–242

Starling, Edmund William, 30–31

Statue of Liberty, 7–8

Stewart, USS, 4

Stimson, Henry, 176, 279, 286, 289, 290

Strait of Gibraltar, 13, 47, 73, 74, 75–76, 87–88, 89–90, 101–102, 105

Strategic Air Forces Europe, U.S., 40–42, 85–86, 91, 93, 286–287

"strong points" concept, 60, 239–240

Stuart, Francis, 64

Sudan, 77–78

Suez Canal, 59

Sumatra, 50

Supreme Allied Commander, 43–44, 60–62, 85, 91–92, 107–109, 111, 114, 243–244, 245, 248, 249, 261, 278, 279–283, 289–290

sword presentation, *137*, 241–242

T

Taiwan, 50, 60, 262

tea time, 241

Teazer, HMS, 90

Tehran, Iran, *135*, 293–294: Big Three meetings and, 205–218, 242–250, 261, 263–266; British capitulation and, 258–262; Churchill-Stalin clashes, 211–212, 214–218, 252–254, 255–256; Conference resolution and, 261; dinners held in, 218, 221–224, 252–254, 267–269, 275–276; final days of conference and, 271–276; German assassination plot, 197–199; JCS preparatory session with Roosevelt, 193–197; joint communiqué and, 275, 283–284; meetings between Stalin and Roosevelt, 200–205, 237–240, 272–273; military conference, 226–236, 242–243; photographs in, *135–143*, 242; poverty in, 189; Roosevelt's visit to Camp Amirabad, *142–143*, 237, 271, 275, 277; travel to, 80, 155–156, 171, 186, 189–191. *See also* Soviet Embassy in Tehran

Thanksgiving, 171–177

Time Magazine, 290

Tinian, 50

Tokyo Raiders, 40

torpedo incident, 35–39

Toulon, France, 47, 88

Trippe, USS, 90

Trowbridge, HMS, 90

Truk, 51

Truman, Harry S., 27, 288–289, 292–293

Tully, Grace, 2, 16

Tunisia, 79–80, 106–115, 164

Turkey, 91, 93, 163, 165, 168, 173, 174, 175, 181, 182, 194, 196, 208, 210, 211, 214, 227, 243, 258, 262, 271–272

Twelfth Air Force, 88

Tyrian, HMS, 90

U

U-boats, 5–6, 8–9, 22, 25, 35, 47–48, 64–65, 74–76, 101, 255

Ukraine, 202

USSAFE. *See* Strategic Air Forces Europe, U.S.

V

Vichy France, 39, 56, 87, 203–204, 221, 223

Virginia Military Institute, 27, 48, 280

Von Karman, Theodore, 31

Voroshilov, Kliment Efremovich, 23, 24, 55, *137*, *140*, 186–187, 211, 215, 226, 231–236, 237, 242, 243, 264

W

warm-water ports, 262

Watson, Pa, 177, 277

West Point, 30

White House, 1–3

Why Do We Fight, 111

William D. Porter, USS, 36, 38, 47

Wilson, Henry Maitland, 182

Winant, John Gilbert, 149–153, 158, 176–177, 191

World War I, 28, 48, 61, 257

Wright brothers, 30

X

"X" factor, 110–111

Y

Yamamoto, Isoroku, 77

Young, USS, 47

Yugoslavia, 14, 57, 58, 91, 97, 98, 165, 166, 168, 175, 181, 195, 196, 211, 214, 227, 228, 242–243, 248, 258

Z

Zangozi, Angelo, 37, 38

Zhukov, Georgi, 201